GOA AND PORTUGAL

Books of the XCHR Studies Series

No.1 : João de Barros: Portuguese Humanist and Historian of Asia/ *C.R. Boxer*

No. 2 : Coastal Western India: Studies from the Portuguese Records/ *M.N. Pearson*

No. 3 : The Black Legend of Portuguese India: Diogo do Couto, His Contemporaries and the Soldado Prático-A Contribution to the Study of Political Corruption in the Empires of Early Modren Europe/ *George Davison Winius*

No. 4 : Health and Hygience in Colonial Goa (1510-1961)/ *Fátima da Silvà Gracias*

No. 5 : Trade and Finance in Portuguese India: A Study of the Portuguese Country-Trade, 1770-1840/ *Celsa Pinto*

No. 6 : Goa and the Revolt of 1787/ *Charles J. Borges* (Ed.)

No. 7 : Goa and Portugal: Their Cultural Links/ *Charles J. Borges* and *Helmut Feldmann* (Eds.)

No. 8 : Goa-Kanara Portuguese Relations 1498-1763/ *B.S. Shastry* and *Charles J. Borges* (Eds.)

No. 9 : Goa's Foremost Nationalist: José Inácio Candido de Loyola: The Man and His Writings/ *Charles J. Borges* (Ed.)

No. 10 : Goa and Portugal: History and Development/ *Charles J. Borges, Óscar G. Pereira* and *Hannes Stubbe* (Eds.)

No. 11 : Conversions and Citizenry: Goa under Portugal 1510-1610/ *Délio de Mendonca*

About the Editors

Rev. Dr. Charles J. Borges, S.J. has been with the Xavier Centre of Historical Research (Goa) since 1981. Besides his own publications, he edited or co-edited books including *Jesuits in India: In Historical Perspective and Goa and the Revolt of 1787*.

Prof. Helmut Feldmann is Director, Instituto de Fstudos Portugueses e Brasileiros and Vice-Director, Centro Mundo Lusófono (University of Cologne). He has lectured at universities in Europe and Brazil and has a special interest in Portuguese and Goan studies.

XCHR Studies Series No. 7

GOA AND PORTUGAL
Their Cultural Links

Edited by

CHARLES J. BORGES
Director, Xavier Centre of Historical Research, Goa

and

HELMUT FELDMANN
Director, Instituto Luso-Brasileiro, Cologne

CONCEPT PUBLISHING COMPANY PVT. LTD.
NEW DELHI-110059

ISBN: 978-81-7022-659-8

First Published 1997

Published and Printed by

Concept Since 1974

Concept Publishing Company Pvt. Ltd.
A/15-16, Commercial Block, Mohan Garden,
New Delhi-110059 (India)
T: 91-11-41101460
E: publishing@conceptpub.com, *W*: www.conceptpub.com

PREFACE

The need for a deep understanding of Goa, capital of the *Estado da India* and headquarters of the Viceroys of the Portuguese in Asia, was felt at the Instituto de Estudos Portugueses e Brasileiros of the University of Cologne, during its decade-long Luso-Oriental research. This resulted in the international seminar on the theme "Portugal and Japan in the 16th and 17th centuries: A Nanban culture" (Cologne, 30 January — 2 February, 1992). One of the first objectives of the Centro Mundo Lusófono, an institute at the University of Cologne, since its inception in 1992 with its multidisciplinary orientation and openness to all Portuguese-speaking countries and enclaves, was to satisfy that need.

I visited as Director of the Instituto de Estudos Portugueses e Brasileiros and of the Centro Mundo Lusófono in 1993 Goa where the well-known specialist in the cultural history of Goa, Prof. Dr. Teotónio de Souza as Director of the Xavier Centre of Historical Research, offered his services to me in the scientific planning of the international symposium on the theme "Cultural Relations between Portugal and Goa" at the University at Cologne (29 May to 2 June 1996). The realization of this project went ahead with the valuable assistance of Fr. Charles J. Borges, S.J., present director, Xavier Centre of Historical Research, of Dr. Shirodkar, director, Directorate of Archives, Archaeology and Museum, Goa, of the late Dr. Joseph Barros, secretary, Instituto Menezes Braganza, who passed away in Lisbon a few weeks preceding the symposium, of Mr. Percival Noronha, an authority on Old Goa, of Prof. D. B. Kapp, director of the Institute of Indology at the University of Cologne, of Prof. Dr. Michael Jansen, director of the faculty of architecture at the Technical University at Aachen, and of Dr. Helmut Siepmann, professor of Portuguese and Brazilian literature at the University of Aachen and director of the Portuguese department at the Centro Mundo Lusofono. I owe much also to my friends Dr. Manfred Prinz, professor at the University of Giessen and member of the diretoria of the Centro Mundo Lusófono, and to Dr. Oscar Pereira, Goan doctoral student at the faculty of education at the University of Cologne. We were able to solve the financial problems involved thanks to the help of the Deutsche Forschungsgemeinschaft, the Comissão Nacional para as Comemorações dos Descobrimentos Portugueses, the Fundação Oriente, the Municipal Council of Cologne and the University of Cologne, respectively. The ambassadors of India and Portugal offered their services and honoured us with their greetings at the solemn inauguration of the symposium. To all these honoured professors, my sincerest thanks.

DR. HELMUT FELDMANN
Director
Instituto Luso-Brasileiro

CONTENTS

LIST OF CONTRIBUTORS

Charles J. Borges is author of *The Economics of the Goa Jesuits 1542-1759: An Explanation of their rise and fall* (1994).

Victor Anand Coelho is an accomplished musician, Professor of music history at the University of Calgary (Canada) and author of *Music and Science in the Age of Galileo.*

George V. Coelho, a social psychologist (Harvard, USA) has written on emigration and is presently working on an anthology of Goan literary works in Portuguese.

Teotónio R. de Souza is author of *Medieval Goa* (1979) and teaches economic and social history at Universidade Lusófona, Lisbon.

Helmut Feldmann is Director, Portuguese-Brazilian Institute (Instituto Luso-Brasileiro) and Vice-Director, Centro Mundo Lusófono, both of the University of Cologne.

Athos Fernandes, formerly with All India Radio, is presently a doctoral student at the University of Macau.

Takashi Gonoi is professor of history at the University of Tokyo.

Fátima da Silva Gracias teaches history at the Dhempe College (Goa) and is author of *Health and Hygiene in Colonial Goa* (1994)

Michael Jansen is Director, Faculty of Architecture, Technical University of Aachen.

Engelbert Jorissen is associate professor at the faculty of integrated human sciences at the Kyoto University, Japan.

Dieter B. Kapp is Director, Institute of Indology and Tamil Studies, University of Cologne.

Maria de Jesus dos Martires Lopes is author of *Goa Setecentista Tradição e Modernidade* (1996) and a writer on Goan history.

Thomas Malten is at the Institute of Indology and Tamil Studies, University of Cologne.

Percival Noronha is President of Friends of Astronomy Club, Goa.

António Nunes Pereira, is scientific assistant at the Aachen Technical Institute, Germany.

Oscar Pereira has specialized in law and social sciences and lectures at the Faculty of Education, University of Cologne.

Manfred F. Prinz is at the University of Cologne and the University of Giessen and a member of Centro Mundo Lusofono.

Fenelon Rebello writes on Indo-Portuguese numismatics and is Director of Italab Agency, Goa.

Prakashchandra P. Shirodkar is editor *Goa: Cultural Trends.*

Helmut Siepmann is Professor of Romanic Philology at the Technical University, Aachen, and author of *The Allegorical Tradition in the work of Clement Marot (1968).*

Thomas Strater is at the University of Cologne.

INTRODUCTION

Goa and Portugal: Their Cultural Links is a collection of twenty-one papers presented at the international symposium on the theme "Intercultural Relations: Portugal and Goa" (*Relações Interculturais Portugal - Goa*) held at the University of Cologne (Germany) between the 29 May to 1 June 1996, and organized by the Centro Mundo Lusófono and the Instituto de Estudos Portugueses e Brasileiros. Those who took part in it included delegates from Germany, Portugal, India, the United States and Canada. The proceedings were conducted in English and Portuguese.

The papers have been grouped together under four main themes: Goa and Portugal and their various cultural relations; Goa in its contacts with Japan and Mozambique; Art, architecture, music and numismatics; and Goa-Portugal ties as reflected in literature.

PART 1: P.P. Shirodkar writes on "Socio-Cultural Life in Goa during the 16th century"; Fátima Gracias on "The Impact of Portuguese Culture on Goa — A myth or a reality?"; Charles Borges on "A lasting cultural legacy: the role of the Society of Jesus in reforming Goan society"; Maria Lopes on "Conversion as a means of cultural adaptation: the catechumens of Betim in the 18th century"; and Oscar Pereira on "Present-Day Goa: Reflecting various legacies."

P.P. Shirodkar begins with 1510 and tells us about Goa and the early life, about the Portuguese who tried to control revenue administration against traditional rights and customs, and about the Afonso Mexia Charter which gave a "twist to the socio-religious life of the Goans besides making revolutionary changes in the village administration". Religious life of the Goans was "totally disrupted and ruined on account of the terrible onslaught on Hinduism and the Hindus" and the introduction of the "most unholy pitiless Holy Inquisition in 1560 was the greatest blow, the Goans could ever imagine", he informs us.

F. Gracias tells us that the pre-Portuguese culture of Goa was a product of a fusion of Jain, Buddhist, Muslim and Hindu influences. It was different from the western culture and in some ways superseded the culture of the West. Portuguese culture left its impress on the attitude and general lifestyle of the Goans, seen in different fields and more prominently in architecture, arts and crafts, education, music, religion and cuisine.

C. Borges believes that the Jesuits rank as one important group that has left an indelible Portuguese mark on Goa. The memory of their presence in Goa since their arrival in 1542 in the person of Francis Xavier and companions has come to stay. All through the centuries in Goa they succeeded in doing many things, one of which was to reform Goan society of the times they lived in. Being the most dominant missionary group then in Goa and having more Portuguese men in their ranks, by their educational methods, popularizing of devotions and art forms, they gave Goan Christianity a dominant Portuguese flavour.

M. Lopes informs us about the institution of the *Pai dos Cristãos* (Father of Christians) which had as its main objectives, the conversion of the population, the teaching of the Christian creed and the protection of the new Christians. The conversion to the Cathoiic faith, the acceptance of Christian names, marriages with Portuguese men, the granting of public offices to new converts, led to a cultural adaptation expressed in clothing, food and manner of living.

O. Pereira believes that the heritage left behind by the Portuguese and Indian rulers led to an Indo-Portuguese culture in Goa. New cultural changes are taking place in Goa today and there is need for a "psychological liberation", the "pledging oneself to the new constitutional order in which Indianness and indigenisation are priorities, encouraging the obtaining of cultural features for a proper Goan society". He refers to cultural identity showing how people often see themselves in danger of being assimilated by other cultures and offers the examples of Goans in Portugal and Germany and their attendant problems.

PART 2: Helmut Feldmann has a paper on "The image of India in *the History of the Church in Japan* by João Rodrigues, S.J."; Takashi Gonoi on "Relations between Japan and Goa in the 16th and 17th centuries" and Manfred Prinz on "Intercultural relations between Goa and Mozambique in colonial and contemporary history: Literary Mozambiquean traces".

H. Feldmann tells us about João Rodrigues, the *Tsuzzu*

(interpreter) who in his celebrated work on the Church in Japan defended the interests of the Portuguese Padroado in the Far East against the Spanish claims. Japan is shown as a second centre for the spread of evangelization of Asia. Rodrigues completed only a small part of his vast project: a general presentation of Japan, its geography and history, its political and social system, its religion and customs—and the narration of the Jesuit mission of Japan till the death of St. Francis Xavier. That the Portuguese nation was effectively the chosen nation by God, he saw confirmed by indications of secular history which lead one to catch a glimpse of divine providence.

T. Gonoi mentions that relations between Japan and Goa which endured for about one hundred years, started in 1548 when the Japanese Anjiro (Yajiro) visited Goa to meet Francis Xavier. Initially there were contacts by the daimyos (feudal lords) of the Kyushu region, followed by talks between the governments of Japan and Goa respectively. Gonoi refers to the introduction of the press in Japan, the acquisition of the printing skill and the influence that *Isopo no Fabvlas*, today known as *Isoppu Monogatari* had in Japan. Goa soon became the point of diffusion of European culture and Christianity into Japan.

M. Prinz refers to Portuguese colonialism in India and in Africa and sees their similarities. The community of the prazeiros was in the 18th century largely of Indian extraction. The impact of the Goans and Indians in East Africa showed the Portuguese community withdrawing itself little by little from Mozambique, considered as unfavourable land that presented serious problems of acclimatization. Prinz speaks of the Indians as portrayed in Honwana's literary work *Nós matamos o cão-tinhoso*. He refers to Indians/Goans in Mozambique from the point of view of their implantation and more effective presence than that of the Portuguese. He ends with a comparison of socio-linguistic problems for Goa and Mozambique believing that the view of speaking and understanding Portuguese well appears in colonial and post-colonial African literature constantly as a criterion of distinction and discrimination of the participants, akin to the peripheral situation of the African countries.

PART 3: Victor Coelho speaks on "Connecting Histories: Portuguese Music in Renaissance Goa"; Antonio Pereira on "Christian Goan Architecture of the 16th Century"; Percival Noronha

"Old Goa in the context of Indian Heritage" and Fenelon Rebello on "Evolution of *Bazarucos* of Portuguese India: Classifications, and an unpublished value of 1748".

V. Coelho says that the influence of Portuguese artistic and cultural traditions in Goa has so far been studied chiefly in terms of the craft, architectural and painting industries. This has been valuable in tracing the cross-cultural exports of Portuguese cultures and aesthetic tastes to India, identifying systems of patronage, and following certain Portuguese cultural traditions as they evolved through contacts with indigenous Goan culture. He discusses functional music, sacred music and musical activities at the College of St. Paul. He asks what can the history of Portuguese music in Goa tell us about the Portuguese in India.

A. Pereira tells us about the earliest chapels in Goa, the very modest structures, built quickly to satisfy immediate religious needs. They were later rebuilt, some of them several times over, so that there is nothing left of the 16th century in them. The foundation of a real Christian architectural tradition did not exist till the arrival of several religious Orders from Portugal. The Basilica of Bom Jesus in Goa shows all the influences from Portugal. One main problem while comparing these churches is to know which building served as a model for the other. In the 17th century the arrival of Orders directly from Italy brought new architectural traditions to Goa, we are informed.

P. Noronha attempts to project Old Goa in the context of Indian heritage, the scope of the presentation restricted to the architectural heritage of India in relation to religious monuments. With the establishment of religious orders in Goa in the 16th century, an intense conversion drive started and at the same time an increasing number of religious buildings were being raised. A gradual transition from the rigid Portuguese Gothic (Manueline) of the early days, through Italian Renaissance style down to the admirable outline of the great gilted Boroque, is noticeable in them.

F. Rebello probes the evolution of *Bazarucos* of Portuguese India, their classifications and value. There are difficulties in assessing them in some cases where the records do not tally or due to the availability of documents without actual coins to support them. Rebello suggests that one follow the changes of the lower denomination coins and arrive at a realistic reclassified evaluation. From 1510 onwards new coinage struck in Goa included the *leal, dinheiro* and *cepaica.* Newer issues both with regard to their equivalent values as well as to composition of the metals used gradually aggravated the Goan situation rather than brought about any monetary stability. A problem that emerges in the study of Indo-Portuguese coins is the uncertainty about the mintings having been executed in accordance with the *Assentos* or decisions of the *Conselho da Fazenda,* since there is evidence that the workshops were not necessarily following orders faithfully.

PART 4: Teotónio de Souza discusses "The Portuguese in the Goan folklore"; George Coelho "*Desassossego* in Luso-Indian Goan Poetry"; Athos Fernandes "Influence of Portuguese Language and Culture in Daman"; Engelbert Jorissen "16 March 1554: Reflections on a mid-sixteenth century scene in Goa"; Thomas Strater "From Peregrination to pilgrimage: Tabucchi's *Notturno Indiano*", Helmut Siepmann "Goa in the novel *O Signo da Ira* by Orlando da Costa"; Thomas Malten "Antam de Proença's *Tamil-Portuguese Dictionary*, printed in India 1679" and Dieter Kapp "Dravidian Borrowings from Portuguese (Kannada and Telugu)"

T. de Souza analyses some Konkani proverbs and a few folk songs which evoke historical events and convey native reaction to those events and the native perceptions of the colonial attitudes implied by them. The folk expressions are seen as filters of the native sensibilities, constituting the sedimentation of the folk memory with references to the Portuguese colonial presence in Goa. These expressions have survived the dulling effect of time. Popular culture is an expression of the historic identity of a people and as such it is a process in constant evolution.

G. Coelho refers to the dominant themes of Goan poetry written in Portuguese in this century. They define complex interacting elements in the Indo-Portuguese cultural crucible that moulded the Goan poetic temper. His essay delineates the salient aesthetic features of Goan sensibility that was influenced by the village *comunidades* and Portuguese education. Goan poets tell their people's story as lived and owned by Goans themselves. They rejoice in the beauty and bounty of their land, river, hill, lake and stream, church towers and palm trees casting a spell over the seashores of the islands of Goa.

A. Fernandes describes Daman, one of the main centres of trade and commerce under Portuguese rule since 1559 and deals with Portuguese culture in Daman as seen in its linguistic form, its dialects, uses, and customs. Daman had many colleges, convents, seminaries and churches which became centres of attraction for neighbouring areas. The influence of Christianity is reflected in the devotion of the people, seen most clearly in the devotion to São Gonçalo de Amarante.

E. Jorissen tells us why 16 March 1554 was an important day in Goa. The morning of that day saw crowds of people as hardly ever before seen in Goa come to see the body of St. Francis Xavier which had been brought to Goa. Among the curious onlookers were Garcia da Orta (1500-1568), Fernão Mendes Pinto (1509-1583) and Luis Frois (1532-1597), all acquainted with Xavier. The three used their literary works as an answer to the negative side of European 16th century expansion. The harsh reality with which da Orta, Pinto and Frois were confronted became a catalyst for them to 'digest' what they had seen in literary forms which they developed over the already existing limits.

T. Strater shows interesting insights into the work of António Tabucchi. He starts with Somerset Maugham's excerpt from his *Notebook* which reveals a foreigner's disparaging remarks about India. Tabucchi's *Notturno* has themes like the quest for identity, mirrors and mirages, and the role of Goa, the real and imagined. The book is about a search for Xavier Janata Pinto, a mix of St. Francis Xavier and Fernão Mendes Pinto. The persons who appear are merely shadows from another world, according to Strater, for the book he says is "a cat and mouse game, a do it yourself kit, a riddle".

H. Siepmann discusses the novel *O Signo da Ira* of Orlando da Costa and says it is not a atemporal novel in the sense of a creation without historicity or of a philosophical construction. Its reference-cover is the time when the Japanese troops were stationed in South East Asia and in Bengal during Second World War, and a village in Goa, where the presence of Portuguese troops excites a certain disquiet within the local population. The scene, the time and the climatic conditions, these are what structure the novel. A certain happening in the village leads to unknown and strange fears which in turn provoke unforeseen reactions. The novel calls for renunciation in favour of an ideal humanism in the world touched by regional and historical elements and Siepmann manages to concentrate in a few figures many aspects and problems of social life in Goa in the middle of the 20th century.

Antam de Proença's *Tamil-Portuguese Dictionary* printed in India in 1679 is examined by T. Malten in the context of the linguistic contacts of the Portuguese with the South Indian Tamil language as exemplified by the earliest printed lexicographical works. The *Tamil Portuguese Dictionary* or *Vocabulário Tamulico (VT)*, printed in the Jesuit missionary station Ambalakad in 1679 is the earliest specimen of a printed dictionary of any Indian language. On the Portuguese side it contains the collected lexicographical knowledge of over 150 years of linguistic contact with the main language and literature of South India and is a first attempt to define a prose standard of Tamil based on text corpora.

D. Kapp shows that Portuguese was the first European language with which the Dravidian-speaking peoples of the Indian sub-continent came into contact. Though the Portuguese period in India was short, its influence, particularly on the languages of the peoples of South India was remarkable. Portuguese was spoken in its pure or corrupt form throughout the whole of India, Malaysia, Pegu, Burma, Siam, Tonquin, Cochin-China, China, Kamaran, and Mecca. One can study sources for loan-words from Portuguese in Dravidian languages, with works available for studies dealing with Dravidian borrowings from Portuguese, and for Tamil.

The above articles offer a rich fare of how Portugal has had a deep influence on the culture of Goa in particular and how through Goa it moved further afield. Has the influence been good? Though inevitable, reactions to it are varied and present day studies point to where one needs to draw the line in various forms of assimilation. In this connection the Afterword of Dr. Michael Jansen serves as a timely warning.

I am grateful to Prof. Dr. Helmut Feldmann, Vice-Director, Centro Mundo Lusófono, Cologne for his guidance in jointly editing this volume. I thank his staff for their assistance in dispatching various notices to the contributors. And a word of thanks to the XCHR Office Assistant Ms. Ernesta Bhobe for her capable typing of the entire text.

31 JULY 1997

FR. CHARLES J. BORGES, S.J.
Director,
Xavier Centre of Historical Research

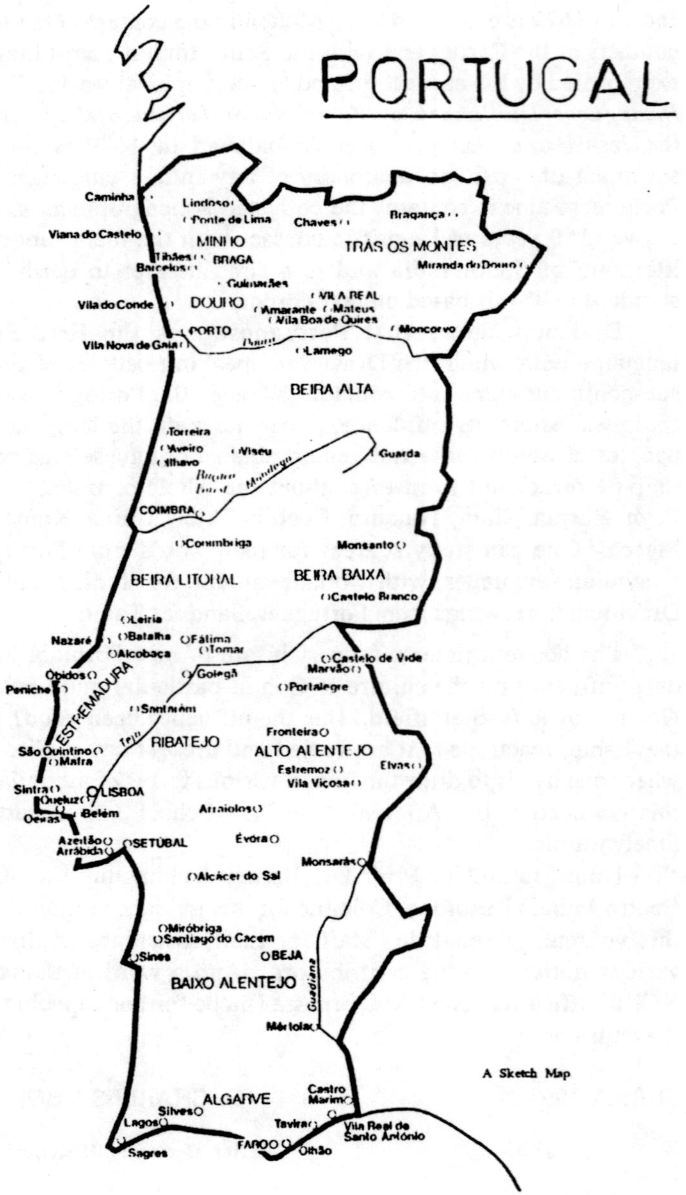

Map 1: Portugal

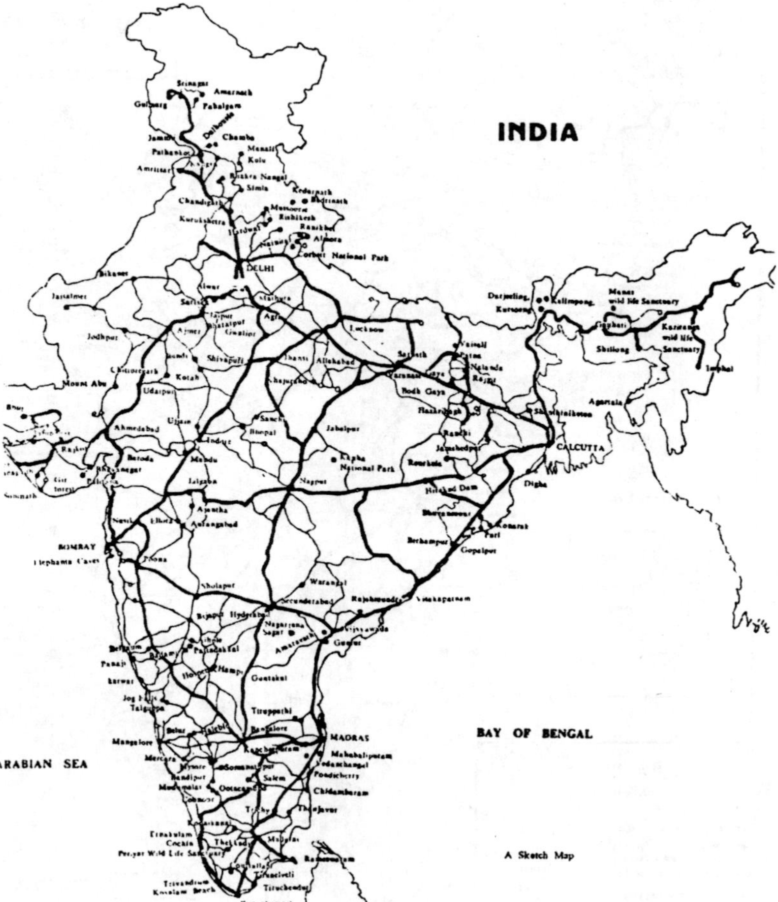
INDIA
Srinagar
Amarnath
Gulmarg
Pahalgam
Dalhousie
Chamba
Jammu
Pathankot
Manali
Kulu
Amritsar
Simla
Kedarnath
Chandigarh
Mussoorie
Rishikesh
Kurukshetra
Hardwar
Almora
Corbett National Park
DELHI
Bikaner
Jaisalmer
Alwar
Mathura
Agra
Jaipur
Ajmer
Gwalior
Jodhpur
Lucknow
Sarnath
Jhansi
Allahabad
Shivapuri
Patna
Nalanda
Rajgir
Mount Abu
Kotah
Udaipur
Khajuraho
Varanasi
Bodh Gaya
Sanchi
Ujjain
Bhopal
Ahmedabad
Jabalpur
Indore
Baroda
Rajkot
Mandu
Kanha
National Park
Ranchi
Jamshedpur
Rourkela
Nagpur
Hirakud Dam
Ajantha
Aurangabad
Nasik
Ellora
BOMBAY
Poona
Konarak
Puri
Berhampur
Gopalpur
Sholapur
Warangal
Secunderabad
Hyderabad
Nagarjuna
Sagar
Guntur
Pattadakal
Hampi
Panaji
Karwar
Guntakal
Tiruppathi
Bangalore
MADRAS
Mangalore
Mercara
Mysore
Mahabalipuram
Pondicherry
Salem
Chidambaram
Ooctacamund
Trichy
Thanjavur
Ernakulam
Cochin
Madurai
Periyar Wild Life Sanctuary
Rameswaram
Tirunelveli
Tiruchendur
Trivandrum
Kovalam Beach
Kanyakumari
Darjeeling
Kalimpong
Kurseong
Manas
wild life Sanctuary
Shillong
Kaziranga
wild life
Sanctuary
Imphal
Agartala
CALCUTTA
Digha
BAY OF BENGAL
A Sketch Map

Map 2: India

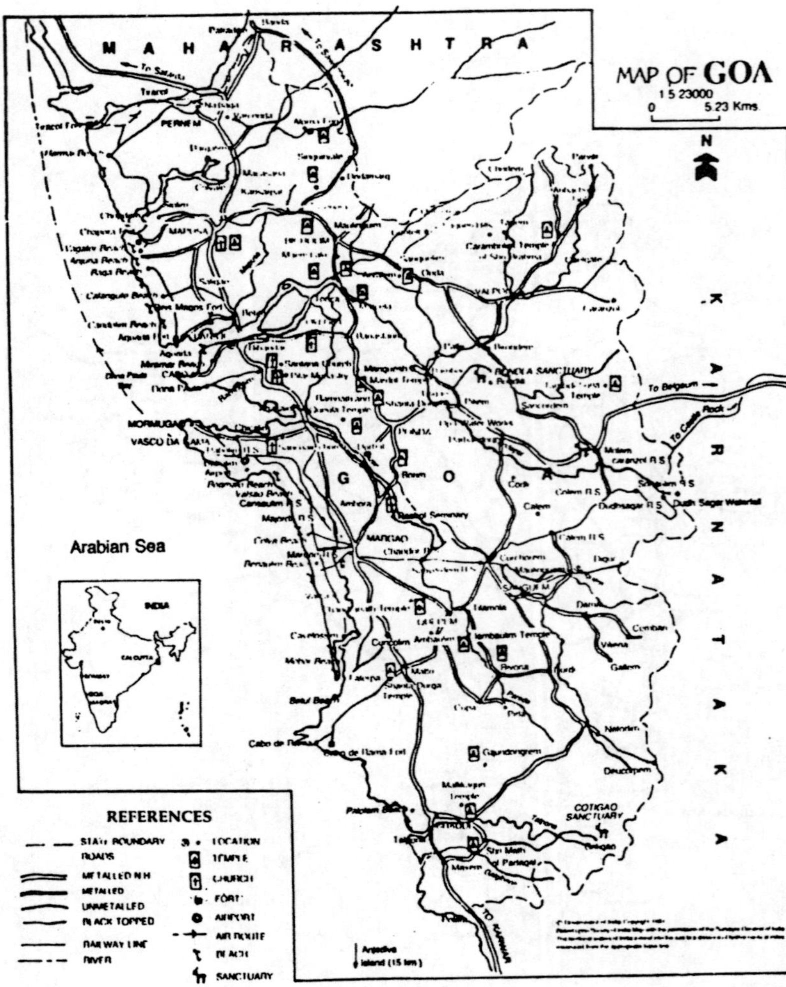

A Sketch Map

Map 3: Goa

PART I

GOA AND PORTUGAL AND THEIR VARIOUS CULTURAL RELATIONS

ONE

SOCIO-CULTURAL LIFE IN GOA DURING 16TH CENTURY

P. P. SHIRODKAR

When Afonso de Albuquerque conquered Goa on 25 November 1510, Goan society which was groaning under the Muslim rule of young Adil Khan beset with internal rivalries, submitted itself to the new fate in store for it under an altogether alien rule of the whites, who were hitherto unknown to it. The new conquerors during the capture of the city of Goem (Old Goa), almost annihilated and exterminated the Muslim soldiers, the pretty widows of some of whom were encouraged by him to have a fresh conjugal alliance with his Portuguese gentry stationed in Goa.

Prior to this queer rehabilitation of the helpless widows, Albuquerque while reducing the imports a bit in the newly conquered Tiswadi islands, assured the residents (mostly Hindus), that they would be obliged to the Portuguese king for their inheritance, rent money, taxes and charges which they used to earlier pay their kings and lords of the land and he would protect their rights and customs.[1] He did not change the existing basic administrative set-up. Gradually, the Portuguese began to introduce their own system of administration and established the *Senado de Goa, Fazenda, Alfandegas, Casa da Moeda*, etc. But at the same time they were extremely cautious not to disturb the age-old existing traditional indigenous institutions like *Tanadaria, Gaoncaria*, the office of *Catual*, etc. since the local populace was very attached to them in carrying out their socio-religious activities.

Nevertheless, Albuquerque boasted of having converted Goa into "the mother of the whole of India".[2] While it is extremely difficult to imagine what made him attribute such a high status to Goa, it may be surmised that Goa being centrally located on the west coast of India with easy access to the Far East and Europe, he must have thought it had the central position in their expected future conquests in the East.

Much reliable information about the life in Goa of the early period of the conquest of Goa is available in *A Suma Oriental* penned by the apothecary of Prince D. Afonso who came to Goa in 1511 as Factor of Drugs. Tomé Pires describes vividly the life and the people of Goa at the time. He reveals that the caravans of fully loaded bullock-carts coming from far-off lands outside Goa brought merchandise and the merchants enjoyed much as compared to the situation they had to face with the Muslims at the helm of affairs prior to the arrival of the Portuguese. Goa, according to him, was a haven for the traders from all the nations and the men with enormous capital had a number of ships with the good port to thrive. The people who plied their ships were the local residents who were good seafarers. Their business being on a grand scale, the revenue earned by Goa in the anchorage as well as duties on goods besides the toll levied through *Tanadarias*, offices of the chief local police with military authority to collect imports and customs levies, was enormous. Thus Goa soon after the Portuguese conquest earned dues from all sources annually to the tune of four lakh *pardaos* of gold each valued at 335 *réis*.

Pires believed that Goa had more rich and honoured citizenry with a lot of fortune and almost the whole land was dependent on them. They lived respectably merrier and luxuriant lives than those of the citizens from Cambay, another important port town on the east coast in the Rann of Kutch. He disclosed that these rich people of Goa had numerous temples with brahmin priests of varied manner, some of whom for generations did not eat any item with blood nor did they consume any food prepared by others. They were held in high esteem all over and their services were also utilized for carrying the goods and letters safely by land. The people of Goa without torture confessed everything that they did and suffered immensely various types of tortures patiently and before death they would confess their determination to keep certain secrets. The women of Goa, according to him had the knack of dressing well and their way of dancing and swinging round and round was much applauded all over. It was customary for a woman to immolate herself on the pyre of her husband. If in case she refused to sacrifice her life on the fire, her relatives were dishonoured and the people would admonish others not in favour of the sacrifice and force them to immolate themselves. Those women who would refuse to sacrifice on any pretext would become public prostitutes and they would earn for the maintenance and the construction of the temples. This gives credence to the not oft-repeated view that the caste of dancing girls of *devadasis* was the creation of the kinsmen of such hapless women not only in Goa but all over India who on account of the male-oriented, selfish, weird tradition forced their own womenfolk to enter into the despicable life. It also implied that the destitute women from all castes and classes in India who abstained from being *sati* were forcibly drawn together to create the devadasi system and in turn the new caste in anthropological terms.[3] However, it goes to the credit of Albuquerque to put a stop to this pernicious and inhuman practice on humanitarian basis,[4] a step which was the first of its kind on the soil of India.

Touching upon other ports in Goa, Pires has recorded that the rice, betel leaves and the areca nuts were in great demand there. The areca nuts of Goa were of very good quality and they were highly rated and exported to far off ports like Aden, Hormuz and Cambay.[5]

But what is infinitely more important is that Goan Hindu society of the period under discussion was not different from its counterparts in the rest of the country. It was a caste-ridden, tradition-bound, conservative, extremely religious-minded, pious, socially well-knit, morally at a higher level, much conscious about customs, rites and rituals and very possessive of its property and deities. As in other parts of India, they strictly followed the *Manusmriti*, code of Manu which was accepted by the Indians as Hindu law and jurisprudence. Since it was older than *Dharmashastras* or Brahmanical legal manuals, it was considered by the Hindus for the last hundreds of years as the most important work after the *Vedas*, though of late it is derided as biased. But in older times, the people of India fully adhered to it because it laid down moral and ethical precepts for the general guidance of the Hindus and formulated the rules and regulations, customs, rites and ceremonies. No Hindu in the country could go against it and hence it was held to be absolutely binding on the Hindus of all castes and creeds. It almost carried the weight of law, giving divine sanction to the institution of caste and endorsing its continuity. This being the general situation in the entire Indian peninsula, tiny Goa was no exception at all though it underwent the ignominy of being ruled by several dynasties and sovereigns over the centuries followed by the Portuguese.

At the time of the fall of Goa in the hands of the Portuguese, its population, majority of whom were Hindus, followed by the Muslims mostly on military duty continued to live in villages with its agricultural communities. Originally these villages belonged to the settlers namely ganvkars, and it is they who managed the village administration from time unknown. This system prevailed throughout the Indian peninsula. The villagers under the system of *comunidades* or *gaoncaria* had their common rights and interests in their occupied lands. They followed the Hindu law of inheritance. Manu determined that the sovereign did not have the right over one-fifth of the gross produce. But, as in Indian mainland, in Goa too the rulers used to extract as much imposts as they liked thereby putting the populace to great hardships. Such was the situation when Adilshah had to give up Goa to the Portuguese, who on conquest assured the populace that they would allow them to pay as much as they did to their predecessors.[6]

But in the meanwhile another scenario which was changing the demographic profile of Goa was gradually emerging. Within a decade and a half in 1524, the Portuguese who married and settled in Goa totalled 450 besides several others including fidalgos, knights and shield-bearers and other individuals of merit who had scattered outside the city with sons and daughters of marriageable age who by their nature were populating the land creating thereby ethnic changes.[7]

Though the Portuguese right from the beginning made constant efforts to have full control over revenue administration against the odds of allowing the traditional rights and customs, it was not so easy for them because of the powerful lobby of the ganvkars. Nevertheless, Albuquerque dared to select his own man João Machado, a Portuguese, as the *tanadar* of the city of Goa in 1515[8] ignoring the claims of the local. However, by 1523, the situation seems to have taken a reverse turn. When Krishna was heading the *tanadaria*, the regimen had been issued giving the clear indication that the rights and customs as per the contract during the conquest of the territory would be continued to be maintained without any changes.[9] But this softening of the stand did not last long. Afonso Mexia, Overseer of the Revenue of India who on his own, independent of the Viceroy or Governor was working on the idea to regulate the uses and customs of ganvkars and peasants of the Tiswadi island. And he did not succeed, when Dom João, king of Portugal duly approved it and it was put into operation from 16 September 1526 in the form of *Foral dos uzos e costumes os gancares e lavradores desta ilha de Goa e outros annexos nela,*[10] (Charter of uses and customs of ganvkars and peasants of the island of Goa and other territories annexed to it).

This Charter was one of the most significant events after the occupation. It not only had the imprint on it of the Portuguese domination and assertion of the rule but also gave a sudden twist to the socio-religious life of the Goans besides making revolutionary changes in the village administration. It empowered Viceroys, chief tanadars, revenue overseers, magistrates of justice to such an extent that their orders, decisions and judgements gave rise to the plethora of social legislations in the years to come thereby raising the influence of jurisprudence in the day to day life of the Goans.

The Charter which had the preamble and 48 articles touched upon civil law, penal and fiscal legislation, and even the rural economy of the *comunidades* and civic issues.

The Charter exhorted (Articles 6-8) the ganvkars of 31 villages[11] to pay the Portuguese administration a certain share of the revenue as per the Charter, which the ganvkars of each village with the help of the scribe distributed and gave in auction to the peasants and persons who had their inheritance within the boundaries of each village and this process would be carried out under the condition with which it was given to each one according to their uses and customs. The said ganvkars were to collect taxes and pay the said revenue whether it swelled or waned. They would bear the loss or increase and it was left for them and the concerned village to compensate the loss or procure a part of the increase for the persons whom it belonged by their customs. Only exception was to be made to the loss in case of war when it was not to be paid proportionately in respect of their loss. The aforesaid increase or loss of each year would be distributed as free pay since every one paid the taxes on the lands or the paddy fields that he held. Some palm-groves and paddy-field growers were asked to pay annually some unspecified *tangas*. In the event of any losses, they were exempted from doing so.

Each one of the ganvkars was asked to give grounds in his village being unoccupied, gratis to put to good use or to be utilized, by the officials of the village, namely, priest of the temple, clerk, porter, tenant, washerman, cobbler, carpenter, blacksmith and *farash* and mistresses of the temple and a jester. Any ganvkar was prevented from giving either any grounds or orchards gratis simply by paying a certain rent except authorized by the ordinance to that effect. If the ganvkar or the person from the village wanted to sell any inheritance in any of the said villages he was prevented from doing so without the permission of all the ganvkars of the village. And thus likewise nobody could buy without the said permission.

If any man being married to two women had four sons from one and one from the other or more or less, though not equal in numbers, then the sons would divide the property of the father and the division would be made in halves. One son would take as much as the four or three sons and no daughter would inherit the property of the father or of the mother.

None was allowed to bring flambeau, palanquin and umbrella without the permission of the revenue overseer or Governor except if it was owned by the one as an inheritance from their fathers and grand-fathers and the said license was to be given to them in two days only on account of the graces of their services. There were two types of such licenses. One was for bringing umbrella and palanquin with the attendants and flambeau and oil at their cost. Another license was receiving the honour by the authorities along with the attendants in which case the cost of the oil was to be paid by the authorities. The male and female dancers who used to go to celebrate the village festival would go first at the residence of the principal ganvkar and subsequently if they desired to visit anyone's house, it would remain open to them. The ganvkars would honour them with betel or any other honour and they would receive them standing together with arms crossed keeping the right hand below the left hand for showing more respect.

During the seeding time and during the time of harvest, the principal ganvkar would have first preference in ploughing and harvesting. Likewise, the main ganvkar would cover his house first by the leaves of the palm-trees namely *ollas*. The village of Taleigao had the prominence and it had the first preference in harvesting of paddy fields. Its ganvkars would come in groups each year with cluster of new crops to present it before the main altar of the Sé. From there, the Vicar would go with them to the trading post and the Factor would honour them with four *pardaos* in *pachodi* putting them around their necks. Whenever there was any invitation for a feast or gathering in which there was a practice of receiving betel or *pachodi*, the principal ganvkar of each village was to receive the honour first followed by others, according to the custom and practice.

It is worthwhile to have a peep into religious life of the Goans of the day which was totally disrupted and subsequently ruined on account of the terrible onslaught on Hinduism and the Hindus. The pre-dominant Goan Hindu society had been greatly influenced by the Nath cult, also known as Yoga, Siddha or Avadhut cults. In this cult, the teacher has an unusual and pre-eminent position. It believes that the Shakti creates the universe, Siva nurtures it and time destroys it and Natha brings *mukti* (freedom). Natha is the only pure soul whereas the rest are mere human beings.[12] It does not recognize the caste system.[13] Perhaps this was the main reason for the attraction to it of the people all over the country, including Goa. The Nath[14] cult must have spread in Goa since the 12th century. The patronage of Kadambas to Saptanatha and its temple at Naroa must have given it a sudden boost leading to its spread all over Goa so much so that most of the temples of Goa in Ilhas, Bardez and Salcete belonged to the larger Saiva sect and Nath cult, the remaining being of the Vaishnavite sect.[15]

It is discerned from the letter of D. João III to the city of Goa that right since the conquest of Goa, there was a practice among the Goans that whenever they wanted to prove something they used to resort to the practice of taking a vow on the betel leaf, cow or buffalo dung and salt. Those who took such vows were considered upright. But the system resulted in several cases of falsehood and several unjust punishments had been meted out thus. Therefore, Governor Nuno de Cunha had issued an *alvará* emphasizing that all such vows should be taken in the Mahalaxmi temple at Bandora, outside the Portuguese occupied territory because that was the only temple where such a practice was in vogue.[16]

While the Hindus were leading their life as per the age-old practices, a consistent effort was on since 1518 by the Franciscans who had already initiated the Christianity anew after St. Thomas, at Anjediv island off Goa in 1505. Friar António had pleaded with the king of Portugal that he should not allow the yogis to enter Goa from the mainland because they brought with them the flowers offered to their deities in the temples and other tokens with the help of which they tried to renew the heathen traditions of the indigenous people.[17] Bishop de Dumenas mentioning about the existence of the 'images of the enemies of the Cross' on the island recommended to the king that it would be a great service to God if the temples on the island of Goa were demolished and in their place churches built. He further suggested that the king should issue an order that anyone desiring to live on the island and have a residence and lands should convert himself to be a Christian and in case he did not opt for it, he should leave the island. He was of the firm belief that none on the island could remain without being converted because if driven out of the island they would not be able to sustain themselves.[18]

Nevertheless, the new orientation was given to religious persecution by Miguel Vaz, the new Vicar General who arrived in Goa in 1532. This was followed by the upgradation of Goa to the bishopric in 1534 though it did not merit it on account of the sparse population of Christians. In 1541 the Church introduced an element of *Rigor de Misericordia* in Goa resulting in the destruction and devastation of all the temples on the island. Further, the important Hindu ganvkars were forced to accede voluntarily the siphoning of the revenue of the lands of the desecrated temples amounting to 2,000 *tangas brancas* annually for the maintenance of the newly-erected churches, chapels and the evangelists thereby depriving the guravs, dancing-girls, brahmins, blacksmiths and other servants of their livelihood. Not only this, but the steps were ordered to appoint native priests as chaplains because the local people could accept them with contentment as they would prefer to learn easily from them on account of the absence of the language barrier.[19]

Tracing the course of events, in April 1541 Padre Miguel Vaz and Diogo de Borba established Confraternity of Holy Faith to render help to the poor Christians and for the upkeep of the churches. It was also instrumental in erecting the Seminary of Holy Faith and the College of St. Paul to impart education for the youth of the East in priesthood.[20] Confraternity also sought preference for the Christians in the government postings. In the following year landing of the Jesuit missionary Mestre Francisco Xavier in Goa on 6 May 1542 gave such a boost to the process of evangelization in Goa and elsewhere in the South as well as in the Far East that the social fabric in Goa was torn giving rise to turbulence in the indigenous population which was virtually uprooted ultimately in the years to come in the wake of the Inquisition which was in store for them within the next two decades.

One of the articles of the statutes of the *Confraria da Conversão a Fé* was that it should take care to see that the gentiles neither re-erected their temples nor built new ones. And it desired to take steps against the brahmins who insulted the Christians. It emphasized that the new converts should be made to work in such a manner that they did not live a bad life with idleness and in case they did not improve, they should be fed from Confraria but their parents should be forced to pay for their sustenance or leave their inheritance for them.[21]

Leaving nothing to chance, Vaz sent a note to the king, which was received by him in November 1545 seeking a special order that on the island of Goa, there should not be any public or secret temple and the violators of it should be punished severely. He recommended that no idols of wood, stone, copper or any other metal should be allowed to be made. He suggested further that no public festival of the gentiles should be permitted and the brahmins from the mainland should be prevented from taking shelter in their houses. He wanted the Crown to allow the authorities of St. Paul to raid the houses of the brahmins and the gentiles if they suspected the existence of the idols there. He also wanted that no unfaithful native (Hindu) should be allowed to earn his living by painting sacred Christian images. He wished that the Goans who went to Bassein and Diu should be driven out from there thereby allowing only the natives from there to live.[22] However, the resentment of the Goan natives is discernible from the letter of Master Diogo de Borba to the Jesuit priest Simão Rodrigues wherein he states that the Indian gentiles neither desired to know nor wanted to hold in high esteem the holy name. With their enormous ways of worshipping idolatry and so-monstrous customs they never wanted to submit themselves to the truth and charity of Jesus Christ.[23]

Realizing the harsh realities, the Crown seems to have acted with vehemence on the recommendations of Mestre Miguel Vaz. He ordered Governor Martim Afonso de Souza to punish severely, even without accepting the appeal those who continued to perpetuate idolatry of any kind and allow the newly-converted to enjoy the exemptions and liberties in payment of duties permitting them to avail of the privileges and honours which the gentiles were accustomed to enjoy before. The Governor was also instructed to exempt the Christians from India from being recruited forcibly in the

Portuguese armed forces thereby avoiding violence. He was further instructed to punish those Portuguese who on buying the slaves at a cheaper rate were selling them subsequently to the Muslims from across the borders at a higher premium. It was desired that such slaves should be converted to the Christian faith. Governor was also urged upon to render assistance to the evangelists in their conversion activity by charging the annual duty of 300 *pardaos* on mosques. The Crown reminded him that it had been informed of the ill-treatment to the newly-converted natives by their parents and friends who deprived them of their houses and possessions violently thereby forcing them to lead a miserable life. It counselled the governor to alleviate their difficulties in consultation with Padre Miguel Vaz.[24]

Keeping in line with the trend, the Crown directed the new Viceroy, Dom João de Castro to treat well and favour the new converts among the natives in such a way that they should be allowed to occupy all the posts in the city of Goa and the villages of the island. He also ordered the Viceroy to establish the schools in those villages where the conversions had taken place to teach them *Doutrina Christa*.[25] In the instructions issued to Padre Miguel Vaz, the king asked him to put his efforts in the mainland carefully without any scandals, by removing all the idols and planting in their places the crosses, where the neo-Christians could be taught whatever possible of the religion so that it could help more conversion.[26]

It is observed that the residents had still the attachment towards the temple lands usurped by the Colégio de Santa Fé. While they continued to procure clandestinely the items produced in those properties, the stringent law was made to imprison them forcing them as well to pay the rent for the entire period during which they indulged in this type of activity.[27] Considering the population of the island of Goa in 1548 of nearly 40,000, one can imagine how extensive could be the offenses of this nature committed in the island. Another noteworthy feature among the Hindus was that though Albuquerque had abolished the practice of widow-burning soon after the conquest, the practice appeared to have continued.[28] It took more than a decade for its total abolition by Viceroy Dom Constantino de Bragança on 30 June 1560 by inflicting the severe punishment to the abettors in the crime by putting them under permanent captivity after confiscating all their estates, half of which would go to the accuser and the remaining half would be spent towards the construction works of the house of Apostle St. Thomas.[29]

In the meanwhile, the Crown had totally stopped the review of granting fresh privileges to certain persons by the governors and captains in India.[30] He had also enforced the rule that the moment the slaves of the Muslims and the Hindus who would convert themselves to be Christians, their owners should sell them immediately to the Christians alone.[31] Worse still, no brahmin or gentile was to hold any administrative post whatsoever. If anyone was found continuing to be so, not only he would lose his posting, he would also be held captive besides forfeiting his estate, half of which would go to the accuser and half would go to the government treasury.[32] The Crown in a shrewd move to give further boost to evangelization ordered that the residents and the natives if converted to Christianity would enjoy the same status in the city and island of Goa as those of the Portuguese.[33] A deep sense of skepticism was pervading the minds of the gentiles when one after the other laws were passed in rapid succession to deprive them of their age-old rights. King D. Sebastião passed one more such law ordering that there should be neither temples nor idols in anybody's houses nor outside it, in the island of Goa and other adjoining areas any more. He also put restrictions on all sorts of festivities by the gentiles either in their residences or outside, besides ban on all types of image-making. Anybody going against this law would lose his estate, half of which would go to the accuser and the remaining half would be utilized for the works of the church under the jurisdiction of which resided the culprit who would be sent to the galleys without any pardon.[34] By another law, the sons, grandsons and relatives were allowed to inherit the estate of their converted parents, whether they be gentiles or Muslims or the other unfaithful persons as per Portuguese law. In case they got themselves converted, they would each inherit third part of the property.[35] The introduction of these prejudicial laws not only created dissensions in the families permanently but also gave severe jolt to the joint family system which was turning apart for long but survived and grew up once again under two different faiths — Hinduism and Christianity.

This alienation of kith and kin and a sense of demoralization in the minds of the Hindus was not only on account of the pernicious laws of unimaginable dimensions but also on account of the deprivation of their temples, shrines, deities and idols in their own residential abodes. It had shaken the Hindu society to such an extent that it had to carve out its own future anew. They had only two options. One was to migrate and the other was to remain in the extremely servile condition accepting the new faith against their wishes.

The introduction of the most unholy pitiless Holy Inquisition in 1560 was the greatest blow, the Goans could ever imagine. The Jesuit Mestre Francis Xavier, who was later on canonized as the patron saint of the East was the first[36] to seek the establishment of the Inquisition in Goa way back in 1546 though it took 14 years for it to take a concrete shape. During 248 years of its existence, which could be cited as the blackest period in Indian religious history had no parallels elsewhere. In the words of Goan historian J.C. Barreto Miranda, "the cruelties which in the name of the religion of peace and love this tribunal practised in Europe, were carried to even greater excesses in India, where the Inquisition surrounded by luxuries which could stand comparison with the regal magnificence of the great potentates of Asia, saw with pride the Archbishop as well as the Viceroy submitted to their power. Every word of theirs was a sentence of death and their slightest nods moved to terror the vast populations spread over the Asiatic regions, whose lives fluctuated in their hands, and who, on the most frivolous pretext, could be clapped for all times in the deepest dungeons or strangled or offered as food for the flames of pyre.[37]

This great cataclysmic blot in history full of abominal tortures and horrendous annihilation of innocent human beings is better summarized in 1912 by the Portuguese author of repute, José F. Ferreira Martins. He pathetically lamented: "Hundred years have elapsed since the Inquisition ceased to exist in Portuguese India. But even today one who reads the history of this terrible institution does not comprehend how a people so heroic with peerless feelings of nobility amply proved and admired by the whole world could give consent to a so horrible Tribunal in Portugal and in her colonies".

"Pity on you oh convicts! Poor victims in sheepskin tunics and sackcloth on, were walking to undergo the final punishment! One by one they were walking to the burning pyres of the Inquisition. They were not allowed even to utter the last goodbye to those who were their dear ones in this world! There were no weepings, no cryings, no tear that might have weakened the rage of the terrible Inquisitors, who at the black covered main altar of St. Francis of Assisi Church at Old Goa were sitting on a throne having at their side the Viceroy, witness of nefarious act! Yes, witness but irresponsible on account of the terrible sentences and other proceedings of savage banditry resorted to under the garb of a false religiosity".[38]

The Inquisition triggered mass migrations as far as the south of the country. Many families were separated permanently. Some left their kith and kin behind to be converted or already converted prior to their escape. Many villages left with their deities and re-established them in the neighbouring Antruz and Sattari regions where they found security and safety. Considering the spate of baptisms in Tiswadi, according to Padre Lucena in one year itself to be of the order of 20,000 and in 1560 according to Padre F. de Souza, the number was 3092,[39] it was not at all surprising that the residents of the islands, Bardez and Salcete opted to flee away from the scene to avoid the ignominy of conversion to a new faith, totally alien to them. Though the Inquisitors prayed upon the neo-Christians who followed their earlier religious traditions and customs, their abettors and those who persuaded them not to embrace the Catholic faith were also subjected to Inquisition. Even a slight whisper against the Holy Office would invite punishment by the Inquisitors.

There is a reason to believe that most of the 159 temples in Ilhas were destroyed by Miguel Vaz after his return from Portugal, in October 1546 with wide powers and provisions.[40] In 1567, Diogo Rodrigues, captain of fort of Rachol razed to the ground 280 temples,[41] prominent among which was the temple of Mhalsa at Verna where the people from South Goa used to take solemn oath to prove their innocence. In the same year, nearly 300 temples from Bardez[42] were demolished by the Franciscans. The destruction of the temples *en masse* created an unimaginable impact on the Hindu populace making a terrible dent on their psyche from which they never recovered even after the abolition of the Inquisition in 1812.

In the backdrop of such a sombre setting, the social life in Goa appeared to be totally different from the day of the establishment of the Inquisition. Within a couple of years, the Crown emphasized to his authorities in Goa that the principal responsibility of the Crown in his conquests was that of conversions of the unfaithful. And being satisfied with the progress on this front, he urged upon them to make vigorous efforts with zeal to see that no unfaithful remained there without being converted.[43] As a shrewd move to entice more, the

Crown further ordered that when the wife got converted, the husband having refused to succumb to the new faith, all her jewellery and garments at the time of her conversion should be handed over to her and she would also have half the share of the movable property and the fields owned by him after the marriage.[44] This obviously led to several matrimonial discords and eventual separations.

Consequent to the introduction of the Inquisition, in 1561 the situation in Goa was such that the entire island was depopulated, the villages were lost, the tilled tracts of lands were inundated choking the river, the old Hindu residents did not desire to return as their properties and estates had been passed over to others.[45] And in 1563, the prescription was reinforced with the penalty of seizure and captivity at the galleys of those gentiles of any category with the exception of washermen, physicians, carpenters, blacksmiths, druggists, and the fiscal renters who were found not prejudicial to Christianity.[46]

Now the growth of Christianity was such that the first Concilio Provincial (provincial ecclesiastical assembly) was held in Goa in 1567. Some of the decrees which it passed created the suffocating atmosphere in Goa. For instance, decree No. 7 stated that those who on being converted induced others to follow the sects and their cults of superstitions would be subjected to grave punishment. This was more applicable to those who could not give up their old traditions in spite of being converted. So also was an offence if anyone impeded the conversion to Christianity of anyone, scandalizing or deriding him for his action or instilling fear in his mind that he would forfeit his castes, would be punished severely (decree No. 8). Taking note of the neophytes resorting to same old practices of worshipping the idolatry, the Synod at this assembly recommended to the Crown to destroy totally the idolatry and the un-Christian cult so that the demon was never venerated. Similarly, it also demanded the destruction of all mosques. It deliberated against all types of ceremonies and festivities and modes of worship, adoration of the demons like deities, cremation of the dead, and several other rites, invocations, fasting, processions, thread ceremony, applying sandalwood paste on the forehead, animal sacrifice, tree worship, etc. (decree Nos. 9-10). It also came heavily on those gentiles who went outside the Portuguese territories to participate in these festivities of the temples or to take part in the religious processions there (decree No. 11). The Synod also desired that in the villages when the plain lands were to be rented they should be given on the rental basis as per the Charter only to the Christians and not the gentiles, and the tax-gathering should be entrusted to Christians only (decree No. 15). It prohibited the Hindu painter to paint the images of divine cult, the goldsmith to make the chalices, crosses, melters and tin makers to make metal objects or tin items (decree No. 28). The synod also touched upon more personal aspects (decree No. 42). It prohibited the neophyte to attach the caste of his son. Nor could he allow his son to marry a Hindu girl. He was prevented from crying while mourning for his dead on the lines he used to before being converted. He was disallowed either to go to any temple or to offer any money. Worse still, if he were to be ill, no Hindu, even his own father was allowed to pay him the courtesy visit. He could neither attend any Hindu festival nor could he proceed in the adjacent territories on the mainland to share the joy of celebrating the feasts with the gentiles (decree No. 42). It advised the parish priest and the chaplain to help the neophytes to bury their dead (decree No. 45).[47]

Most of these decrees were legalized by the Viceroy D. Antão de Noronha.[48] As an incentive for the boost of Christianity, his successor D. Luis de Ataide removed the customs duties on the clothes which were to be distributed in the form of alms to the neo-Christians by the authorities of the College of São Paulo.[49]

Strange as it may seem, in spite of all the orders from the Crown or the Viceroys, the gentiles continued to carry on their old traditions of worshipping the idols as before even after two decades of the Inquisition. The situation therefore, forced the Crown to issue the fresh order in 1580 to stop the 'abominable mistakes' which were prejudicial to the conversions.[50]

In order to dissipate the continuous veneration of the 'false gods' the king instructed the viceroy to ensure the non-raising of the temples, prevention of the ceremonies and the public rites of the Hindus as well as Muslims. In the meanwhile many Portuguese, taking advantage of the weaknesses of ganvkars had unjustly usurped the gaoncarias thereby impoverishing the rightful holders of them violating the *Charter of Uses and Customs* of 1526.[51] The Crown realized the serious mischief committed by the Portuguese individuals and ordered the viceroy to restore those gaoncarias and the lands to the proper holders.[52] With a view to augment the conversions further, the neophytes were given the concession of non-payment of tithes for 15 years from the date of their conversion.[53] Besides, all the regulations and the privileges in favour of Christianity and conversions were confirmed with regard to all the Christians in the Portuguese-occupied territories.[54] Further, in a bid to soothe the ruffled feathers of the neophytes, the Crown allowed them to hold a public office.[55] Further, the posts were henceforth reserved only for the Christians and the brahmins and other gentiles were deprived to hold any public post under canon law.[56]

The 4th ecclesiastical assembly which was held in Goa in 1592 took serious note of the entry of the Hindu priests, astrologers, yogis, preachers and kurumbins into the city of Goa through the passes of the island, taking shelter in the houses of the Hindus and native Christians reminding the old and new Christians about their old rites and customs, feasts, thereby acting against the Christian faith. Hence, it recommended that such individuals should not be allowed in the city and if found should be jailed and punished and anyone giving them shelter should be fined 50 *cruzados* besides the punishment for the crime.[57]

If the above was the picture of the 16th century, by the end of the 17th century, the Portuguese with the help of the Church had succeeded to a great extent in converting a substantially large part of the Goan population to Christianity, mostly against their free will, thereby weaving a new fabric of the society at the cost of the gentiles who underwent innumerable odds and hurdles, suffered ignominy, lost their dear ones at the altar of the Inquisition, faced the galleys and deportation for the sake of sticking to their traditions, rights, customs and religious beliefs. No other sections of the Indian society must have suffered as much for sticking to assert their rights during the European expansion in India. The Inquisition would continue for many more years hanging like a Democles' sword over the head, and more pernicious laws were to follow under which the generations of Goans had to carve out their own destiny.

NOTES AND REFERENCES

1. Historical Archives of Goa (HAG): Monções do Reino (MR): *Foral dos uzos e costumes dos gancares e lavradores desta ilha de Goa e outros annexes ella*, No. 76, fl. 48 ff.

2. *Relatorio Annuário de Administração do Concelho da Ilhas*, Panaji, Imprensa Nacional, 1904, p. 762.
3. Armando Cortesão (ed.), *A Suma Oriental de Tomé Pires e o Livro de Francisco Rodrigues*, Coimbra, Univ. of Coimbra, 1978, p. 14.
4. Quoted by A.K. Priolkar, *The Goa Inquisition*, Mumbai, Univ. of Mumbai, 1961, p. 52.
5. No. 3, p. 218.
6. Antonio da Silva Rego (ed.), *Documentação para a História das Missões do Padroado Portuguez do Oriente*, vol. 4, Lisbon, Agencia Geral do Ultramar, p. 304.
7. *Ibid.*, p. 37.
8. Felippe Nery Xavier, *Colecção das Leis Peculiares das Comunidades agricolas dos Concelhos das Ilhas, Salcete e Bardez*, Panaji, Imprensa Nacional, 1852, p. 102.
9. *Ibid.*, p. 103.
10. *Ibid.*, p. 104; J. M. Teixeira Guimarães, *As Comunidades Indianas das Velhas Conquistas*, Panaji, Imprensa Nacional, 1885.
11. Neura o Grande, Gancim, Ella and other villages.
12. *Marathi Vishwakosh*, vol. 8, Mumbai, M.R. Sanskrit Mandal, 1979, p. 481.
13. L.M. Joshi, *Shri Navnath Tatvadnyan ani Upasana*, Mumbai, Gajan Book Depot, p. 41.
14. P. Shirodkar, "Nath-cult in Goa", *Goa: Cultural Trends*, ed. Shirodkar, Panaji, DAAM, 1988.
15. Priolkar, *op. cit*, pp. 69-70, 79-84.
16. Rego, *op. cit.*, vol. 4, pp. 208-210.
17. *Ibid.*, vol. 1, p. 354.
18. *Ibid.*, pp. 452-453.
19. *Ibid.*, pp. 292-303.
20. *Ibid.*, vol. 3, pp. 13-14; Anthony D'Costa, *The Christianisation of the Goa Islands*, Mumbai, 1965, pp. 32-33; A. Lopes Mendes, *A India Portuguesa*, Lisbon, Imprensa Nacional, 1886, p. 149.
21. Rego, *op. cit.*, vol. 3, p. 6.
22. *Ibid.*, pp. 203, 223-224.
23. *Ibid.*, p. 241.
24. *Ibid.*, pp. 316-317, 319-320.
25. *Ibid.*, pp. 323-324, 327, 329.
26. *Ibid.*, p. 261.
27. J. H. Cunha Rivara, *Archivo Portuguez Oriental*, fasc. 5, New Delhi, Asian Educational Services, 1992, pp. 218-219. (reprint)
28. Rego, *op. cit.*, vol. 4, p. 36.
29. HAG, No. 9529, *Provisões a favour de Christandade*, fl. 78v.
30. HAG, No. 8791, *Livro Vermelho da Relação*, fl. 29.
31. *Ibid.*, fl. 29v.
32. Rivara, *op. cit.*, pp. 319-320.
33. *Ibid.*, p. 387.
34. No. 30, fls. 41-42.

35. *Ibid.*, fl. 44v.
36. Rego, *op. cit.*, vol. 3, pp. 351-352.
37. Quoted by Priolkar, *op. cit.*, p. 30.
38. *História de Misericordia de Goa 1621-1910*, vol. 2, Panaji, Imprensa Nacional, p. 43.
39. Caetano F. de Souza, *Estudos Históricos Archaeologicos Instituições Portugueses de Educação e Instrucção no Oriente*, Mumbai, 1890, p. 40.
40. Francisco de Souza, *Oriente Conquistado a Jesu Christo*, Mumbai, Examiner, p. 15.
41. *Ibid.*, p. 15.
42. Rego, *op. cit.*, vol. 5, 1951, p. 408.
43. *Ibid.*, vol. 9, pp. 41-42.
44. *Ibid.*, pp. 47-48.
45. F.N. Xavier, *Bosquejo Histórico das Comunidades das Aldeas dos Concelhos das Ilhas, Salcete e Bardez*, vol. 1, Bastora, Rangel, 1903, p. 107.
46. *Ibid.*
47. Rivara, *op. cit.*, fasc. 4, pp. 11-14, 17, 24-25, 30-31.
48. *Ibid.*, pp. 69-75.
49. Rego, *op. cit.*, vol. 11, pp. 6-7.
50. Rivara, *op. cit.*, fasc. 5, pp. 967-969.
51. *Ibid.*, pp. 977-978.
52. Rego, *op. cit.*, vol. 12, p. 725.
53. *Ibid.*, pp. 726-727.
54. *Ibid.*, pp. 730-731.
55. HAG: *MR*, No. 93, fl. 351.
56. Rego, *op. cit.*, vol. 12, pp. 750-751.
57. Rivara, *op. cit.*, fasc. 4, p. 189.

TWO

THE IMPACT OF PORTUGUESE CULTURE ON GOA
A Myth or A Reality?

FÁTIMA DA SILVA GRACIAS

The pre-Portuguese culture of Goa was a product of her long interesting history; the result of being under the sway of various Muslim and Hindu dynasties. The pre-Portuguese culture of Goa was a fusion of Jain, Buddhist, Muslim and Hindu influences. It was different from the western culture and in some ways superseded the culture of the west.

The Portuguese when they conquered Goa from Adilshah of Bijapur, brought along their own culture which was also a blend of cultures mainly Latin and Moorish. We imbibed some elements of the Portuguese culture but at the same time maintained many existing elements of our rich culture. B. B. Borkar, Goan poet and writer referring to Goan culture says, "The virility and vitality of this quiet, soft-mannered and peace loving society's culture were tested and proved beyond doubt when in the sixteenth century the Portuguese conquerors of Goa tried fanatically to uproot it completely. Though partially impaired under the onslaught of superior arms and administrative machinery, it not only outlived it but even absorbed some good and progressive features of their Latin culture".[1]

By culture, we mean human creations that is all that man has made in the form of material goods, all that man has elaborated in the way of attitudes, beliefs, ideas and judgements, codes, institutions, arts, sciences, religion and philosophy.

The unique Goan identity or non-identity has been in focus in recent years and has been subject of much discussions. The opinions or views have differed regarding the impact of the

Portuguese rule on Goa.

These views could be divided in three categories: that which believes that the Portuguese rule left no impact or rather a superficial impact, second view is of those who feel that the Portuguese culture left a powerful impress on Goa and yet a third view that points out that the Portuguese culture only touched a particular community and that too only people of higher social status and not the majority of Goans.

Those who hold the first view feel that over 450 years of Portuguese rule were in vain and that there was only a superficial impact of Portuguese culture on Goa. According to them Goa is like the rest of India. One has remarked, "Goa is an extension of Maharashtra (a large neighbouring state) — an extension of the rest of India minus its grinding poverty, illiteracy and teeming population. The differences if any are only superficial. The core of Goa is very Maharashtrian — except for the Portuguese rule and its adverse consequences".[2]

However, a Brazilian architect-visitor to India, Ana Cristina Santos Parreiras, refutes this view. She says, "Goa is more like Brazil rather than rest of India. The lifestyle differs between Goa and rest of India specially when it comes to the ways of dealing with the people, table manners, clothing and more so Goans have a great sense of humour not found, for instance, in south of India".

Manohar Malgonkar remarks, "Goans are markedly different from other Indians. In part, of course, it is the legacy of their language Konkani but to greater extent, it is the influence of the convivial and informal ways of the Portuguese national character that has taken root and grown strong in the soil of Goa".[3] The statement that Goan ethos owes little to the Portuguese influence might not sound convincing to those who feel that Goa's unique character sets them apart from rest of India. Among those who believe that the Portuguese culture left a significant impact on Goa is the Goan architect Lucio Miranda. Saryu Doshi writes, "The Portuguese have left their impress on the attitude and the life styles of the people of Goa and given the place a definite, identity of its own".[4] Among those who hold the third view is Prabhakar Angle. Angle writes that "with exception of *descendentes* and a very small section of affluent Christians who adopted European habits, the rest of the population of Goa is not different from rest of India. Hindus and Muslims did not suffer any modifications in their lifestyles by their contact with the Portuguese".[5]

Some of my Hindu colleagues do not accept the view — that the Hindus have not been influenced by the Portuguese culture. They state they have been touched by the Portuguese culture. The Konkani language they speak at home has many Portuguese words. In addition, they say that the Portuguese influence has made them in some ways more liberal and sophisticated than their counterparts of same social status elsewhere in India.

Given the fact that eastern and western cultures parleyed for a considerable length of time in Goa, it is but natural that Goan culture should be influenced by the culture of the rulers. Goa has a distinctive culture and it can be certainly attributed to the Portuguese to some extent. Although the Portuguese influence is more pronounced on the Christians, the Hindus are nonetheless influenced by Portuguese way of life. Goa is perhaps the first place in this globe where the East met the West — where there has been mingling of both cultures for the first time. This cultural encounter had both positive and negative impact. In many ways it has contributed to enrich our culture.

Several major factors have contributed to the formation of Goan identity and spread of Portuguese culture in Goa. The most important, it is the Catholic Church. The Catholic Church played a significant role in Goa not only in spreading a new belief but also in shaping the Goan identity and spreading the Portuguese culture. Therefore, naturally the Christians were more influenced than other communities.

Goan intellectuals contributed to the spread of the Portuguese culture too. In the early centuries of Portuguese rule, the intellectual life in Goa was dominated by European clergy and it was church-oriented. As result Goan intellectuals were influenced by European thought and models of the day. In the later period, education became more secular. Goans were brought in contact with liberal ideas which made them conscious of their rights.

The Impact of Portuguese Culture

The Portuguese culture has left its impress on the attitude and general life style of the Goans. The impact of the Portuguese culture was felt in different fields and more prominently in architecture, arts and crafts, education, music, religion and cuisine.

The influence of Portugal is seen in art and crafts. Some of these works of art were brought from Portugal, while others were inspired or copied from models brought from Portugal by receptive Goan artisans. They were made for the local use and for the courts of Indian rulers. In course of time Hindu, Mughal and other oriental designs and elements were incorporated. Our artisans made beautiful objects using gold, silver, brass, mother-of-pearl, stone, wood, ivory, bone, copper and similar material. Diogo Couto, the first archivist-historian of Portuguese India, has left a scathing account of the works produced at the time. Describing the home of the *Vedor* after his retirement he writes: "If you should walk into one of their houses you will find the verandah full of tailors, some making mantles of silk and satin, others rich quilts. Inside, craftsmen hammered out silver carafes, Chinese style tankards, chains and bracelets for wives and daughters, other men trimmed caskets with tortoise shells, silver and coconut from the island. Below, in the courtyard, turners and carpenters were busy at orders for pleasure boats of all varieties, desks in marquetry work and wardrobes for commercial use."[6]

Many of the objects made right from early period are still seen in Goan churches, temples, and private homes as well as in other parts of India and museums abroad. Goan artisans evolved a new art which came to be known as Indo-Portuguese art — an art that incorporated elements of Portuguese and Indian art.[7] The Portuguese brought European architecture to Goa — including the Renaissance architecture. They built grand churches and convents. The churches of Goa, specially the churches of Old Goa represent a fusion of Indo-European elements. European architectural influence can be seen not only in religious architecture but also in military and civil architecture. The Portuguese were responsible in teaching our masons this architecture which still exists in Goa. The progeny of the masons who were artistic and trained to build churches and grand monuments in different European styles, used these styles for domestic houses and produced beautiful houses for both Christians and Hindus. The art was passed from generation to generations of masons.

Today, we have about 200 grand houses from the Portuguese period depicting various aspects of the architecture brought by the rulers.[8] These houses and many big churches are characteristic of Goa. One does not see them in other parts of India — the result of the western influence, which resulted in a special kind of architecture known as Indo-Portuguese architecture. Lucio Miranda is of the opinion that modern architecture of Goa is making marks based on Indo-Portuguese architecture such as arches, tilled roofs, verandahs and other decorative elements. However, architect Dean de Cruz feels that the Indo-Portuguese architecture is slowing disappearing because it is not being incorporated in modern architecture of Goa. Further he says that unlike Indo-Portuguese architecture, modern Goan architecture does not have sense of space and details.[9] Some temples of Goa are unique with beautiful architecture. It is true a considerable number of the Goan temples were erased by the Portuguese rulers but some were rebuilt in the 18th century. The rebuilt temples mainly of Ponda have many aspects of counter-Reformation church architectural style.[10]

A look at the paintings in many of our convents and churches scattered all over Goa, specially the Convent of St. Francis of Assisi and Convent of St. Monica at Old Goa, provides information about the impact of the western culture in this field. In modern times Goan artists Angelo Fonseca, Newton de Souza, Gaitonde and Laxaman Pai have shown the capacity to synthesize eastern and western styles.

Western education introduced by the colonial rulers helped the Goans in course of time to master several European languages. Learning of Latin made the Goans better prepared to think in Latin based scientific terms, rational thinking and to adjust better to the western world. It opened new avenues for Goans outside their land when they started migrating in large numbers to British India and Africa. Goans who migrated returned home for holidays every few years. They brought along new ideas, new things and outlook as result of contact with other cultures. In addition contacts with Portugal and her colonies such as Brazil, Mozambique, Macau and others made it possible the transfer of ideas, technology and goods which enriched the material culture of the people and strengthened their sense of identity.

The Portuguese established in Goa, the first Medical School of western medicine in Asia.[11] The graduates of this school have carried pioneering work in different parts of the world. They were able to blend the eastern and western medicine.[12] The first printing press in India was brought by the Portuguese in Goa. It helped the dissemination of culture through the printed word.

The use of Roman script to write Konkani created bigger

interaction between languages of the East and the West. The Portuguese language had its impact on Konkani — the mother tongue of the Goans. The Konkani spoken both by Christians and non-Christians has many Portuguese words. Even today one finds Portuguese words in the Konkani texts (devanagri script) prescribed in Goan schools for instance words such as *herdeiros, carreira, escola, calção, codigo, bolsa, sabão* and *passeio*. In many cases the last syllable has been dropped as for example in case of *janel, codel, mez, vestid* or *cop*. The Portuguese language also left its impact on Marathi language in Goa and words such as *saban (sabão), chavi (chave)* and *Mez (meza)* are not unusual in this language.

One of the lasting Portuguese influences was on Goan cuisine. The dietary habits of the Goans changed when they converted to Christianity. Beef and pork became a part of their diet cherished of upper and middle classes. The Portuguese not only introduced some of their food habits but also brought along Chinese food habits from Macau and Malacca.[13] Several Portuguese dishes became a part of Goan Christian cuisine which is a blend of eastern and western cuisine. Some of the Portuguese dishes in Goan cuisine were modified to suit our needs, tastes and availability of ingredients.[14] Apparently, western cuisine, did not leave its impact on cuisine of non-Christian Goans.

Before the Portuguese conquest of Goa, the dress of the inhabitants was to a great extent uniform but soon after the conquest, the natives who embraced Christianity were required to use European style clothes to distinguish them from non-Christian. In course of time Hindus began to wear western style clothes.

The Portuguese introduced the Civil Code which benefited Goans of all communities including women. Today efforts are being to extend a similar code to other parts of the country. The Portuguese issued a considerable volume of legislation to prevent gender discrimination and improve the conditions of women.[15] In some instances conversion was the motive.

The church in Goa played an important role in popularization of western music even to the lowest village level. In most parishes in Goa village children were taught rudiments of western music in the church or schools attached to the church. They were taught solfaggio, to play violin and to sing hymns, psalms and *ladainhas*. Singing of *ladainhas* is still done in Latin with hymns in Konkani and Portuguese languages. Church music in its turn influenced secular music in Goa. Parish schools were the nurseries of a number of Goan musicians and music teachers of Goa. Goans learnt to play various western instruments which helped them to find employment as musicians in different parts of the world and mainly in British India or on board of passenger liners.

Methods Used to Spread Culture

How did the Portuguese go about spreading their culture? The Portuguese used various methods to spread their culture. Soon after the conquest of Goa, Albuquerque introduced a policy known as *Politica dos Casamentos*. This was marriage alliances between his countrymen and native women. This policy helped to spread the Portuguese culture among a section of Goan population. Native women who married Portuguese men learnt to speak Portuguese, embraced the Christian religion and many of their customs and traditions. Culture was also spread through a series of legislation enacted by the state. The Portuguese government issued decrees banning people from following their cult, customs and other practices, for example in the 16th century, the Hindus were forbidden to move about on horses or palanquins.[16] They were also forbidden to have their weddings celebrated in public specially in the presence of Christians.

Force as well as incentives were used to introduce the new culture of the rulers.[17] For example in the 17th century the State issued an order to all native Christians not to observe Hindu customs regarding festivities to be performed after the birth of a child.[18] Those who refused were humiliated, harassed and punished. The punishment prescribed often was the confiscation of their property. At other times they were forced to leave their ancestral home and go in exile elsewhere.

The Church through Church Councils, pastoral letters and Holy Inquisition issued wide ranging prohibitions, injunctions and restrictions covering various aspects of life styles of the people.[19] Decrees were issued to prevent the Christians from following non-Christian customs and prevent Hindus from following many of their customs and traditions.[20] After the conversion Goan Christians were expected to make a clean break with their Hindu past. The personal names, food habits, customs and the dress had to conform to the ways of the Europeans. In their attempts to introduce their culture the rulers tried many times to destroy the existing culture specially in the field of art, literature, religion and architecture.[21] Various measures were introduced to separate the Christians from others. For example, the first provincial council held in 1567 prevented Christian women from seeking help of non-Christian *dai* at the time of delivery because they used non-Christian rituals and witchcraft.[22]

The Holy Inquisition imposed a variety of restrictions on both Christians and non-Christians making it difficult for them to practice many of their customs and traditions including customs observed at time of birth, marriage and death. For instance in 1736 the Holy Inquisition banned several practices including the practice of massaging the bridal couple with oil, ground saffron, coconut milk, rice flour and powder of abolim leaves.[23] The same decree forbade Christians from eating boiled rice without salt as done by the Hindus. Furthermore, the same tribunal banned Christian men from wearing *pudvem* and women from wearing *choli* as was done by *gentios*.

Throughout their rule in India, the Portuguese issued decrees banning some practices and introducing new ones. In the fourth decade of the 20th century, the State ordered that Goans should appear wearing pants in all towns of Goa, in headquarters of the New Conquests and ferry wharfs of Betim, Durbate, Rachol, Sanvordem, Dona Paula and Piligação.[24] However, non-Christians were allowed to wear a coat along with *pudvem* instead of pants.[25] This was a symbol of amalgamation of two cultures.

Bans were imposed to alienate the natives from their culture and bring about a change. The natives often resisted these changes.[26] Despite restrictions and all kinds of punitive measures the Goans were able to maintain many aspects of their culture.

Bans and punitive measures were not the only means used by the rulers to bring about changes. At times incentives were provided for the people to embrace the new religion and customs of the rulers. In early centuries of Portuguese rule in Goa widows and orphans who converted to Christianity were entitled to their husband's and father's property.

The colonial policy succeeded to certain extent. The impact of the Portuguese culture had a mixed impact on Goans. Although there was a phase of ruthless oppression caused by the Holy Inquisition and policy of the State there was also a great deal of interaction as we have seen between native and alien culture which is reflected in art, literature, language and various aspects of culture. This strengthened the cultural traditions of Goans. There is no doubt that Portuguese culture has left an impress on Goan culture. We admit that the impact was felt more by one community than the other but one cannot accept the view that the impact was superficial and that it touched only a particular community.

Today, Goa is a part of Indian Union. Attempts were made to merge Goa with a larger neighbouring state or to form a new state incorporating other Konkani speaking areas in dispute. Attempts were also made to subvert the Goan culture and identity.

Are we losing our identity and culture today? Ms. Parreiras says that Goa is unique and Goa will never be like the rest of the country.

Contacts with rest of India, tourism and the globalization of the world into a big village has led to greater interaction between Goa and rest of the world. As result Goan cultural life has assimilated new and fresh elements from other cultural patterns including the rich cultural heritage of rest of India. This has further enriched Goan culture. But many Goans today are disturbed about the influxes of various ethnic groups in their State who have come with their services looking for job opportunities. They fear that their culture may be invaded by varied cultural patterns. The speedy industrialization, the starting of Konkan railway — a coastal railroad passing through Goa linking it with Maharashtra, Karnataka and Kerala and plans for a free port are likely to attract more people to this tiny State. This is the price Goans have to pay for development. Given these circumstances it may not be easy for Goans to maintain their identity but as poet Borkar says: "To face them tactfully and draw the best out of them without letting our culture suffer in its essentials shall be our task of the tomorrow".

NOTES AND REFERENCES

1. *Goa, Then and Now 1961-1981*, Goa, Information Depart., 1981.
2. Patrick Ferdinand, "Drama a social reality in Goa" (seminar on "Drama as Social Reality", Goa Univ. , 22 September 1995).
3. *Inside Goa*, Goa, 1982, p. 18.
4. *Goa: Cultural Patterns*, Mumbai, Marg Publications, 1983, p. 1.
5. *Goa — Concepts and Misconcepts*, Goa, 1994, pp. 31, 57.

6. *O Soldado Pratico*, Portugal, Publicações Europa-America, p. 52.
7. This impact is also seen on exquisite embroidery work executed on bedspread and liturgical vestments in churches and convents of Goa.
8. These houses are spread over 45 large villages of Bardez, Ilhas, Salcete and Murmugão. There are also some houses in New Conquests.
9. This could be due to lack of awareness, lack of craftsmanship and the builders desire to economize in the cost of construction.
10. The temples depict a blend of east-west such as arches, graffito techniques, the tripartite division of mandappa, Venetian chandeliers and lamps. The lamp towers in some Goan temples are inspired by the Portuguese Christian Art (Gritli Mitterwallner, "The Hindu Past — Sculpture and Architecture" in *Goa Cultural Patterns*, ed. Saryu Doshi, p. 38).
11. F. da Silva Gracias, *Health and Hygiene in Colonial Goa 1510-1961*, New Delhi, 1994, p. 175.
12. *Ibid.*, p. 209. Both these systems were practised in the Royal Hospital and others in Goa.
13. Many of our popular dishes such as *Vindalho, balchão, caldeirada, cabidel, feijoada, sorapatel, guisados* was introduced in our land by the Portuguese. In addition they brought a number of sweet dishes such as *dedos de damas, pasteis de Santa Clara, bolo podre* to name a few.
14. *Vindalho* was modified version of *Vinho de Alhos, sorapatel* is modified version of Portuguese dish *Sarabulho*. It is believed that *Balchão* came from Burma and Malacca. In Macau this dish is known as *Balichão*. The Portuguese also brought to Goa new ingredients and fruits from other parts of the globe including their colony Brazil.
15. F. da Silva Gracias, *Kaleidoscope of Women in Goa*, New Delhi, Concept, 1996. The Portuguese issued a number of legislation to improve the condition of women. They banned the practice of sati, child marriages, polygamy, practice of tonsuring the widow. They also encouraged widow remarriages.
16. Historical Archives of Goa (HAG): Ms. 9529 - *Provisões a favor de Cristandade*, fl. 1; HAG: Ms. 93 - *Monções do Reino*, fl. 363.
17. HAG: Ms. 7795 — *Livro das Posturas*, fl. 25.
18. It was a custom among the Goans to celebrate the birth for eight days with entertainment and lots of food. Those going against the order had to pay a fine of 100 *xerafins* for the first time. Second violation invited exile either to China or to Mozambique.
19. Arquivo Nacional da Torre do Tombo (ANTT): *Conselho Geral do Santo Officio (Inquisição de Goa), Maço - 33*, no. 18.
20. HAG: Ms. 9529.
21. J. Wicki (ed.), *Documenta Indica*, Rome, 1969, pp. 387-396. A Jesuit report of the 16th century says that the Portuguese erased temples *emblemas do cultu gentilico* and burnt books in vernacular languages because they contained non-Christian doctrines.
22. V. de Paiva Manso, (ed.), *Bullarium Patronatus in ecclesiis Africae, Asiae atque Oceaniae*, Tomo 1, Lisbon, 1889, p. 69; Gracias, *Health and*

Hygiene in Colonial Goa 1510-1961, p. 155. The same Council decreed that Christians should not ask non-Christians to paint their idols neither ask Hindu goldsmiths to make candlesticks, crosses and other Church requirements.

23. ANTT: CGSO-IG: 36/23; Gracias, *Kaleidoscope of Women in Goa*, p. 62. The inhabitants of Ilhas, Bardez and Salcete were also forbidden from using mouth organ at the time of marriage and from singing *vovios*.
24. Persons disobeying the order were required to pay fines.
25. *Legislação Relativa ao Estado da India, 1934*, Panaji, 1936, pp. 136-137.
26. For example during the time of Viceroy Dom Constantino, Hindus were banned to perform certain rituals at the time of their weddings. The Hindus protested, the merchants closed their shops, some sent their families to the kingdom of Adilshah and farmers opened *valados* causing floods.

THREE

A LASTING CULTURAL LEGACY
The Role of the Society of Jesus in Reforming Goan Society

CHARLES J. BORGES

Introduction

Many were the groups that have left an indelible Portuguese mark on Goa. Among them as one important group figure the Jesuits. The memory of their presence in Goa since their arrival in 1542 in the person of St. Francis Xavier and companions has come to stay. Today they form a much smaller group than before yet their influence though less vocal is significant. All through the centuries in Goa they succeeded in doing many things, one of which was to reform Goan society of the times they lived in.

I intend to show here how they went about their tasks, either alone or with the help of government and other religious orders and how significantly they could rework Goan society to their plan. They were largely Portuguese in number and though they had Italians and Spaniards in their ranks their outlook was mainly Portuguese. Two important ways in which they reformed Goan society prior to their suppression in 1759 was by their educational institutions and teaching and by the popular religious devotions that they helped propagate.

Education in Goa

When the Jesuits came to Goa it was to convert a people who had not known about Christianity. Their strategy was the education of the young and it proved very successful. At Old Goa, the

Confraternity of the Holy Faith set up a college, later to be renamed the College of St. Paul's and intended initially for the Portuguese and local youth, but it soon opened its doors for others too. Governor Dom Garcia de Castro writing in 1543 had remarked that it was edifying to see the boys serve mass so well. He was confident they would become good preachers of the divine word and would bring forth much fruit in the places they had come from. The boys at the College prepared themselves for missionary work. They studied grammar, good habits, and the mysteries of the faith. They would take part in the solemn high masses on Sundays, attend funerals, and religious processions. Their regular daily exercises included meditation, spiritual reading, examination of conscience, and the recitation of the Rosary. As matter for table-reading, they had the history of the missions and lives of outstanding missionaries. They confessed their sins once every fortnight, went frequently for communion, and did an annual retreat.[1]

Children soon loved singing the doctrine they learnt and those who attended St. Paul's sang it on their way to and from school. In the villages, they could be heard doing the same. Once a group of baptized children brought their cattle out to graze, and seated in sight of one another, they formed two choirs and intoned the catechism alternately. A Portuguese fidalgo who witnessed this sight was soon moved to tears and stood there a long while taking in the sweetness of the moment. At other times, children playfully climbed trees and alternately sang their catechism in two groups. It was soon a daily practice with them to sing it in the evening at Angelus time. By 1561 the first Portuguese catechisms with a Konkani version of them appeared containing the Sign of the Cross, the Profession of Faith and the place of Jesus Christ in God's plan for mankind.[2]

Among the Jesuit educators was an important Jesuit official known as the *Pai dos Cristãos* who had to take care of orphans and those in the process of being baptized. He was reminded by his superiors in their instructions to him that he had to stay near the settlements of the people so that *todo o tempo lhe pudessem falar os cristãos* (the Christians could have easy access to him). He had to punish those who took part in the festivals of Holi or Durga (termed *idolatrias*). Orphan children were brought to his home and kept off any harm (*procure que não conversem nem falem com elles infieis ou outras pessoas que os possão dessuadir de ser cristãos ou perturbar nisso*). They were to be given regular instructions twice daily (*das couzas de nossa santa fee e da falsidade de suas seitas e idolatrias*). And the children had to be vested *conforme a sua calidade e officio ou casta.*[3]

Popular Devotions

The popularizing of devotions went on at the parish level on a regular basis with greater recourse to these devotions during feast days or in moments of stress. The converts and others too performed them. A Jesuit Report of 1557 mentioned that it often happened that Hindu parents would bring their sick children to the church and placing them in the centre would raise their hands to heaven, saying that they come to offer them to St. Paul in order that he would cure them. They occasionally brought candles or oil for the church lamps. In 1560 a large group of village elders was seen chanting the catechism as it made its way towards St. Paul's to ask for baptism.[4]

Having recourse to the persons of Jesus and Mary meant the final act of allegiance to the faith, many were told. A Portuguese once saw a young man drowning in a tank. He called out to him to invoke the name of Jesus and next jumped in himself and swam to the drowning man's rescue. Such was the impression made on the young man that from then on he constantly invoked the name of Jesus, and later became a Christian. A dumb Muslim boy was taught by signs. When the moment arrived to test whether he could be baptized, he showed his belief in God the Creator by pointing to heaven and earth, and his belief in the Crucified by pointing to his feet and side.[5]

There were devotions which were similar to the local traditional ones. People used blessed water and relics in time of illness, venerated the Cross and holy pictures and used images and beads. Converts on their deathbeds would ask for a Cross to be placed in their hands. Many a home would have a Cross painted in the front rooms. People would show their fondness for sacred articles by pestering new arrivals from Europe for these. The Jesuits would regularly receive many such articles for local distribution. Tin crosses were popular among children. People had a special attachment to the Mother of God. They had a practice of passing Saturday nights in the poaches of her shrines. This practice which gave rise to abuses was eventually forbidden by the first Provincial Council. Lent saw the enactment of the *passos* or representations of various stages of Christ's passion and death. What was clear was that emotions played a large part in these devotions in tune with the spirit of the late Middle Ages which in contrast to the intellectualism of the preceding period, emphasized sentiments in devotional life.[6]

Local traditional feasts were merged into the people's Christian life. It had been the practice for the village Hindu astrologer to bless the rice-harvest which the people brought in procession to offer at the temple. A Jesuit letter describes how the recent converts of the parish in the Divar village in Goa at harvest time, requested their parish priest to bless their new yield. They had come carrying a banner with the names of Jesus and St. Paul on it and the sheaves of rice to the accompaniment of music and dance. These the priest accepted and placed on the altar-steps.[7]

In an article "Popular Religiosity in Catholic Goa"[8], I have described the forms of popular devotion in Goa in the 16th century. Various reports of the period speak of the variety of religious expressions of the people. Being recent converts from Hinduism they needed these devotions to help them feel at home in their new-found faith and events like processions, baptisms, feasts, and conversions helped in this process. These expressions of their religiosity did not differ very much from the Hindu practices of the time. The church in Goa allowed them to unfold lest the new converts feel the absence of their former practices and revert to them. The new converts needed these to bring about an amalgam of the mind and heart in themselves.

These Christian religious devotions, the processions in particular, marked an important time in their lives. They had very little else to look forward to in normal days and longed for the special days when the processions to mark the *Corpus Christi*, the rosary, and the Passion of Jesus, came around. The impressive larger-than-life statues which went round the city on these occasions were artistic and caught their fancy. Popular folklore formed part of these. Preachers used many realistic props to heighten the effect of remorse during their preachings that accompanied these events. Flagellations during Lent, for instance, were common yet bizarre with men whipping themselves and Jesuits treating them with medicines afterwards. The Easter processions were generally more joyful. Overall, the accounts of the miraculous show the desire on the part of many to prove the efficacy of their new faith.

One may wonder how these practices persisted for so long. There is the fact that the presence of local elements in these festivities and practices from the earliest times made them popular. The sense of the mystery of God and his inscrutable ways led many then as now to attempt practices in the hope of cure or protection. Yet the clergy of the time and the civil authorities suggested by their tacit approval of these practices that only supernatural intervention could solve their problems thus preventing the people from using their natural freedom to improve their economic and social world in any disturbing revolutionary manner. In a way it went well with the Hindu idea of divine destiny.

Cultural Background of the Jesuits and other Missionaries

But if Jesuits did work strongly at reforming Goan society educationally and religiously, what were their own cultural and religious backgrounds? It is true that those who went in search of new lands in the West in the 15th and 16th centuries hailed from the Iberian Peninsula which itself had developed a culture which was an ensemble of various other cultures (Phoenician, Carthagenian, Greek, Celtic, Visigothic, Jewish, Moorish and Roman) over the centuries. With this it formed a further mixed culture in the new world. It was originally a rich culture and travelled across the Atlantic undergoing changes in its encounter with the cultures of other lands. One historian remarks that "the simple most important contribution to the West was the introduction of the redeeming message of Jesus Christ with its own world of symbols and rituals, which seems to have been incorporated into the religious and spiritual drives of the natives with relative ease". It is hard to agree with this view totally and with his further point that with the redeeming message of Jesus Christ came the Christian principles of the sacredness of the human person which would ultimately be the foundation for the principles of human rights and social justice. Instances of Christian hardness and intolerance over the locals is all too evident in history.[9]

Yet it must be said that generally missionaries who came to the East or the West were free volunteers and committed men to their missions in terms of sufferings, sickness and death. One can recall the life of St. John de Britto who had always had a deep desire to die a martyr in Madurai. For him as for most of the Jesuits coming to

Goa the mission was most important (*negotio da cristandade como couza principal da Companhia nestas partes).*[10]

Some of the Jesuits were academically brilliant as their biodatas (found in Jesuit annual reports reveal), yet they and their other confreres were unable to come to terms or grips with the social reality of their time, and with regard to the caste system at least they had their own understanding of it. They had come with their own idea of nobility of blood and its gradation, all from a European point of view and saw in the caste system an equation of the same. Aware that working with the lower castes would demote them in the eyes of higher castes they sought converts from among the latter convinced these would establish the faith on a sounder footing.

In the 16th century at least, the Portuguese province in Europe did its best to guide the Indian province (which functioned under its control) according to its own spirit. During discussions for the appointment of a Father Visitor to India in the 16th century, it decided that in the eventuality of a person being chosen for the post who was not a Portuguese, he would have to be young enough to allow himself to be guided in his administration by the views of the Superior General of the Order as well as by the Portuguese superiors in Portugal and India.[11] Fr. Alessandro Valignano, eventually chosen as Visitor was an Italian, but in spite of his initial ideas to rid himself of most Portuguese controls, he had to submit to some. He collected his forty two recruits for the Indian mission for a strict course of training in an isolated part of the College of Saint Roque in Lisbon. Here they all spent time in prayer and reflection, served in prisons occasionally and in learning Portuguese. One consequence of the Indian mission's dependence on Portugal was that all Jesuit missionaries had to travel to the mission by way of Portugal where they were subjected to a thorough scrutiny, and at times either taken off or sent to Brazil instead.[12]

For all his yeoman activities Fr. Valignano did much harm to the Indian missions. He once wrote, "A trait common to all these people is a lack of distinction and talent. As Aristotle would say they are born to serve rather than to command. They are miserable and poor beyond measure and are given to low and mean tasks". But many an Indian ruler was born not to serve but to command and in some armed attacks Portuguese pride was ground to dust. A look at the *Décadas da Asia* of João de Barros gives one an idea of the valour and skill and pride of the Indians.[13] The Visitor had termed the stories he had come across of Indian gods "ridiculous and obscene", a view not shared by all Jesuits. Strangely he had a high opinion of the St. Thomas Christians in South India. But if he had had a better insight into India's ancient culture, he would probably have judged otherwise the intellectual capability of the people and the missionary methods he proposed might have been radically different.[14]

The Conversion Process

Conversion among other things came to mean a clean break with the past way of living. Taking Indian names and the wearing of nose-rings for women, were considered incompatible with Christianity. Not everything Indian was considered wrong. One of the Portuguese Jesuits who worked at demolishing Hindu temples in a letter of 1567 wrote of the high quality of the temple architecture. The inspiration for the temple-destructions had come from the first provincial council in Goa which believed that an excellent way of bringing the Christian message to non-Christians was to build churches in their midst and to keep there priests of good and exemplary lives.[15]

The Portuguese destroyed much of the ancient Goan temple art along with its literature after their arrival here in the 16th century. The same report mentioned above spoke of how "some of the temples were burnt down, others were heaped as garbage and others razed to the ground, nearly two hundred and eighty of these being big and some of these very sumptuously done and of exceedingly fine workmanship". These were repositories of literature of a mainly religious nature and were centres of learning and teaching.[16]

The destruction of temple and temple art in the 16th and following centuries led to the emergence of Christian art as an expression of Portuguese Baroque in the splendour of the Indo-Portuguese Baroque, believes one art historian. Foreign and Indian craftsmen recreated Spanish and Portuguese Baroque and Rococo styles in the many Jesuit churches of Goa. The influences were from Italy and France initially but Indian craftsmen saw to it that their creations were not mere imitations of the original. Rather they were an elaboration in new forms with local materials and local sense.[17]

Archaeologist Gritli Mitterwallner had explored the various remains of Hindu temples in Goa. She refers to the tripartite *linga* of Shiva from the razed temple at Moira and which was later used as a stand for the holy water basin in the Catholic village church. A pillar of another temple became a prop for the holy water basin in the church of St. Francis of Assisi at Old Goa. She refers to the ceiling of the cemetery chapel at Piedade which consisted of a *vitana* of basalt stone carved with a fine *padmasila* in the centre. Her article describes how Goan temples in turn drew from the Portuguese building techniques of the time and how they made use of the graffiti technique popular in Italy during the Renaissance.[18] And another archaeologist, Henry Heras describes how in the cemetery chapel of the church of Piedade (Goa), the full ceiling and a lattice work-screen of one of the windows came from an ancient Hindu temple. The artists at the Mughal court, while reproducing Christian subjects (as a result of Jesuit presence there), sometimes copied from the old masters and introduced Indian features.[19]

Christian themes were painted on the walls of the tomb of the Mughal emperor Humayun at Delhi, and were said to have been built with the help of about 200 European craftsmen. This accounts for the mix of European Renaissance, Turkish and Persian overtones in Mughal style in architecture and painting with Persian motifs predominating in the decorative panels. In the Mughal territories Christian art became a means of evangelization. Thousands would be attracted in Lahore and Agra to the exhibition of the crib and religious objects. Jesuit records speak of images and reliquaries brought from Portugal for new converts. The Mughal emperor Akbar was said to have always worn one such around his neck and it had an image of Mary on one side and the Lamb of God on the other.[20]

Together with the open reforming of art and architecture, went another process, that of a general reforming or destructuring of Goan society. By way of comparison to Goa, I refer to a recent paper of mine in which I have described the destabilizing of Sri Lanka as a missionary enterprise. The religious Orders (Jesuits, Franciscans, Augustinians and Oratorians) used their powers well to de-structure Sinhalese political and religious systems to bring about a society patterned on and beneficial to Portuguese colonial interests and culture.[21] Conversions to the Christian faith brought problems for the local situation.[22]

F. Houtart in his *Religion and Ideology in Sri Lanka*[23] has analyzed well the role of colonization in the destruction of a native society. Christianity could only exist by destroying the meaning and the organization of the existing religious systems. Many of the kings who converted to Christianity realized that if they wished to retain their power, they had to adopt the conqueror's system of meaning. At the religious level, there was a definite destructuring of Buddhism, a destruction of symbols so as to weaken the system of meanings and the elimination of the religious organization. Christianity could only exist by destroying the meaning and the organization of the existing religious systems. In Goa too the Jesuits made Hinduism appear in a bad light while in their conversion drive.

Local Church or Universal Church?

'The true church is universal', wrote a church historian. "It is not restricted to any definite country or nation, it is not tied down to any particular culture or civilization, it is not identified with any distinct race or people . . . . is ready to adapt itself to all sane customs, climates and conditions of life. Everywhere it can find itself at home. And in the church all men, all nations, all cultures, all values, can find and achieve their perfect fulfilment". Written forty years ago they reflected the mood of the time. Pope Pius XI had once said that the principal duty of the papacy was to plant the church in all countries of the world. But it had all along being a Western church.[24]

The planting of Christianity began in a India of rich cultural diversity. All said and done the Jesuits and the other missionaries could not bring about the same kind of religious and cultural synthesis that the Thomas Christians and Syrian Christians brought about themselves for these moved well beside the cultural world of the Hindus. But conflicts over doctrine soon arose in the contacts that the Portuguese had. The Religious Orders in particular, failed to understand and tolerate the natural peculiarities of the Indian-Christian communities.

There was a strong ecclesiastical structure,[25] and the right of patronage gave widespread powers to the priests to announce the gospel. It advised them to ask the unbelievers to give up their idolatry, their diabolic rites, and customs and come over to the faith of Christ, adding "so that in this manner all might be united and joined together in charity of law, and love, since we are created by one (common) Creator and redeemed by one Redeemer But if the people are stubborn as to reject the true faith they should be put to fire and steel". And Pope Leo X had asked King Manoel of Portugal in 1515 to "receive this warlike sword in your always victorious and warlike hands. With this you will wage wars under the most happy auspices, you will subject the enemies of the Faith, as you have done up to now. . . . may you use your force, strength, and power against the fury of the infidels; may you consecrate, not only your most religious spirit, but also the kingdom itself, and the forces of the kingdom, to the giver of them, to God the best and the greatest, so that having received through this gift the help of heaven in battles, you may bring back abundant spoils and most famous triumphs."[26]

Conversions and Reactions to it

Conversions led to divisions among the people of Goa themselves. My work[27] shows the tension-ridden relationships that existed between the Jesuits and the local clergy on the one hand, and with sections of the local population on the other.

As in Latin America, Jesuits founded small settlements of new converts in Goa around their churches the better to protect them from contamination with their fellow Hindus. This spirit of separation continues with Catholics reluctant to join in cultural and social celebrations of the Hindus for fear of contamination.

Missionary accounts do not speak much of the lives and times of the converts they worked for. Recent writings have corrected this and stressed what one historian calls "the historiography of the voiceless". Were the Jesuits killed in Goa in 1583 martyrs of Cuncolim or were they Europe's martyrs, is a query he makes.[28] The names of the two native boys who were accompanying the priests on their temple-destruction mission and who were killed along with the Jesuits have never figured in the church list of the blessed of Cuncolim. The Portuguese with their interest in their own national religion created their own saints.

One author believes that in Goa one notices traces of Portuguese forms of worship. The city became a "second Lisbon" and church festival days corresponded to those observed in Portugal with her national saints like St. James, St. Sebastian and St. Anthony making a lasting appearance here. The same could be said of Travancore in south India where the churches were miniature reproductions of those in Portugal and seemed to supply an incurable nostalgia for the land where their architectural style belonged. This tendency, observes he, "to feel a permanent debt to Europe and to imitate her ways and customs has remained a dominant trait in all Goan Christians and this fact may explain why so many inhabitants of Goa seem unable to feel that they are true citizens of India".[29]

In studying the psychology of the "discoverer" and of the "discovered" while analyzing the colonial process, a psychologist has spoken about the dynamics of interaction between the two.[30] The trampling on local sensibilities and on age-old cultural traditions, psychologically, were the most debilitating to the collective identity of a people. This led to their degeneration, conquest and humiliation. "However, benign and noble the colonizers may have claimed themselves to be,' he adds, "the very act of colonization is brutal and destructive. Since the colonized had to learn to live according to the rules drawn up by the colonizers, they had of necessity to develop psychological-coping mechanisms, the more common being that of submissiveness".

In spite of a mass of critical thinking on the issue, there are some who think otherwise of missionary methods and a comment captures this well. "Missionary expansion was not an easy affair. There were many hurdles on the way. . . . This is the great galaxy of Catholic martyrs, who sacrificed their lives for the sake of missionary expansion, and enabled the Catholic faith to gain a firm foothold in the East. . . ."[31]

Conclusion

There will always be mixed feelings towards the work done by missionaries during the colonial period. With a strong government to back them, a stable financial base and a sense of mission, the Jesuits, for instance, during their stay prior to their Suppression in 1759 reworked Goan society according to their own ground plan. The Society of Jesus being the most dominant missionary group then in Goa and having more Portuguese men in its ranks, by its educational methods, popularizing of devotions and art forms, gave Goan Christianity a dominant Portuguese flavour. Its mark on Goan culture is accepted but the debate about its importance will continue.

NOTES AND REFERENCES

1. Carlos M. de Melo, *The Recruitment and Formation of the Native Clergy in India (16th-19th century): An Historico-Canonical Study*, Lisbon, Agencia Geral do Ultramar, 1955, pp. 77, 81, 195.
2. Anthony D'Costa, *The Christianization of the Goa Islands*, Mumbai, Heras Institute, pp. 154-155, 179.
3. *Documenta Indica* (1595-97), ed. Josef Wicki, Rome: Institutum Historicum Societatis Iesu, 1988, vol. 17, doc. 21, pp. 83, 86; *O Livro do Pai dos Cristãos*, ed. J. Wicki, Lisbon, CEHU, 1969.
4. D'Costa, pp. 155-160.
5. *Ibid.*, pp. 166, 175.
6. *Ibid.*, pp. 182-184.
7. *Ibid.*, p. 187.
8. Charles J. Borges, "Popular Expressions of Religiosity in 16th century Catholic Goa", *Souvenir of the Holy Family Chapel*, Goa, 1992.
9. Ricardo Ramirez, "The Question of Columbus: Evaluation of the Result", *Boletim Cehila* (São Paulo), nos. 43-44, January 1993, p. 33.
10. *Documenta Indica*, vol. 17, doc. 21, p. 82.
11. Josef F. Schutte, *Valignano's Mission Principles for Japan*, Anand, Gujarat Sahitya Prakash, 1980, vol. I, part I, p. 46.
12. *Ibid.*, p. 81.
13. *Ibid.*, p. 131; Borges, The *Decadas da Asia* of João de Barros: A Portuguese view of India and Asia during the Discoveries", 1994 (unpublished paper).
14. Schutte, *op. cit.*, p. 135.
15. D'Costa, *op. cit.*, pp. v, 11-12.
16. Teotónio de Souza, "Christianisation and Cultural Conflicts in Goa 16th—19th Centuries", *Boletim do Instituto Menezes Braganza* (Panaji), no. 170, 1994, p. 65. His quotation is from *Documenta Indica* (Rome), vol. 7, p. 391.
17. José Pereira, *Golden Goa*, Mumbai, Marg Publications, 1980, p. 3; "The Art Historiography of Baroque India", *Indica* (Mumbai), vol. 23, nos. 1-2, 1986, pp. 159-170.
18. "The Hindu Past", *Goa: Cultural Patterns*, Mumbai, Marg Publications, 1984, pp. 21-40.
19. "Indian Christian Art", *Examiner* (Mumbai), Nov. 19, 1949, pp. 681-682.
20. Thomas Mulackal, "The Christian Paintings in Arab-ki-Sarai" in *Examiner*, Feb. 22, 1975, p. 89.
21. Borges, "Goa's role in the destabilizing of Sri Lanka: A Missionary Enterprise", 1994 (unpublished paper).
22. Houtart, *Religion and Ideology in Sri Lanka*. Bangalore, TPI, 1974.
23. V. Perniola, *The Catholic Church in Sri Lanka* (The Portuguese, Dutch and English Periods 1505-1844). Dehiwala (Sri Lanka), Tisara Prakasakayo, 1989-1992. *passim*
24. Melo, *op. cit.*, p. xxv.

25. François Houtart & Genevieve Lemercinier, *Genesis and Institutionalization of the Indian Catholicism*, Louvain-la-Neuve, Univ. Catholique de Louvain, 1981, pp. 82, 86.
26. Melo, *op. cit.*, pp. 17-18.
27. Borges, *The Economics of the Goa Jesuits 1542-1759: An Explanation of their rise and fall*, New Delhi, Concept, 1994. Worth seeing is the document in *Archivum Romanum Societatis Iesu, Fondo Jesuitico* (Rome), 1443/9, file 23, *Goa* 22, I, fls. 59-65.
28. T. de Souza, in *Jesuits in India: In historical perspective*, eds. T.R. de Souza & C. J. Borges, Macau, Instituto Cultural de Macau, 1992, pp. 37-47.
29. Felix Plattner, *Christian India*, London, Thames & Hudson, 1957, p. 56.
30. Anthony da Silva, "The Discoverers versus the Discovered: Psychological perspectives on Portuguese-Goan Prejudices in the 16th-18th centuries", *Discoveries, Missionary Expansion and Asian Cultures*, pp. 45-54.
31. Joseph de Barros, "Discoveries and Martyrs of Missionary Expansion in the East", *Discoveries, Missionary Expansion and Asian Cultures*, p. 88, 90.

FOUR

CONVERSION AS A MEANS TO CULTURAL ADAPTATION
The Catechumens of Betim in the 18th Century

MARIA DE JESUS DOS MARTIRES LOPES

The study of religion has lately been appraised by modern historiography as an important element of social groups. This aspect is undeniable in Goa where three major social and religious communities (Christian, Hindu and Muslim) while co-existing, each has its own way of living.

As it concerns a multi-religious society which comprised a great number of Gentiles living together with the Christian community, certain principles regarding paganism had to be defined. It can be said, on this subject, that from the second half of the 16th century, the policy of freedom of religion initiated by Albuquerque gave way to bigotry. In Portugal, at that time, because of the Counter-Reformation, a policy of religious intransigence was enforced in order to transform the *Estado da India* into a Catholic state and Goa into the Rome of the East.[1]

As regards the subject of religious practices, the Portuguese government did not allow the performing of Gentile ceremonies in public in order to avoid scandal in Christian lands as well as the religious corruption of the Christian population. Therefore, while the Catholics were allowed to attend religious ceremonies in public places, Hindus and Muslims had to perform their cults privately.[2] However, there were times when this policy allowed for more religious freedom to the Gentiles. During both Count of Alva's (1754-56) and Pombal's government, the Gentile community performed its religious festivities in public with many instruments, chants and dances.[3] Owing to the annexing of the New Conquests and the cultural ambiance of the *Luzes*, a change in the religious policy was called for. However, it was precisely on these historic occasions, that one of the main characteristics of Goa was forged: the pacific co-existence of different creeds and beliefs.

As it happened in other territories in the Orient, there was in Goa the institution of the *Pai dos Cristãos* which had three main objectives: the conversion of the Gentile population, the teaching of the Christian creed and the protection of the new Christians. As regards the first objective, as in India the conversion was not only carried out through preaching and teaching, but means had to be used: idolatry had to be prevented, its followers had to be punished, favours had to be denied to the Gentiles and granted to the Christians in order to compel other religious communities to embrace the Christian faith. Thus, the need for the *Pai dos Cristaõs* to be well-informed on all governmental orders issued for all Christendom.

Indeed, since the 16th century, either the Portuguese or the Goan government issued several charters in order to protect the new converts. During the 17th and 18th centuries, these documents were copied and very often included into more recent ones. These documents although numerous are also more or less scattered in several official registers. However, two ancient manuscripts, comprising only the regulations pertaining to the protection of the new converts and currently known as the *Livro do Pai dos Cristãos* can be found in the Historical Archives of Goa.[4]

Until 1762, those who were meant to embrace the Roman Catholic faith were taken into custody at the Jesuit school of S. Paulo-o-Velho. At that time, Viceroy Count of Ega, moved the House of the Catechumens from that unhealthy location to Betim which besides an healthier environment, had also a panoramic view over the cove of the river Mandovi. He also endowed his establishment with financial support thus allowing it to be financially independent.[5]

But who were the neophytes and how many were they in the 18th century? Which was their social as well as their professional status? From which country did they come? What were the motives that made them embrace another religious creed? The records of the christenings as well as the marriages and the registrations of the catechumens clear up some of the doubts concerning these interesting as well as c mplex issues.[6]

From 1733-52, 812 catechumens were christened showing an

average of 40.6 christenings per year (5%) while in 1737 a maximum of 74 christenings (9.4%), and in 1733 a minimum of 14 christenings (1.7%) was recorded.[7]

During the quinquennium of 1740-44, its numbers were always lower than the annual average. What caused this situation? Was it the conquering of the Province of the North by the Marathas which meant the acquisition of a very rich part of the *Estado da India* and the beginning of a social as well as financial crisis in Goa, which caused a lesser number of christenings? We must remember that a number of catechumens came from Bassein or from its surrounding areas.[8]

Generally speaking, it may be said that there has been a great disparity in the number of christenings performed each year. There was a great number of ceremonies some years, while in others there were but a few.

While the number of conversions may not be very significant within the social as well as religious context of India, it is nonetheless very important for the study of the Goan population. Indeed, it must be stressed that during the second half of the 18th century, the Christian community in the New Conquests was much larger than the other ones. It is a well-known fact that it was a century later, and owing to emigration, that the Christian community was outnumbered in Bardez and Ilhas by the gentiles.[9]

According to the above-mentioned examples, the number of Christians living in Goa was due to the fact that many Hindus embraced the Catholic church. Indeed, most of the neophytes were originally Hindus. Of the 812 catechumens that were baptized between 1733-52, 627 were Hindus (77.2%). Therefore, from an average of 40.6 christenings each year, 31.4 were former Hindus (5.0%).

During the years when a larger number of conversions had taken place (1734 and 1737), 63 Hindus were christened in either year which amounts to 10 per cent of the converted Hindus. The year 1737 must be stressed as it includes two important facts: it was the year where the largest number of christenings, either from Hindus or from other native communities, is listed. 1733, on the other hand is the year where the least number of Hindu conversions (10 christenings, that is 1.6 per cent of the converted Hindus) as well as with regard to christenings in general (only 14 which means 1.7%), is filed.

TABLE 4.1

Year	Hindus	Moors	Parsis	European Protestants	Agnostic Portuguese	Caffrarians	Chinese	Christening
1733	10	—	—	—	—	4	—	14
1734	63	—	—	5	—	3	—	71
1735	36	—	—	—	—	4	1	41
1736	28	1	—	—	1	9	—	39
1737	63	4	—	1	—	7	1	76
1738	33	—	—	—	—	12	—	45
1739	57	3	—	4	—	5	—	69
1740	23	—	—	—	—	7	1	31
1741	16	1	—	—	—	1	—	18
1742	26	—	—	—	—	—	—	26
1743	27	—	—	1	—	—	—	28
1744	22	—	—	—	—	1	—	23
1745	30	—	—	—	—	7	—	37
1746	39	—	—	—	—	11	—	50
1747	24	1	—	—	—	11	—	36
1748	26	—	—	—	—	5	—	31
1749	16	—	—	—	—	8	—	24
1750	21	—	—	—	—	23	—	44
1751	23	—	—	—	—	18	—	41
1752	44	2	1	—	—	21	—	68
Total	627	12	1	11	1	157	3	812

The *caffrarians* (slaves) follow the Hindus in percentages (19%) and in yearly averages 7.9 (1.0%). They came from Africa and practised their own religion. In 1750, 23 slaves were christened which represents the largest number of christenings during 1733 and 1752. On the other hand, not a single ceremony was performed in 1742 and 1743. Although scarce, several Muslims were also listed (1.5% of all the catechumens, with 12 christenings which represent 0.6 ceremonies performed each year (0.08%).

Protestants from England and Holland were also christened in India (11 christenings or 1.4% from all the catechumens with 0.6 christenings each year (0.07%). There were also three followers of Chinese rites. They were only three and all of them were prisoners, as well as one Parsee and one Portuguese agnostic who embraced the Christian faith.

We will now analyze at length the baptized Hindus as they represent a significant parcel of the catechumens. They belonged to different castes with a predominance of the following: Kurumbin (11.7%), sudra (9.7%), Maratha (7.8%), fisherman (7.5%), chardo (7.3%), brahmin (6.9%) and faraze (3.2%). However, there is a slight dominance of the so-called lower castes: sudra, kurumbin, fisherman and faraze. Their adherence to the Christian faith — an equalitarian religion could also mean a manner of social promotion and a better way of life.[10]

Many other castes are also mentioned: dancer, balagateer, bandhari, gauddho, pandit, prabhu, rajaputra, savana, etc. and even if their numbers are not high, the diversity in the social origin of these catechumens should nevertheless be mentioned.

Besides what the authors failed to tell us regarding the motives for these conversions and human nature being very complex, it can be said that it was mainly due to stray circumstances that these people embraced the Christian faith. A number of persons entered the College of St. Paul's or the House for Catechumens either for reasons of health or need. Some women came for food (*para dar conta da barriga*) and ended up as Christians.[11] Many young children as well as old people about to die were also baptized.

Sometimes, they were sent by the authorities such as the Viceroy, the Archbishop, the Inquisitor or the priests. There is also an explicit mention of a spontaneous adherence of many who came *por sua livre vontade* (of their own free will and with their own people) *sem condução de pessoa alguma.*[12] In a very significant case, a forty-year old Hindu Brahmin, imprisoned for his failure to pay his debts, decided to be christened against the will of his family *"contra a vontade de todos os seus parentes gentios graves"* and not minding the promises made by his family to pay off his debts *"não fazendo caso de muitas promessas e partidas que faziam os ditos gentios com ele em ordem de pagar a sua divida".* His six-year old daughter followed his example.[13]

Very often the christenings of one member was followed by the conversion of other members of his or her family.[14] Very often it was due to the action of a catechumen, friend or protector that the conversion took place. That is why these people were often chosen as godfathers. Their difficulties were sometimes decisive for the conversions: illegitimate, unwanted and orphan children, or the sick, all these unfortunates contributed for these conversions and christenings.[15]

Gentile orphans and illegitimate children of gentile mothers (boys twelve years or below and girls sixteen years or below) were sent to the *Pai dos Cristãos* in order to be taught and baptized. However, the fact that these children were christened against the will of their families as well as of their gentile mothers (when related to the illegitimate children) caused a certain amount of controversy. A number of laws were passed in order to clarify doubtful situations and justify religious, moral and social principles that directed the regulations. In either one, it was ordered that in the proceedings used towards these children, understanding and respect for a different creed should be used. Their age as well as their free will should be taken into account.[16] As the catechumens were taken care of and instructed within the Christian faith in the school of St. Paul's, they were, of course, christened in the church of the school. This state of affairs would undoubtedly change with the founding of the House of the Catechumens in 1762.

In order to bestow more dignity to the ceremony and because of the number of converts, several high-placed dignitaries were invited to attend the christenings, among them the Archbishop, the Inquisitor of the Holy Office, the Superior of the Professed House of Bom Jesus, and the *Pai dos Cristãos* who would be represented by another priest (usually a Jesuit) should it be impossible for him to be present.[17]

Godfathers were chosen of sound and ancient stock who were also good Christians in order to protect the new converts to whom

Christian names were given as was proclaimed in *Constituições do Arcebispado de Goa* (Constitutions of the Archbishop of Goa). Their family names came from their godfathers who very often came from important and influential Portuguese families.[18] Many catechumens chose either their Master, *Pai dos Cristãos*, the Archbishop, the Viceroy or a Jesuit, to be their godfather. Since the early days of the 16th century, the office of the *Pai dos Cristãos* was taken up by priests of the Society of Jesus which helps us to understand even better the earnest striving of the Jesuits in their religious tasks.

However, it is also possible to see as godfathers of these catechumens, people from other less-important social groups such as tailors, barbers, jailers, tenants, shoemakers, church-clerks, and so on. This fact is undeniable when related to the slaves as they chose other members of their social group to be their godfathers in order to protect them.[19] We may therefore conclude that the neophytes chose very often as godfathers the same people who led them to embrace the Christian faith.

It is also noteworthy the important role played by women in the conversion of these neophytes: Gentile women newly-converted leading their children from far countries to the school of St. Paul's or to the House of Catechumens and persuading other members of their families to share the Catholic creed.

One should emphasize for her militancy the example of Esperança, a newly converted woman, the godchild of Inquisitor António de Amaral Coutinho who persuaded several gentiles from Goa and Bhonsale to embrace the Christian faith. Other women received their godchildren in their own homes, feeding and protecting them.[20]

This programme of moral and religious training was complemented by a social welfare assistance lent to the neophytes as can be verified in the book of *Matricula dos Novos Convertidos (1761-1765)*. These catechumens were given food (mostly rice), cloth (from Balghat, Cambay and Diu), suits, dowries for their marriages, medicines, money for their support, transport, funerals and even for their Christmas lunch. Money was also given to those wishing to be christened on the same day as others. The *baptismos gerais* (common baptisms) were a common custom at that time when many people were baptized at the same time.[21]

The conversion of the gentiles to the Catholic faith, the

acceptance of Christian names belonging to families from Portugal, their marriages in some cases with Portuguese men, the granting of public offices to new converts, led to a cultural adaptation as they began to use other kinds of clothing and food, granting a certain way of living.[22] Then, the catechumens began to dress up in breeches, robes and to use neckties and wrist-studs with jewellery, shoes and hats. They even had a Christmas supper during Christmas just like the Christian community.

However, their Indian background and their social contacts with other gentiles and Muslims to whom they were bound by family ties, established certain habits where the interpenetration of Christian as well as Hindu elements was very strong bringing forth a more or less harmonious synthesis.

NOTES AND REFERENCES

1. Luis, F.F. *Reis Thomaz, De Ceuta a Timor*, Lisbon, Difel, p. 253; E.R. Hambye, "Goa", in R. Aubert (ed.), *Dictionnaire d'Histoire et de Géographie Ecclésiastiques*, fasc. 121, Paris, Letouzey & Anè, p. 286.
2. J.M. dos Martires Lopes, *Goa na Segunda Metade do Século XVIII: Esboço de um Ensaio Cultural*, Lisbon, 1993, pp. 421-23.
3. Letter from the king to the Count of Alva, 27 March 1756. AHU, India, ms. no. 86 (107).
4. J. Wicki (ed.), *O Livro do Pai dos Cristãos*, Lisbon, Centro de Estudos Ultramarinos, 1969, pp. ix-xv.
5. Letter from Belchior J.U. de Carvalho to the Count of Ega, 15 January 1763, AHU, Monções do Reino, Book no. 135, fls. 567-572v.
6. AHU, Codex no. 1554, fls. 649, 1824.
7. The amounts found either in 1733 and 1738 are fragmented. It seems that they do not cover the whole year.
8. AHU, Codex no. 1554.
9. Lopes, *op.cit.*, pp. 127-166. An analysis concerning the native population.
10. Mariano Feio, *As Castas Hindus de Goa*, Lisbon, 1979; Sebastião R. Dalgado, *Glossário Luso--Asiático*, vols. 1-2, Coimbra, 1919, 1921; Hobson-Jobson, *A Glossary of Colloquial Anglo-Indian Words*, New Delhi.
11. AHU, no. 1554, fls. 54, 61v, 64, 88.
12. *Ibid.*, fls. 26, 47, 49, 98v.
13. *Ibid.*, fl. 73v.
14. *Ibid.*, fls. 36v, 73v, 88, 89v.
15. *Ibid.*, fls. 45, 47, 47v, 48, 67v.
16. Lopes, *op.cit.*, pp. 426-428.

17. A number of multiple christenings were performed during the years 1734-37 and 1748-52 (AHU, Codex no. 1554, fls. 9v-12, 13v-14v, 15v-17v, 21-24, 33-33v, 41-41v, 52-55, 56v-57v, 78-79).
18. Constituições do Arcebispado de Goa, Book 1, Title 3, const. 3, p. 19.
19. AHU, Codex no. 1554, fls. 30, 30v, 60, 62, 86, 88, 88v-89.
20. *Ibid.*, fls. 54v, 55, 58, 69.
21. Matricula dos Novos Convertidos (Codex no. 1824). A great variety of clothes are mentioned that are very important for a study of Indian textiles as well as for their everyday customs mainly pertaining to their way of dressing.
22. Wicki, *op.cit.*, pp. 109-110, 208-209, 255-256, 319-320. Among the public posts offered to the new Christians there is the post of "escrivão da catuália e avenças" for three years, as well as of interpreter of the "Ouvidor Geral do Civil", of "Naique", of the "jiuxo da Ouvidoria", of "Mocadão escrivão" of the village, medical doctor and so on.

FIVE

PRESENT DAY ADMINISTRATION IN GOA*

A Reflection of Past Legacies

OSCAR PEREIRA

The aim of my paper is to try to analyse if the legacies left by the Portuguese and by the Indians has led to the historical birth of an Indo-Portuguese culture in Goa. At the same time, it will probe if this Goan culture can be considered as the cultural profile of Goans, marking their genuine and separate identity from other ethnic groups. In the second place, the paper will throw light on this cultural identity asking if it is a consequence of the acculturation of past generations. It will study if there are any hypothesis for its preservation, paying attention to administrative and actual situations in Goa.

At the outset it will be necessary to clarify the theoretical concepts of culture and identity. But first I would like to mention some opinions with respect to this problem. On my last visit to Goa, I saw that the issue of a Goan cultural identity was fairly real, since it is a situation in which one community thinks that it runs the danger of losing its cultural autonomy. It is natural that its members pledge themselves to the preservation of their identity and space within conditions where this can be done well. This is the actual situation in Goa. There is one group that supports emotionally the presence of a Goan identity, proving this with arguments and attesting to facts that unmistakably point to its cultural nature. On the other hand, there are those who while arguing about a unique and decisive heritage that had bound and continues to bind Goans, insist on an Indian culture.

* Translated from the Portuguese by Charles J. Borges.

In view of these opinions, cultural identity is either only an unsupportable myth or a historical fact. This divergence of opinions and the actual situation, moved me (although this is not my field of professional research) to study this topic in the hope that perhaps I may be able to come across some clues.

Well-settled Goans one encounters abroad are 'shocked' by the new cultural changes during their visits to Goa. These changes are a result of the difference of cultural traditions in which the Goan community is involved in since the liberation of Goa in 1961. For these Goans, their cultural identity lacking the contact or ongoing links with Goans in Goa, their cultural values of an age prior to the liberation, remain in static moulds. For these Goans, their cultural identity becomes a desire unrealizable like all their personal difficulties of accommodation.

The better to raise this cultural conflict, I will present the opposing published views of two Goans resident in Goa. Carmo Noronha, a Catholic, is in favour of the presence of a Goan cultural identity and calls it 'Goanidade' (Goanness): ". . . . the signs of intelligence, imagination, and sensibility, all the results of work and industry which may be typical and genuine creations of Goan talent and imagination and over which some can reassert their rights of authority and ownership".[1]

Prabhakar Angle, a Hindu, speaks against the existence of a Goan identity[2] mentioning what "an illustrious personality of Goa, Josè Rangel, told him, "We are Indians by blood, but our culture is Indo-Portuguese. This mixed culture was created over centuries. It cannot and must not disappear". His comment on this opinion is "What is the percentage of Goans who would subscribe to this view? Will even half a dozen Goan Hindu families claim that their culture is Indo-Portuguese?"[3] and "Goa is a typical example of the refusal of being blown off one's feet. Its culture has remained basically Indian in character in spite of winds of alien culture blown about its land".

I want to make a reference to the third current that exists in Goa supported mainly by those who think that the Goan cultural autonomy is weakening and for this reason see the necessity of putting an end to illusions and gathering proper traditions, customs and usages, starting a culture and civilization rooted in the midst of one's local setting.

In this context one speaks of a 'psychological liberation' which consists in shelving wholly "Saudosismo", "Sebastianismo" and "Missionismo" and pledging oneself to the new constitutional order in which Indianness and indigenisation are priorities, and encouraging the obtaining of cultural features for a proper Goan society.[4]

'Culture' may connote various inter-disciplinary areas like philosophy, psychology, anthropology, sociology and geography. A more relevant and interesting perspective in this study is an anthropological viewpoint, since in its forms, culture cannot be judge of values, that is, one culture is not nor can be superior to another.

It is not right to discuss this theme in terms much in vogue, but turn to the fact that Portugal was founded in 1084, a time when India had already a history of 1,000 years, and that in 1510, the year of the conquest of Goa by Afonso de Albuquerque, the geographical area of Goa enjoyed great material and moral prosperity.[5]

In this context I would like to make a reference to ethnocentricism or may be to a super valuation of one's own culture. To me this is no reason to be and is incompatible with the essence and definition of one's culture.[6]

I have tried in the following lines to involve the definition of culture in general terms that would be valid for other areas also since culture can be defined, according to W.E. Muhlmann, "as the typical form of a people, its mentality, and in a special way, the orientation of its values".[7]

Culture is always dependent on a geographical area defined in relation to a global society in which individuals take part in the same traditions of behaviour. Other cultures can exist in other adjoining geographical areas, and thus one can have cultural units side by side. In general, the essence of culture consists in ideas, abstractions and behaviour.

We have to identify the elements that could be determinants of Goan culture, elements such as (Konkani and Indo-Portuguese furniture, for example)[8]; abstraction (the total exclusion of material things — in this case religion whether Catholic or Hindu); behaviour (the way of acting as one unit by Goans and their reactions in the social milieu). Here I would like to show the intercultural liberty of 'live and let live' which is the attitude of Goans and which is the expression of religious liberty and of multi-cultural and multi-social conviviality. The components of culture present in the Goan cultural tradition are popular theatre, music and poetry, Catholic and Hindu religious culture, fine arts, cuisine, and architecture.

These components were passed through generations. Religion can be defined as a mental attitude with a very special emotional content in Catholic and Hindu Goans. The intrinsic special values which inspire the orientation and human behaviour of a Goan imply that his cultural autonomy may be recognized whether in Goa or elsewhere.

The social life of Goans abroad, which is very popular, shows itself in these meetings. I refer especially to the Goan associations in England and in the Former British colonies.

The components cited did not exist before the Portuguese presence in Goa and are without doubt the product of a historical process from 1510 to 1961. These historical events began from the day of conquest of Goa and started the organization of administration according to the Lisbon model, the establishing of laws and tribunals of justice of the same type, the minting of Portuguese currency, the tolerating at the same time of religious beliefs, and the prohibiting of the practice of *sati*. This marked the beginning of a historical process of interaction between two cultures with different cultural ingredients and with mutual difficulties of participation, a process that can be considered a preliminary stage of acculturation. The flourishing Portuguese commerce that turned Lisbon into a grand commercial emporium, and then the decline of the Portuguese empire in the East in 1595, were also economic factors that influenced the society of that time.

I will overdo it were I to relate the history of Goa in detail although I think it is fit to say that the history of Goa and of Portugal show an interdependence, not hindered by their territorial distance especially since Goa was the point of Portugal's interests in the East. Already by 1559, Goa, Daman and Diu were termed the Portuguese state of India, Goa being the capital. Till the end of the 1950s, Portugal always considered Goa as a symbol of its legacy in Asia and an integral part of its constitutional territory.

I must in this context also mention the important role of the missionaries who learnt Konkani and introduced the press, the first in Asia. They were the principal carriers of Portuguese cultural traces, serving a most important place in the social cultural process. Other significant events were the conversion of the Hindus and the consequent concessions of certain privileges to all those who helped the Portuguese administration as well as the Inquisition in Goa (introduced already in 1560), and the imposition of the Portuguese language by the Viceroy in Goa during the years 1681 and 1686. The initiatives and the political liberalism of Marquis of Pombal in 1749 gave Goans the same rights as the Portuguese and these were the events that influenced this historical process.

Equally important were the era of the Felippes of Spain from 1580 to 1640, the setup of the Republic in Portugal in 1910, the new state and its colonial policies from 1932 to 1974, the independence of Portuguese colonies in 1974, and the recognition of the sovereignty of India over Goa, Daman, Diu and Nagar Haveli on 31 December 1974.

These are the additional historical facts that influenced as much the inhabitants of Goa as those of Portugal regarding their cultural past.

This interrelation gave rise to cultural traditions shown by the members of the Goan society, giving this society a coherence and continuity different from its culture.

This social process in which the conquerors and conquered in Goa tried to reach through generations and centuries a culture with its own personality, is the product of a fusion of two cultures, Indian and Portuguese. These two cultures are founded in a proper culture known as Indo-Portuguese or Luso-Indian culture. This process of the miscegenation of two culture is a historical fact which cannot be denied.

Identity is the inherent dimension of a human person, which can be considered substantial and elementary. UNESCO defends and supports in its projects the proclamation of cultural identity as an inalienable right. Identity seen under the psychological aspect, is the capacity of an individual to maintain his continuity through time and not lose his "I". Social identity is defined as the capacity of a person to satisfy and relate to the expectations of the members of his society maintaining his same social identity.[9]

What remains now is to define cultural identity which is the capacity to live and move in a defined culture and to feel as being in one's own home.

The failure of an individual to adapt to his cultural environment would result in an identity crisis which can rise from the fact that an individual cannot identity with himself or with his social milieu.[10]

Pertaining to the complexity of civilization of our times and the constant horizontal mobility of workers, cultural identity is an important consideration. It is known that people see themselves in danger of being assimilated in the country of their work. As said earlier when one ethnic group sees itself in danger of losing its identity, although this risk can be subjective, it automatically appears motivated enough to obtain the protection or the space where its cultural autonomy can be preserved and defined. The organization of social life and their folkloric activities, are for example, signs of this desire. I will describe the Goan social life of Goans in Lisbon. Till 1974 Goans did not feel the necessity of having an association seeing themselves a group numerically small but without the danger of discrimination, and on the contrary, feeling well-accepted and defended by Portuguese society.

After the great influx of people from the former colonies, Goans came to feel the necessity for starting in Lisbon a collective association with the object of giving a stamp to their cultural identity and set up the Casa de Goa, an association with its internal rules which read in Article 3, line 2B: "to organize conferences, colloquiums, debates and other forms of Indo-Portuguese cultural programmes or those related to it". In the next line D: "to start and help post-graduate and doctoral studies for theses on Indo-Portuguese culture in Portuguese, Indian and other universities". I can cite many other associations whose statutes have the same objectives.

A look at the present cultural conflicts in Germany will perhaps help show that the fight for identity and for cultural space is a very real phenomenon and absolutely normal. What one sees in Germany is seen in other continents too. In Germany one discusses vividly the problem of social integration of foreigners. There are 62,51,523 foreigners including 4,38,191 Asians,[11] the result of agreements for recruitment of workers between the German government during the 1950s and 60s with those of Greece, Italy, Yugoslavia, Morocco, Portugal, Spain, Tunis and Turkey. The number of citizens from these countries resident in Germany rose to 37,83,096 and the citizens from the European Union resident in Germany are 14,83,766.[12]

In these circumstances the German government sees itself confronted with a dilemma. To resolve the problem of integration of ethnic peoples in German society it has the following options: to maintain the identity of ethnic groups turning Germany thus into a multi-cultural country or to assimilate foreigners into the German cultural tradition.

While ethno-centricism is gaining influence, the government presents its policies for foreigners without satisfactory solutions. The reply of the government is to define the term integration as a process of peaceful co-existence, in which Germans and foreign groups respect mutually their cultural traditions, hoping that after some generations there may possibly be an assimilation.

The foreign groups of the first generation fight to safegurd their identity while the second and third generations of foreigners accept the divergent cultural traditions of their countries feeling themselves strangers as much in the countries of their work as much as in their own. Would this perhaps be an inevitable process in Goa?

The study of the growth in Goa after the liberation will give us an idea of the relevant happenings that influenced and continue to influence its cultural autonomy. The tension in which Goa found itself from 1961 till the Opinion Poll (16 January 1967) was fairly intense. At that time Goa ran the risk of losing its existence as a Union Territory. The loss of its existing frontiers before 1961 would have as consequence the loss, more or less latent, of its cultural identity. I would like to mention also that the cultural autonomy is only possible if there would be a territorial demarcation well-defined. It is a sociological fact that culture can only grow and have its own dimensions in such a setting.

With the liberation of Goa, Daman and Diu on 19 December 1961, Goa turned a page of its history on another continent abandoning its definite links with Portugal. Geographically it is on the west coast of the Indian sub-continent, 600 km. south of Mumbai, encompassing an area of 3,701 sq. kms. extending along a coast of 105 kms., reaching into the interiors of the country till about 65 kms. and with about 13,00,000 inhabitants in 1991.[13] To the north it has borders with the huge state of Maharashtra which has 3,07,400 sq. kms. The capital is Mumbai with 45 million people and Marathi is the mother tongue. The border to the south is formed by the neighbouring state of Karnataka (until 1972 called Mysore) whose capital is Bangalore, which extends over an area of 1,92,000 sq. kms. and has 46 million inhabitants, where officially Kannada is spoken.

We can easily understand that the administrative change of a small enclave of Goa since its independence on 19 December 1961 had to pass through a self-affirmation against these huge and powerful states if Goa wished to continue to maintain its own identit, which was not going to be easy. Speaking of this cultural identity, there existed the necessity of focusing on the judicial aspect of the liberation of Goa although there were Goans of the opinion that "it was the invasion of Goa by the Indian troops" and it gave rise to the loss of judicial identity under the guise of constitutional and international right. This fact cannot be considered in my view as a loss of judicial identity, seeing that Goa maintains itself as a separate state of the Union with the same boundaries of 1961 and with Konkani as the official language.

I would like to mention however that the Indian government had to put into effect soon after the liberation a plebiscite to come to know the opinions of the inhabitants. The plebiscite deciding in favour of maintaining Goa as a state separate from the Union and its antecedents, are events in Goan history that made possible the continuation of its cultural and territorial identity. The question started on 12 March 1962 the date on which the 12th Constitutional Amendment was introduced in the Lok Sabha[14], according to which Goa, Daman and Diu became part of the Indian Union.

The political evolution shown below in a general way gives an idea of a situation in force in Goa after the liberation. On 24 September 1962, the Central government nominated a civil governor for Goa along with a consultative group made up of 29 persons. The Governor was a native of Maharashtra who gave rise to conflicts from the moment in which he tried to merge Goa into Maharashtra. It was only on the 9 December 1963, that the first free elections took place for the local assembly of 30 members. The Maharashtra Gomantak Party (MGP) which wanted the merger of Goa with Maharashtra was the winner in the elections getting 14 seats while the United Goans Party which defended the state of Goa separate from the Union could get only 12 seats. The assembly nominated the Chief Minister and members of his cabinet. This group had only consultative functions although all decisions were taken in Delhi.

On 14 March 1962, Prime Minister Pandit Jawaharlal Nehru declared in the Lok Sabha that "we would like to clarify that Goa should maintain its identity, its individuality. It is more than 400 years that Goa had its own identity that the historical process gave it. Let us not try to change or end this identity. In fact some persons counselled us that the Constitution should be amended and Konkani be considered as one more official language of India".

On this day it was decreed in the Lok Sabha that Goa, Daman

and Diu could constitute a local assembly with 30 members and that 2 of the elected members could be sent as representatives to the Lok Sabha which happened on 9 December 1963. On 22 January 1965 a group of members of Parliament made a proposal in the Assembly of Goa, Daman and Diu that Goa should be merged into Maharashtra. On 10 March 1965, the Chief Minister of Goa confirmed this proposal alleging that the integration would pay attention to the economic well-being of Goans and that the religious, educational and cultural legacy of all groups of Goans would be safeguarded and that in future it would continue and grow. Maharashtra would do everything to realize these objectives. Besides this, the decision of integration with Maharashtra would consolidate the Indian Union. However, all that was left was the petition that the Constitution could be changed for this.

I would like to underline that soon after the liberation of Goa there was no doubt on the part of the politicians that Goa had a unique culture. As regards the declaration of the Prime Minister seen at that time, it shows this position.

One of the historical events which defined the existence of Goa as the state of the Indian Union and that gave continuity to its territorial autonomy was the plebiscite, which, as I have just referred to took place on 16 January 1967. The Opinion Poll had to options: in favour of integration with Maharashtra or of continuing to be a state of the Union. It will not be a speculation on my part to declare that in case the decision was in favour of merger with Maharashtra, not obtaining all the promises of the government of this state, Goa would have run the risk earlier than later of its cultural identity going to ruin.

The following were the results of the Poll:

Total number of votes	3,88,382	
Valid votes	3,17,633	(81.7%)
Votes for non-merger	1,72,191	(54.2%)
Votes for merger	1,38,170	(43.5%)
Invalid votes	7,272	(2.3%)

Goa was able to maintain its territorial identity and continues to safeguard its cultural autonomy.

It was a great pledge with which the Goan community completed this plebiscite. A comparison with the voting patterns for the Assembly elections in 1963 show that in all the talukas (old Conselhos) there was a higher percentage, more than in the first local elections in 1963. The participation in the plebiscite was 81.7 per cent. In certain electoral zones it reached 90 per cent, while in the 1963 general elections the massive turnout was only 74.85 per cent.

A comparison of the results in the Old and New Conquests shows that the Hindus and the Catholics had in their majority voted in favour of a separate state. It indicated that the Goans decided to keep their status not purely for economic or linguistic reasons but also because of their cultural heritage.[15]

The other point that deserves to be looked into is the linguistic problem in Goa which came up on the occasion of the choosing of an official language. It is an indisputable fact that a language, like a religion, has elements that also define the cultural identity of a community.

I wish to show the existence of the following linguistic structure in Goa in 1960.[16]

Language	No. of speakers	percentage
Konkani	4,97,227	84.3
Marathi	9,142	1.5
Portuguese	8,972	1.3
Urdu	7,883	1.0
Hindi	1,143	all less than one per cent
Gujarati	926	
Kannada	813	
English	441	

I have not obtained the actual given statistics to be able to make a comparison but I was able to verify that 3 per cent of the Catholic families spoke Portuguese in 1991.[17]

The fight for Konkani spoken by the majority of Goans, as an official language instead of for Marathi is one more proof that Goans managed to demonstrate the importance of the principal element of their culture. The result of this fight was the decision of the Central Government in January 1987 to consider Konkani in the devanagri script as the official language.

With the official recognition of the sovereignty of Indian over Goa, Daman and Diu on 30 December 1974[18] there is an indication of a new phase of rebirth in the relations between Goa and Portugal. The Indo-Portuguese cultural accord of 30 May 1980[19] will offer a cultural relationship stronger than ever between the two countries. The opening of the consulate general in Goa as well as representations of organizations of the State and private bodies like the *Instituto Camões*, the *Fundação Càlouste Gulbenkian*, the *Fundação Oriente*, etc. have come to reinforce the ties that one thought were not to be seen. This new relationship has motivated the setting up of many other associations in Goa with the objective of forwarding and investigating into the relationship that existed between Portugal and Goa. In this context I could mention the Xavier Centre of Historical Research, the Indo-Latin Centre, the Academy for Portuguese and the Association of Culture and Portuguese language studies, among others. Actually with these institutions Goans face anew a current of a Portuguese cultural profile which is going without doubt to strengthen the respective cultural legacies.

Finally, I would like to underline that the Indian Constitution shows that the states of the Union have a proper constitution (with the exception of Jammu and Kashmir), the organization of the legislature, executive and judiciary, approved in the Constitution of the Union and according to the principal statutes of the same.

The existence as separate states and their respective boundaries are not guaranteed by the Constitution, a new territorial formation is possible through a Constitutional Amendment, which can be approved by a two thirds majority in both houses of Parliament.

Parliament can also make laws in the area of competence of the states when the government recommends so with a two-thirds majority, and when the concerned states are in agreement, or when a state of emergency is declared.

The concerned legislatures deal with a list of 200 items distributed between the Central and local governments. Some items are exclusive for the Centre (foreign affairs, defence, finance, atomic energy, commerce, transport) and some for the states (police, health, agriculture) while some are joint items (civil and penal law, health, economic planning, and price control) in which the central legislature has precedence. This division of items can change through a constitutional amendment approved earlier by half the members of the respective assemblies.

When the President accepts that the execution of functions of the government of one of the states is uncertain, (e.g., when it is not possible to form a coalition government) he can appoint an administrator to the State. However, this provision is to be approved by Parliament within two months. Without being pessimistic this situation can some day, although hypothetically, be valid for any state in India as much as for Goa.

Conclusion

The historical process that bound Portugal and Goa for centuries gave rise to a unique and marked culture and the genesis of an Indo-Portuguese culture. This is a process of acculturation that identifies Goans culturally. There exists in Goa actually a latent necessity to discuss the problem of cultural identity, paying attention to the actual socio-political circumstances. This necessity results from the fear of losing one's identity and of seeking a space where this can be saved.

Indian policies soon after the liberation of Goa did not put in doubt that Goans may not have had a unique identity. The plebiscite in Goa decided in favour of being a state of the Indian Union and came to maintain a territorial unity and helped safeguard for a long time Goan cultural identity.

The active associations of Goans are signs of its maintaining its cultural identity. Seeing the concept of culture not as a static concept, the cultural values of Goans today are signs that these are not identical to those of the 1960s soon after the liberation. Based on a population statistic[20] of inhabitants who also use other cultural traditions, one believes that there will arise one culture with a symbiosis of cultural traditions and precisely for this reason a discussion of the problem of cultural identity is going to gain an important position in Goa.

With the recognition by Portugal of India's sovereignty over Goa, Daman and Diu in 1974 after a long period of silence, a phase of rebirth between Goa and Portugal was started and with this a new cultural understanding. With the recognition of Konkani as the official language, the unique Goan identity came to be asserted.

TABLE 5.1: Population in Goa and India: 1941-1991

Year	Population in Goa	%`	Population in India	%
1941	5,40,925	7.05	31,85,00,000	14.20
1951	5,47,448	1.21	36,10,00,000	13.34
1961	5,89,997	7.77	43,91,00,000	21.63
1971	7,95,120	34.77	54,78,00,000	24.78
1981	10,07,749	26.74	68,38,00,000	24.80
1991	11,68,622	15.96	84,39,00,000	23.50

TABLE 5.2: Population break-up in Goa, Daman and Diu in 1971/1981

	Total	Rural	Urban
1971			
Goa	7,95,120	5,91,877	2,03,243
Daman	38,739	21,422	17,317
Diu	23,912	17,698	6,214
1981			
Goa	10,03,141	6,80,929	3,22,212
Daman	48,557	27,554	21,003
Diu	30,419	22,399	8,020

TABLE 5.3: Hindu-Christian Population in Goa

Year	Community	Figures	%
1851	Hindus	1,28,824	35.5
	Christians	2,32,189	64.5
1900	Hindus	2,60,144	49.76
	Christians	2,62,648	50.24

(Contd.)

TABLE 5.3 *(Contd.)*

Year	Community	figures	%
1910	Hindus	2,70,105	50.16
	Christians	2,68,398	49.84
1921	Hindus	2,74,187	52.56
	Christians	2,47,478	47.44
1931	Hindus	5,40,443	50.29
	Christians	2,47,570	49.71
1940	Hindus	2,86,414	53.81
	Christians	2,45,858	46.19
1950	Hindus	3,07,127	56.10
	Christians	2,30,984	42.20
1961	Hindus	3,84,378	59.92
	Christians	2,27,202	38.07
1971	Hindus	4,96,389	62.43
	Christians	2,70,126	33.97
1981	Hindus	6,46,986	64.20
	Christians	3,15,902	31.25

TABLE 5.4: Percentage of literates 1961/1971/1981

	1961	1971	1981
Goa	30.8	44.8	57.0
Kerala	46.8	60.4	69.2
Delhi	52.7	55.6	61.1
Maharashtra	29.8	39.2	47.4
Karnataka	25.4	31.5	38.4
All-India	24.0	29.5	36.2

TABLE 5.5: Indices of Economic growth in Goa

	1960	1980	1982
Industry			
- units	50	2,535	2,416
Mining			
Exports (lakh)	66.37	129.89	136.79
Power			
Consumed (lakh Kwh)	78.7	3,408.30	2,519.79
Per capita Consumption (%) (Kwh)	13	302	232
Communication			
No. of post offices (No.)	81	236	236
No of letter boxes (No.)	219	708	716
No. of telephones (No.)	548	9124	10287
Literacy and Education			
Literacy (%)	30.77	55.86	57
Schools (No.)	593	1873	1904
Students (No.)	52755	250066	260677
Teachers (No.)	1768	8925	9299
Students Univ. Colleges (No.)	475	4703	6959
No. of colleges	—	17	18
Public Health			
No. of Govt. hospitals	17	33	32
No. of health centres	20	161	167
Vital Statistics			
Birth rate (%)	31.39	24.15	24.15
Death rate (%)	13.39	7.60	7.60
Infant Mortality Rate (%)	69.77	32.64	32.64
Tourism			
No. of hotels	25	196	207
No. of Guests	6608	435839	513012
Banking			
No. of Banking offices	5	229	242

Sources: Tables 5.1 to 5.5 are from Prabhakar Angle, *Goa: An Economic Review*, Mumbai, The Goa Hindu Association Kala Vibhag, 1983.

NOTES AND REFERENCES

1. Carmo de Noronha, *Contracorrente*, Goa, Fundação Oriente, 1991, p. 20.
2. Prabhakar Angle, *Goa: Concepts and Misconcepts*, Mumbai, The Goa-Hindu Association Kala Vibhag, 1994, p. 20.
3. *Ibid.*, p. 31
4. Noronha, *op. cit.*, pp. 3-15.
5. M. J. Gabriel de Saldanha, *História de Goa — Politica e arqueológica*, vols. I & II, New Delhi, Asian Educational Services, 1980, p. 36.
6. In Germany we frequently face the problems of ethnocentricity about which I have made references below.
7. W. E. Muhlmann, "Kultur" in *Dicionário da Sociologia*, Bernsdorf, 1969.
8. Percival Noronha, "O Mobilário Indo-Portuguez" in *Revista de Macau a Goa*, p. 53.
9. H. Bausinger, *Zur Kulturalen Dimension der Identitat*, Stuttgart, 1971; *Kulturelle Identitat*, Bonn, 1982.
10. The problem of second and third generation foreigners in Germany has been well-discussed. They feel strangers both in the country of domicile and in their own native ones.
11. *Statistics of the Ministry of Social and Public Works*, January 1993.
12. *Ibid.*
13. *Statistical Pocket-Book of Goa, Daman and Diu*, Panaji, Directorate of Planning, Statistics and Evaluation, 1991.
14. The Indian Parliament consists of two houses (Rajya Sabha and Lok Sabha). Goa has two elected members represented in the Lok Sabha for a period of five years, and one nominated member in the Rajya Sabha.
15. See Tables 5.3 and 5.4.
16. *Annuário Estatistico de Goa*, 1960.
17. Robert Strasser, "Paradies am Indischen Ozean-Goa", *Verlag Indo-Culture*, 1992.
18. Decree No. 206/75, 17 April 1975.
19. *Diário da Republica*, No. 125, 30 May 1980.
20. See Tables 5.1 and 5.2.

PART II

GOA IN ITS CONTACTS WITH JAPAN AND MOZAMBIQUE

SIX

THE IMAGE OF INDIA IN THE HISTORY OF THE CHURCH IN JAPAN BY JOÃO RODRIGUES, S.J.

HELMUT FELDMANN

João Rodrigues was born around 1561 at Sernancelhe (Lamego, Portugal). He went to Japan as a servant of a Portuguese trader in 1575-76 when he was only about 15 years old. In 1580 he entered the Society of Jesus and matriculated at the College of St. Paul's which had just been founded at Funai. He was ordained priest in 1594 at Macau. On returning to Japan in 1596 he became an interpreter to the Japanese in their commercial activities. In 1608 he published his *Arte da Lingua do Japão* (The Art of the Japanese Language) at Nagasaki, which is the first description of the Portuguese language by a westerner. He was nicknamed *Tsuzzu* (the interpreter). In 1614 he was forced to leave Japan and returned to Macau where he died in 1634 without having been able to return to the land of his special love.

At Macau he worked at the editing of the *História da Igreja do Japão* during the years 1620-34, years when the Portuguese commercial empire in Japan was coming to an end. These were also the years of growing persecution for the Jesuits in Japan culminating in their expulsion and in the death of many Christians. This decline of the military, commercial and religious power of Portugal in the Far East conditions the peculiar perspective of the *História*, impelling Rodrigues to show, with ideological and juridical arguments, that the only European nation with the right of presence in the Far East was Portugal.

Initially the churches of Japan and China were linked to Goa, giving the Jesuits the monopoly of evangelization of the two countries. Till 1580, no one questioned the primacy of the archbishopric of Goa over the missions of China and Japan, or the monopoly of the Jesuits given by the Pope and confirmed by the Portuguese Crown. With the ascent to the throne by Felippe II and his upholding this *status quo*, the Spanish Franciscans in the Philippines did not accept the supremacy of the Portuguese Jesuits in the Far East and entered Japan being welcomed benevolently, though temporarily, by Hideyoshi. Along with the friars came the Spanish merchants seeing the rich Chinese-Japanese trade. Both wanted Manila to be a substitute for Goa as Church leadership in the Far East and to have a share in the Sino-Japanese market. In 1608 Rome authorized the route to Japan via the Philippines.[1]

João Rodrigues defended the interests of the Portuguese Padroado in the Far East against the Spanish pretences, and the rights of the Society of Jesus in Japan and in China, but favoured the administrative disassociation of the Church of Japan and China from the archbishopric of Goa. It appears that he was never in Goa. He sets his *História* the task of showing the independence of the province of Japan and its importance as a second centre of the spread of evangelization of Asia. The work is divided in two parts: the missioning of Japan and of China. Right at the beginning of the text, Rodrigues explains the reason why he was led to include China in his history of the Japanese mission "as the mission of China (...) belongs to the Province of Japan because it was founded and designed as a mission by the Superiors of the Society of Jesus in Japan (...) in 1582 (...) the foundation of this mission belongs to the general history of this Province as well as the progress it had during the 37 years it was under Japanese administration". Goa and India, too, appear in the *História* as an important point in the ideological justification of Portuguese and Jesuit presence in Japan.

The *História da Igreja do Japão* remained incomplete. Everything shows that Rodrigues completed only a small part of his vast project: a general presentation of Japan, its geography and history, its political and social system, its religion and customs — and the narration of the Jesuit mission of Japan till the death of St. Francis Xavier. It is strange that he did not complete the work although in Macau he probably may not have lacked the time needed. We do not know which were the obstacles, moral or material which stood in his way.[2]

Rodrigues was not the first to write the history of the

missionary movement in Japan. His more important predecessor was Fr. Luis Frois, author of the voluminous *História do Japão.*[3] According to Fr. Wicki, editor of the work, Fr. Alessandro Valignano, the Visitor, had entrusted Frois in 1583 with the writing of the history of the Japanese mission. He accepted the charge. However, the Visitor later showed little satisfaction with the work. About an annual letter from Frois, he remarks that "*Frois no tiene tanto miramiento en escoger lo que es bien que se escriva*" (his criterion in choosing what was to be published did not correspond always with the interests of the Society of Jesus). Indeed, Frois gave little prominence to the grand religious and national feelings of the period of the Discoveries, acting before it like an empirical, objective and critical observer of the missionary activities of the Jesuits in Japan. It seems that the Visitor halted the publication of the *História do Japão* and the manuscript was sent neither to Lisbon nor to Rome. The Society of Jesus, years after the death of Frois, gave Fr. João Rodrigues the task of bringing out an edition of the history of the mission of Japan more in line with its interests. The result is the *A História da Igreja do Japão*.

An essential difference in the structure between the two works is the chronological orientation of the work of Frois and the organic vision of Rodrigues. In his *História,* Frois returns often to the annual letters edited by him, while Rodrigues refusing to report by "fragments" (p. 10) inserts episodic informations of the mission in the context of the universal history where they received their inner significance. It appears that his predecessors, including Frois, did not always have respect for historical truth.[4]

But what is historical truth for Rodrigues? He considers divine providence to be the fundamental law of universal history, whose roots would be the building up of the city of God in the world, the salvation of humanity. Although divine providence had fixed from eternity the coordination of universal history guaranteeing that it culminates in the victory of Christianity on this planet, the path to the realization of this objective is long and hard, due to an equally strong opponent — the devil. Thus, universal history for Rodrigues is essentially sacred history, revealed and written in the Old and New Testaments as well as in the doctrine and actions of the Catholic Church. Historical truth does not deal with the reality of profane events but turns to them only when the facts of profane history allow one to see the hand of divine providence. And Rodrigues accepting the official thinking of the Discoveries, knows how to see the hand of divine providence whenever the historical roles of Portugal and of the Society of Jesus demanded it.

That the Portuguese nation is a chosen nation by God, Rodrigues sees this confirmed by indications of secular history which allows one to catch a glimpse of divine providence. For example, the fact that "St. Francis Xavier was born in the same year in which India was discovered by the Portuguese, and that he arrived in India the same year that Japan was discovered by the Portuguese (...) So it appears that Our Lord has waited for the arrival to India of Fr. Francis in order to allow Japan to be discovered". Such indications allow him to see the discovery of Japan by the Portuguese, as "a work purely of God and not a human one".

Bearing in mind Rodrigues' idea of universal history, it is logical that he should see the role of the devil in all the actions contrary to the interests of the mission, who is no less omnipresent than divine providence. Universal history shows itself in this way as a continuous war between God and Satan for the conquest of humanity; it is a war in which the missionaries understand themselves as God's army at war against the vast army of the devil.

The *História* starts with a geographical description of Japan and the whole of Asia, from the Red Sea till the Molucca archipelago. Rodrigues reinforces the major importance of Asia in the plan of sacred history. "In this part were made the first things of the world, in it God made Paradise and the first parents of the human family, and man was redeemed (...) It was here that the cult and the religion of the true God flourished ahead of any other place (...) In it flowered the patriarchs and prophets, and the human race was saved from the great flood and turned to inhabit the world again, and in it were written the histories of Old Testament and a large part of the New. In this part was completed the first and oldest scriptures, the sacred text written by Moses (pp. 15-16, 17).

Rodrigues distinguishes two phases of the Christianization of Asia: the phase represented by St. Thomas, apostle of Jesus Christ and first apostle of the East, and the phase represented by St. Francis Xavier, second apostle of the East, separated from the first by a gap of approximately 1,500 years, during which time the devil had succeeded in stopping in large measure the missionary work of St. Thomas, leaving St. Francis the task of recovering lost land and starting the Christianization of the whole of Asia.

The format of the description of the beginnings of the arrival of Francis Xavier into Japan is based fundamentally on the parallels of St. Thomas and St. Francis Xavier. The title of the third book of the *História* in which "is contained as a start to the preaching of the Holy Gospel in that kingdom by the holy Fr. Francis Xavier, second apostle of the East", has in the margin a note of João Rodrigues, the following observation "having to treat of the second apostle of this Christianity, reason calls that first we speak of the first person, the glorious apostle, St. Thomas and of the places in which he preached and where afterwards also preached the second person, as he had foretold". The parallel between the life and work of St. Thomas and St. Francis is not an invention of Fr. Rodrigues, but integrates the ideology of the Discoveries. According to Rodrigues it was king Dom João himself who sent out an expedition to India to inquire into "the life, death and miracles of the holy apostle Thomas (p. 7).

Asia is represented by Rodrigues as being the continent which withstood being christianized. Jesus knowing the difficulties, would choose St. Thomas, the unbelieving apostle, to spread the faith in Asia. Allowing him to put his hands into his wounds and thus converting him, unflinchingly into the reality of resurrection, he would prepare him for his difficult mission. St. Thomas considered, according to Rodrigues, India to be the cradle of Buddhism, conqueror of China and Japan (p. 27), and the platform from which ought to begin the conversion of the Asians to Catholicism. That St. Francis is to imitate by divine providence this important movement, Rodrigues considered revealed by the fact of St. Francis being sent to Goa in 1542, the year in which the first Portuguese arrived in Japan (p. 86). St. Francis Xavier is considered thus by Rodrigues as being the direct successor of St. Thomas.

Rodrigues tries to show the model function of the mission of St. Thomas. In India, St. Thomas converted, according to Rodrigues, first the king of Malabar and many of his subjects, by moving along the whole of the Malabar Coast. "And from there he went to Mylapore, being the greatest, richest and most powerful city of the whole of India, in which he converted the king and many of the people by his preaching". He cites various sources that allow him to affirm that St. Thomas founded eight bishoprics in India and that he embarked from Mylapore for China in a Chinese vessel. According to him, St. Thomas disembarked at Canton, thus opening the door where 1,500 years later the Portuguese would enter China. Many persecutions followed, according to Rodrigues, those first centres of Christians in India and in other parts of Asia, till the arrival of the Portuguese. (p. 6)

It is highly significant according to Rodrigues that St. Francis Xavier went on pilgrimage to Mylapore on the east coast of India, a city where "the Portuguese found the sacred body and tomb and the place where St. Thomas was killed. He wanted to visit the very place of the martyrdom and sacred relics in order to be inflamed in more ardent desires and through this to attain that which might be the divine will". He passed, according to Rodrigues, four months in the house of the Apostle where "he was greatly persecuted by the devil that a great service to God was shown by what the Saint had to do [ ], however the Saint overcame him and frightened him so much so that he always had a fear of St. Francis Xavier (p. 32). Later as he always writes, in a letter cited by Rodrigues, "Our Lord wanted to give me a feeling within my soul of being served by me going to Japan." The enemy worked much to stop my going. (p. 57) And Rodrigues comments: "from these words of the Blessed Father, this resolution clearly shows itself to be in conformity with the divine will and order that expressly ordered him to go there". (p. 57)

Rodrigues shows in many cases during the narrative of the *História*, the parallel between the life and works of St. Thomas and St. Francis. He searches for signs in the first Christian communities in India and the neighbouring countries. He dedicates two years of investigation to collect Christian vestiges of the countries around China and of China itself, in order to show that the recovery of those old groups of Christianity and the continuation of the evangelization fell to Portugal.

Rodrigues sees in the various prophecies that Portugal is the nation chosen by God to recapture and continue the work of St. Thomas and that St. Francis is the second apostle of the East. He affirms that in the maritime city of Mylapore which during the time of St. Thomas was some leagues from the sea, the same St. Thomas foretold "that when the sea would come close to the Malabar Coast, from the West would come a white people who would preach the very law that he had preached" and he comments "that prophecy has been fulfilled, for that white people are clearly the Portuguese who through oceans that nobody had travelled before, were sent as navigators to India by the Most Serene and Imperial kings of Portugal from the far West, with the authority of the Vicar of Christ our Lord on earth, in order that the Gospel preachers might be introduced in the East and be protected, and that by their value and blood, they might plant everywhere the true standard of the Holy Cross of Christ our Saviour, as Father Francis had done with immortal fame and memory continuing the work done by the holy saint". (p. 3)

He refers to the modern theologians who show the divine character of the mission of St. Francis Xavier and of the Portuguese people with prophecies from the Old Testament "Ite, Angeli veloces ad gentem convulsam, et dilaceratam, ad populum terribilem, post quem non est alius".[5] And the theological interpretation according to Rodrigues is: "It seems that the angels are the preachers like Blessed Father Francisco and those of the company of apostles of Japan".[6] The missionization of Japan by the Portuguese is in this manner an important stage of the universal history conceived from eternity by God.

Summing up we can affirm that India plays two essential ideological roles in the *História da Igreja do Japão*.

1. It allows João Rodrigues to show St. Francis Xavier as the successor and direct heir of St. Thomas thus giving a higher legitimacy to the presence of Portugal and of the Society of Jesus in Asia generally and in Japan in particular.
2. It proves that by the will of divine providence the discovery of Japan and the coming of St. Francis Xavier to India are interconnected, the evangelization of Japan being thus by the will of God the exclusive mission of the Society of Jesus.

NOTES AND REFERENCES

1. João Paulo Oliveira e Costa, "A rivalidade luso-espanhola no Extremo Oriente e a quereia missionológica no Japão" in *O Século Cristão do Japão*, ed. Roberto Carneiro & Teodoro de Matos, Lisbon, 1994.
2. The written fragments remained unedited during the centuries. There are two manuscripts at Madrid and Lisbon (at the Palácio da Ajuda containing 236 folios). Till now there had been an incomplete edition of about two-thirds of this manuscript but without the missionary work of St. Francis Xavier *História da Igreja do Japão*, edited by João do Amaral Abranches Pinto in *Noticias de Macau* (Colecção Noticias de Macau, vol. 13, 1954). The title is misleading, it has been already published solely with the description of the Overseas of this, the edition is not critical, limiting

itself to a transcription of the codice at Lisbon and leaving, although the manuscript may be often difficult to read, the notes or comments, and the very introduction. Abranches Pinto, having worked on this transcription when he was ambassador of Portugal in Japan, did it as an amateur of documents related to the Portuguese presence in Japan. The edition is very rare, the work having been practically unknown till now, at least in the West. There is a good edition in two volumes, in Japanese with a introduction and with critical notes.

3. Published in five volumes by the *Biblioteca Nacional de Lisboa* (1980 1984).
4. Preface to the reader, p. 10.
5. Isaias ch. 18.
6. Rodrigues, I, p. 89.

SEVEN

RELATIONS BETWEEN JAPAN AND GOA IN THE 16TH AND 17TH CENTURIES*

TAKASHI GONOI

Relations between Japan and Goa which endured for about one hundred years, started in 1548 when the Japanese Anjiro (Yajiro) visited Goa in order to meet Francis Xavier. During this period the contacts between Japan and Goa were largely political and diplomatic.

First Phase

Those who took part in the first phase of the contacts were some *daimyos* (feudal lords) of the Kyushu region. In the autumn of 1551, Otomo Yoshishige, one of the important feudal lords of the time sent a fidalgo as his delegate to the Viceroy of India accompanied by Francis Xavier. The objective of this mission was to establish friendly relations with the King of Portugal. In 1553 the same fidalgo was sent again to Goa. When Fr. Balthasar Gago returned to Goa from Japan in 1560, Otomo sent Dom Sebastião of Portugal, as a present, a dagger with a scabbard encircled by a golden serpent with the object of bringing their relations closer together. In return he acquired some artillery pieces (*kuni-kuzushi*) and saltpetre, material for the making of ammunition to consolidate his military force.

One of the daimyos of Kyushu, Shimazu Takahisa, according to the letters sent in 1561 and 1562 also requested Fr. Provincial of the Society of Jesus and the Governor of India to send Portuguese vessels to his port.

* Translated from the Portuguese by Charles J Borges.

Second Phase

The second phase of relations was between the governments of Japan and Goa, the Governor of Goa having taken the initiative to do so. Viceroy Duarte de Menezes sent Fr. Alessandro Valignano, Jesuit Visitor of India as his ambassador with a letter dated April 1587 to Toyotomi Hideyoshi, to ask for protection for the missionaries, according to a request of Fr. Gaspar Coelho, Vice-Provincial of Japan. This letter which has its date changed to 1588, is presently kept in the temple of Myohoin and is considered as a national treasure of Japan.

The case of the Portuguese ship sunk in the creek of Nagasaki on 6 January 1610 (*Nossa Senhora da Graça*) led to the suspension of commerce with Japan during seventy years beginning from 1540, and this affected the economy of Macau. In the summer of 1611, the authorities of the same city sent Dom Nuno Soutomaior as delegate to Japan. Governor Edo-Bakufu (or the governor of Edo) gave him a document with a red seal to carry out business as before, in which it was clearly mentioned that this delegate had come from Goa. A little later Horatio Narete (chief captain who was to arrive in Macau from Goa in 1612) was sent as delegate from Goa to Japan.

After the revolt of Shimabara, when the commercial relations with the Portuguese in 1639 were snapped due to politics of isolation and restored the independence of Portugal, the Portuguese Governor sent Gonçalo de Siqueira as ambassador of Japan in 1644 to try to help the economic situation in Macau. However, Gonçalo de Siqueira had to return to Goa, and left for Nagasaki in 1646. Siqueira came to Japan to inform the Governor Edo-Bakufu about the restoration. However, the Governor informed him that he would not be able to return to Japan. The Governor of Goa would be unable to do anything for his own country and the city of Macau.

Various Groups

We can refer to the seventeen Japanese whose identities can be confirmed against their proper or baptismal names. They are:

1. The catechumen and those accompanying him.
2. Students on their way to Europe and aspirants to the priesthood.

3. The four ambassadors sent to the Pope and their escorts.
4. The delegate sent by Otomo to the Viceroy of India.

The first group met Anjiro (Yajiro) who had visited St. Paul's College at Goa coming from Malacca with his two servants. The baptismal name of Anjiro was Paulo de Santa Fé. He had worked with Francis Xavier in the compilation of the Japanese catechism and had helped in the propagation of Christianity in Japan. Joanne and Antonio, their servants who converted to Christianity, after they had returned to Japan, went to Hirado with Xavier and in November 1551, returned to Goa accompanying him. Their mission was to accompany other new missionaries to Japan. In the following year António went with Fr. Balthasar Gago to Funai, capital of the kingdom of Bungo. Joanne too went along with Fr. Melchior Nunes Barreto, Vice-Provincial of the Province of India, who having left Goa in April 1554 arrived in Bungo in July 1556.

Anjiro, António and Joanne, have thus contributed towards the coming of the Jesuits, pioneers of Christianity in Japan. They also distinguished themselves both as students of Japanese as well as of Japanese customs and habits.

The six persons who belonged to the second group visited Goa as non-Jesuits, en route to Europe after their ordinations. The two young persons, Bernardo and Mathias who came with Xavier in 1552, wanted to go to Portugal to study but Mathias died in Goa. Bernardo left Goa for Portugal alone at the beginning of 1553. He entered the Society of Jesus and studied at the College of Coimbra. Arriving in Rome in January 1555 he entered the Roman College to continue his studies. In February of the following year he returned to Coimbra but died there in February 1557.

The four other persons also went to Rome via Goa to be ordained in the 17th century. However, it is not clear when they passed through Goa. Araki Tomas, ordained in 1612 in Rome returned to Nagasaki as a secular priest in 1615 but after four years was imprisoned by the Governor of Nagasaki, reconverted to Buddhism and joined in the anti-Christian movement of Bukufu.

Besides these, there were three dojukus (dojucos) of the Society of Jesus who helped the missionaries as catechists. After the autumn of 1614, those who passed through Macau were not able to study in the respective college due to the poor response that Fr. Valentim Carvalho, Provincial of Japan, got from the Japanese. For this reason they wanted to be ordained in Rome. Pedro Kibe Casui who left Macau in 1616, would arrive in Goa the following year. Passing through the Persian Desert, he visited Jerusalem, the Holy Land and arrived in Rome about 1620. After he was ordained priest in November of the same year, he entered the Society of Jesus, arrived in Goa via Lisbon on 28 May 1624, and returned to Japan in 1630. But nine years later he was imprisoned in the region of Tohoku, and sent to Yedo where he died as a martyr.

Miguel Minoes who went to Portugal via Goa obtained the title of Master of Arts having completed the course of philosophy at Evora in four years time. In 1621 he entered the Society of Jesus in Rome, having been ordained in 1626, but before his return to Japan, he died in Lisbon in 1628.

Konishi Mancio arrived in Rome in 1623 via Goa and Lisbon and entered the Society of Jesus there. In 1627 he was ordained and returned to Goa in the autumn of 1629. He returned to Japan in 1632, and having being imprisoned in 1644 at Osaka, he was martyred. After his death there was no other missionary in Japan. Of the five who belonged to this group and who came in touch with the Christian culture in Europe only three returned to Japan and involved themselves in the propagation of Christianity.

The third group was part of the ambassadorial committee sent to Europe. The sending of the embassy to the Pope on the advice of Fr. Visitor Valignano marked the beginning of the cultural interchange between Japan and Europe. The remaining three Japanese accompanied the four ambassadors as advisers and to complete other matters. In the middle of November 1583, they arrived in Goa and on 20 February of the following year they went from Cochin to Lisbon. On 29 May 1587, they returned to Goa where they spent eleven months till the 22 of April of the following year. Bro. Jorge de Loyola who was instructor of the four Japanese ambassadors, was to die in Macau. Meanwhile the five persons except Augustinho, entered the Society of Jesus after coming back from Japan. All of them except Chijiwa Miguel were ordained.

The official ambassador Chijiwa Miguel who meanwhile left the Society of Jesus in 1601, afterwards served Omura Yoshiaki, daimyo of the state of Omura and his cousin. In 1606, when Omura banned Christianity, he also followed him, having started to move towards his own destruction.

Ito Mancio another official ambassador studied moral theology from 1601 until the summer of 1604 at Macau and was ordained by Bishop Luis de Cerqueira in 1608 at Nagasaki. He died in November 1612 at Nagasaki.

One of the other members of the committee, Hara (Campo) Martinho, who had a talent for languages coming from Rome on his return to Goa greeted Valignano in Latin in the name of the ambassador. In 1608 he was ordained priest and turned into a central figure of Japanese Jesuits. For this reason he was not supported by the European Jesuits to carry out the functions of secretary of Father Provincial. As he could not stay in Japan he had to go to Macau in November 1614. At Macau he helped Fr. João Rodrigues *Tsuzzu*, author of the *História da Igreja do Japão*, where he died in October 1629.

Yet another member of the committee, Nakaura Julião started his theological studies in 1601 at Macau having being ordained in 1608 at Nagasaki. After the exit of the missionaries of Japan in November 1614 he substituted them in this activity in the region of Kyushu. In 1632 he was imprisoned in the city of Kokura, and on 18 October of the following year he was martyred at Nagasaki.

One of the missions of the ambassadorial committee, particularly of Constantino Dourado and Jorge de Loyola was to acquire a European printing press. Constantino Dourado entered the Society of Jesus in October 1595, studying Latin and instrumental music in the Seminary. We can consider him as a cultural intermediary between Japan and Europe. Leaving Macau in 1614 he was ordained at Malacca in 1617. In the following year he took charge as Rector of Seminary at Macau where he died in July 1620.

Bro. Jorge de Loyola too learnt the art of printing in Lisbon and perfected his technique during his stay in Goa. At Macau he helped in the publication of the book *De Missione Legatorum Iaponensium ad Romanam curiam, robusq; in Europa, ac toto intinere animaduersis dialugvs...* written by Fr. Eduardo de Sande, and started to translate it into Japanese. Meanwhile he could not complete this work because he died in 1589. With reference to Augustinho one knows little about him after his return from Japan. I have spoken below about the contribution that this group made in the cultural interchange between Japan and Europe.

The fourth group had a fidalgo of Otomo Yoshishige. As I have said he went to India in the capacity of delegate of Otomo accompanied by Fr. Francis Xavier. In 1552, he was baptized as

Lourenço Pereira having as his godfather Afonso de Noronha, Viceroy of India. In October 1553 he went once again sent by Hirado as delegate accompanied by Bro. Pedro Alcaçova arriving in Goa on 16 March 1554. He will be remembered as the promoter of relations between Otomo, the Viceroy of India and the king of Portugal.

The attitude of the Portuguese Governor in relation to Otomo was revealed through a letter dated 16 March 1558 sent by Dom Sebastião, king of Portugal to Otomo. On the other hand the gratitude of Otomo Sorin for the king of Portugal is confirmed by the dress of his second son Chikaiye called Dom Sebastião, his baptismal name, which took place in 1576. One cannot deny that the mission sent by Otomo to the Viceroy of India had the objective of getting military material, as well as to propose the cementing of relations with the royal house of Portugal. It seems that Otomo Sorin intended to promote his position and dignity of legitimate daimyo of the lineage of Kamakura, strengthening the relations with the royal house of Portugal.

Following this, I will speak of the objectives of the third group in the context of the cultural interchange between Japan and Europe, more specifically, and the introduction of the press in Japan, the acquisition of the printing skill and the influence that *Isopo no Fabvlas*, today known as *Isoppu Monogatari* had in Japan.

One believes that Fr. Diego de Mesquita bought a press of movable types in Lisbon, between January and April 1586, although the preparations had commenced soon after the return of the embassy from Lisbon, coming from Rome in November 1585. Bro. Giovanni Battista Pece, an Italian, accompanied the same embassy to Goa and would learn the printing from the old João Rodrigues during the eight months. Dourado as well would learn this technique from him.

The first text made by the hand of Dourado, done in the press with movable types which had been brought from Lisbon, is dated 1588. It was a text of discussion of Hara Martinho to Fr. Valignano in June 1587. It is the first Japanese work printed and published by a Japanese press. One believes that the *Edição Crista* of the Jesuits, that is, *Kirishitan-ban* in 1612, reached about hundred titles of books and sheets. The larger part of these works came off this press. Therefore, the discourse of Hara Martinho, namely *Oratio habita a Fara D. Martinho Iaponio, sua et Sociorum nomine, cum ab Europa rediret*, and *Patre Alexandra Valignano Visitatore*

Societatis IESV, Goae in D. Pauli Collegio... was the first experimental work of *Kirishitan-ban*. In Goa, it gave the first step for the printing of *Kirishitan-ban*. In 1590 after two years the second book came off the same press. It is *A viagem dos enviados japoneses à Europa* written by Fr. Eduardo de Sande as I have already referred. This work was naturally the responsibility of Constantino Dourado in which Augustinho had also taken part.

As soon as those sent to Europe had arrived at Nagasaki in July 1590 a press was installed at Kazusa in the Peninsula of Shimabara, starting the editorial activities. A new type of Japanese letters was cut and cast. They made matrices of characters of *Kata-Kana* and printed some pages with this new type of characters. However, in the following year this activity was suspended. They went back to making characters *Hira-Kana* and Chinese characters and started to print them with Japanese and Chinese characters. As in the European alphabets they introduced three sizes of Latin letters in Japan, namely big, medium and small and their respective matrices. In 1594 a third type arrived in Japan having being used at the press of Amakusa. In the same year the Grifo type was made in Japan. It seems that this whole process of preparation of types and Japanese characters, Chinese and Grifos was directed by Constantino Dourado.

Regarding *Kirishitan-ban* only 32 titles of books and sheets are known. Except for the books of classical Japanese literature, dictionaries and grammars, the book better known is, *Esopo no Fabvlas* published at Amakusa in 1593. This book is only found in the British Museum. Under the title of *Esopo no Fabvlas*, one reads the phrase "*Latinvo waxite Nippon no cuchito nasu mono nari*". This shows that it is a translation from the Latin into Japanese. This bound volume included two other books: *Feique no Monogatari* and *Qincuxu*. Each of these three books has the transcription with Roman alphabets, but one part of *Qincuxu* is written in the literary form. The reason why a volume with three books was written and published after the first phase of the editorial activity of *Kirishitan-ban* was so that the European missionaries could use expressions of courtesy and precision to win over persons of the intellectual class. The systematization of the language had as its objective to help the missionaries and to advance little by little in the comprehension of terms for their homilies.

The first objective of *Feique no Monogatari* was to show the normative language spoken and for this it adopted the main history in Japan during this time. As regards the *Esopo no Fabvlas* the aim was to present concretely the variety of expressions of the Japanese language and thus allegories useful for preaching were presented. The *Qincuxu* presents the maxims and famous expressions derived from Chinese which the *Bonzes* (Buddhist priests) used, and which for this reason it obtained in order to deepen.

As the authorship of the translator of *Esopo no Fabvlas* from Latin into Japanese is not certain it is usual to suggest the names of the Japanese brothers Fabião, Yofoken Paulo and Takai Cosme. However, it is not figured whether they might have had linguistic knowledge sufficient to translate an original Latin work. Bro. Fabião according to the catalogue of Fathers and Brothers of the Society of Jesus of the Province of Japan, of January 1593, stayed some years to attend the first class of Latin. As regards Yofoken Paulo and Takai Cosme, although they might have mastered Japanese well they have never studied Latin. For this reason the three brothers referred to could only have changed to Japanese the lessons and oral explanation of the Latin text done by the European fathers. It is natural that we think that the Japanese translation may have been done by the Japanese brothers with knowledge of classical Japanese literature with the foundation in the oral narrative of the missionaries. Besides this it is not impossible to imagine that Bro. Jorge de Loyola who learnt Latin may have been occupied in the Japanese translation of the *Esopo no Fabvlas* during his voyage to Macau on orders of Valignano.

The book in Latin *Esopo no Fabvlas* printed at Amakusa in 1593 consists of two parts with 70 fables. On the other hand the Japanese edition *Isopo Monogatari* published in the time of Keicho-Genna, namely between 1596 and 1623 for the first time, was also re-edited in 1639 (in the 14th year of the era Kan'ei) 1659 (according to the year of era Manji) and 1677 (year five of era Yenpo), etc. Thus the work had in all nine editions. The translation is literary and the edition in three parts has 94 fables. However, only 25 fables are together in the edition of Amakusa. For this, we think that it might have had in the beginning a literary translation from the original Latin, afterwards changed into Japanese characters under the title *Isopo Monogatari*. With this text as base the book *Esopo no Fabvlas* was compiled in an oral version. The oral language used in the translation was the oral language which was used in Kyoto during that time.

It is evident that the Jesuit missionaries brought the original Latin of *Esopo no Fabvlas* to Japan. The initial literary translation appears to be the authorship of the missionaries, later translated into Japanese by the Japanese brothers. One thinks that the Society of Jesus decided to print this translation in the oral language and in the Roman alphabets so that the European missionaries could use it in preaching using allegories, episodes and narrations. One can attribute to Fr. Valignano the decision to print *Esopo no Fabvlas*.

In spite of the prohibition on Christianity by the government of Tokugawa, a Japanese version of *Isopo Monogatari* had nine editions and many copies which proves that the Japanese did not identify this work with Christianity, a work that they liked. On the other hand the Japanese also liked the habit of spirit, humour and satire that characterized these stories. The book printed in 1659 (second year of the era Manji) has 13 illustrations. This shows that the readers of the book included the general public. For this we can confirm the influence that *Isopo Monogatari* had on Kana-Zoshi, a culture that spread in the beginning of the Edo period. *Gigen-Yoki-shu* published during the era Genna (1615-1623), *Kasho-Ki* published in the 19th year of era Kan'ei (1642), and *Iguchi-Monogatari* edited in the second year of era Kanbun (1662), all modeled on the book *Isopo Monogatari* with stories and parables directly taken from the text. The aim of these books of Kana-Zoshi was to orient the people towards the enriched material.

Thus, the art of printing that the Japanese delegates who visited Europe during the era of Tensho, brought to Japan and the edition of *Kirishitan-ban* was one efficient means for the spread of Christianity and conversion of the Japanese. The *Esopo no Fabvlas* carried into Japan as an original book of *Kirishitan-ban*, was the epoch in which the Christian faith was prohibited, was received as a model book by the population, and it exercised incontrovertible influence on the manner of life of the Japanese.

Conclusion

It is important to underline that Goa was for Japan one type of passage between Portugal and the Catholic world, acting the part of intermediary for both in various ways. In this context, politically, the government of Goa promised the consideration of ties of friendship between the government of Portugal and the principal daimyos of the region of Kyushu, and also exerted itself to improve the relations with the central government of Japan.

Regarding the cultural point, Goa was the base of diffusion of the European culture spread in Japan, and it was also in the line of promotion and diffusion of the culture in Japan. As has already been affirmed, the European culture of Christianity was transplanted through Goa to Japan. It is important to note that Fr. A. Valignano who was in Goa, the principal spirit for the introduction of European culture into Japan, carried the policy of Japanese mission, before the first visit to the lands of the Rising Sun. He was the one who opted for a systematic introduction of the European culture necessary for the missionary activity. He was also the one who advanced the introduction of the translations of European books and of the press. And all these decisions were taken during his stay in Goa. The execution of the policy was already decided on the occasion of his return to Goa, coming from Japan, with the young legates of Kyushu on the way to Europe.

EIGHT

INTERCULTURAL LINKS BETWEEN GOA AND MOZAMBIQUE IN THEIR COLONIAL AND CONTEMPORARY HISTORY

Literary Mozambiquean Traces*

MANFRED F. PRINZ

Portuguese Colonialism in India and in Africa: Some Similarities

Gilberto Freire, the Brazilian sociologist believes the Portuguese colonizer had a Christocentric and an anti-racial attitude leading to a ethnic-cultural miscegenation. He goes on to speak of the ambiguous colonizer.

"Within a Portuguese there was always a tussle between the Christian and the Muslim — the man of the hot climate, the unfaithful — who was and who would justify perhaps his religious strictness of new conversion. Uncommonly though at the very time that they made efforts in the process of extermination of the native religions and culture of Goa, the Portuguese put into practice a policy of integration entirely new in Europe of the time.[1]

This feature of Portuguese colonization resulted in "an ethnic-cultural inter-penetration", a mutual acculturation of dominant and dominated cultures, "based on a situation anthropo-sociological which soon established itself in relations between Portuguese and non-Europeans; the inter-penetration of races and of cultures", denoted in its specification, according to Gilberto Freire as "Luso-tropicalism".[2]

Besides this feature, this accepted attitude gave rise to a type

* Translated from the Portuguese by Charles J Borges.

of the one who "lives in or beyond the limits or frontiers of civilization", termed "across-borders", seen in the *lançados* on the Guiné Coast, the *sertanejos* of Angola, the *prazeiros* of Mozambique, and the *sertanistas* of Amazonia.[3] With reference to the case of Mozambique, the term *prazeiro* is still current and refers to the "owners of the old prazos, the "leased properties", given out in 1675,[4] "in the context of colonial maritime expansion these figures are defined as persons of European ascendancy who established themselves permanently there at the limits of western society. They include merchants, hunters, mercenaries, deserters, and social outcastes. Due to the relatively reduced number, due to the lack of women of the mother country capable of procreation, and to their total isolation from European institutions of sociability, they were progressively absorbed by the dominant indigenous population.

The *prazeiros* occupied the royal *prazos* with royal assent for the feudal rights which defined a relation highly structured in which the *prazeiros* remained subordinate to the government. The non-acceptance of the rules meant expulsions from the lands. From the 17th century the *prazeiros* constituted the base of Portuguese colonial rule, they extended it till present Zimbabwe reaching noteworthy proportions. The Portuguese Crown created *prazos* for the natives or *mestiços* faithful to her on condition that they would marry with the Portuguese women. In spite of this control the *prazeiros* make the law in Mozambique, live in small palaces, gather all the refinements of Africa, Asia and Europe available at the time, raise taxes in gold, ivory and slaves, and have harems of concubines.[5] They disposed in many cases, like that of the descendants of Sismando Bayão, through the gradual expansion of the web of matrimonial ties of "personal empires that in the case of the Bayão family, included in the middle of the 18th century, nine *prazos*, many thousands of fighting slaves and a substantial amount in taxes." Although Portugal may have tried to avoid the cross-breeding between the *prazos* and the first families, may have preserved consciously, the racial exclusiveness and cultural Portuguese identity, the *prazeiro* community was neither in the beginning nor later homogeneous, neither in composition nor in lifestyle. The Portuguese being an insignificant minority tried to uphold through the *prazeiro* system their economic, commercial and military superiority before the majority of locals represented in the local traditional authorities. The typical colonial situation in the words of Georges Balandier is one not already seen in a pure form in the Portuguese system:

> "la domination imposée par une minoritée étrangère racialement et culturellement différent, au nom d'une supériorité raciale (ou ethnique) dogmatiquement affirmée, à une majorité autochtone matériellement inférieure".

The economic superiority shows itself fully through the feudal system of the *prazeiros*, being ethnically and culturally merged, but dependents of the Crown, controlling the market and negotiating with the local authorities.

The community of the *prazeiros* was in the 18th century, largely of Indian descent. They who received *aforamentos* or titles to property, were residents of a lower status in Portugal, inhabitants of Zambeze, poor, *degredados*, mulata women of European soldiers and Asians of Goa.

The image of the Zambeze Valley as an unhealthy region certainly discouraged the immigration of many Portuguese families. They preferred the alternative of the more desirable climates of Brazil, Goa or other parts of Africa. This fact shows itself clearly in the demographic composition of the inhabitants of Sena and Tete in 1777, a year about which precise statistics exist. Of the 713 Christians of the two principal cities, only 95, or may be 12 per cent were born in Portugal. In this small group, there was clearly a scarcity of the presence of reproductive women. In Sena there were 17 men of Portugal, and no woman. Thus, the adverse picture of Mozambique reduced the number of potential immigrants.[6]

One sees the growing presence of Indians and the predominance of them in the market (ivory, gold, against cloth and *mussingas*) with East Africa already before the Portuguese colonialization during the century, in the Gulf of Cambay, through Daman and Diu in the commercial contacts that were associated with the foundation of the Muslim sultanate of Gujarat in 1392, the sultanate that attained the zenith of its authority at the end of the 15th century, during the reign of Mahmud I, which started in 1458.[7] The Portuguese, after they had eliminated the Swahili Arabs of the African market with the support of the leading Africans, continued rivals of the Indian merchants in such a way that between 1640 (year of the independence of Portugal from Spain) and 1752 (year of the reforms of Marquis of Pombal, giving independence of Portuguese East Africa from the Viceroy of India) the Portuguese Crown conducted a commercial policy between a free market and a commercial monopoly.[8]

In the elimination of the Arab-Swahili influence, the collaboration with the local African kings was essential: when the Portuguese climbed the Zambeze till Sena, Manica and the kingdom of Monomotapa, they obtained from Monomotapa (Muenemutapa) permission to proceed in the excavation of the gold area. The more ambitious plan of the Portuguese, of taking over the gold mines, was realized in the second half of the 16th century. It was through the Christian mission from Goa, that Portugal was directing its political and economic interests in East Africa. In this connection, the Provincial of the Jesuits in Goa, Fr. de Quadros ordered missionaries to be sent to the region of East Africa: Frs. Dom Gonçalo da Silveira, André Fernandes and André da Costa arrived from Goa on 4 February 1560 on the present coast of Mozambique with the objective of converting Monomotapa to Catholicism. It was Gonçalo da Silveira who would pay with his life in 1561 in trying to convert Monomotapa to the Christian faith. This murder was the pretext for an expedition, planned by D. Sebastian in 1569 and sent to the area of the mines, as much for the propagation of the faith, especially against the Islamic influence, as for the revenge for the death of the missionary (who was killed by king Monomotapa as a result of an intervention of the chief religious Muslim Mingame who informed the king and his advisers of the danger of growing influence of the Portuguese). The intervention of Mingame was described by Fr. Francisco de Souza 150 years later in the following manner:

> "Let us go to the Monomotapa who is an inexperienced young man. Let us pretend that we are very much interested in the good of his monarchy, and let us convince him that the priest is a spy sent by the Portuguese to find out about the strength of his army, the accesses and exits of his lands, to gather information about the inclinations of his government, to buy against him hearts of his vassals with gifts and promises (. . .) that he is a famous magician and that the water he pours on the heads is a powerful charm to win over the hearts of the men as is the salt he puts in the mouths, the saliva he applies to the noses and ears and that only by his death can these charms be

counteracted and these spells be broken".[9]

Monomotapa was the name of the king and of the kingdom in the present area of Zimbabwe and Mozambique. His descendents went in the following decades to be formed priests at the seminaries of Goa which is testified in an epitaph on a tomb stone in the cathedral of Goa. There was a custom, besides, that the *prazeiros* constructed big churches in their kingdoms, and many sent their sons to Portugal or Goa, for a good Catholic education.[10] This incident of king Monomotapa in the century shows the gamut of political, economic and religious interests as well as the inter-cultural composition of individuals and of society involved in this process.

The Arabs who already had an influence in the 15th century, from India along with the Indians, and the Portuguese who from the 16th century extended their domination against the Arabs both used the authorities and local African societies of the region. The Portuguese benefited from all the requirements, inspite of and because of the limited human potential at their disposal in order to preserve and extend their influence in the same territory.

The impact of the Goans and Indians in East Africa underlines in the first place numerically the fact of the Portuguese community withdrawing itself little by little from Mozambique, considered as unfavourable land that presented serious problems of acclimatization. The Goans formed a growing community, marrying with those of Portugal and entered through miscegenation into the group of *prazeiros*, all this from the start of the 18th century.

> "In 1750 the Governor of Rios de Sena still regretted the virtual absence of white colonial entrepreneurs, that he thought were necessary for the out living of the Portuguese community. In trying desperately to maintain a nominal presence in Zambeze, Lisbon started distributing land to all, independently of origin, capacity or loyalty. Those who received the *aforamentos*, or titles to property, were residents of a lower status in Portugal, inhabitants of Zambeze, poor, *degredados*, mulata women of European soldiers and Asians of Goa".[11]

The Portuguese preferred the more agreeable lands of Brazil, Goa and other parts of Africa, while the Goans, mainly after the independence of East Africa from the Viceroy of India in 1752, and the abolition of the customs system, extended their commercial power to the Zambeze Valley, establishing an important economic position.

> "Of the small numbers that went to Zambeze during the second half of the eighteenth century, the majority was of Indian descent.(. . . .) During the period between 1722 and 1802, the white population decreased from 300 to 282, of which a substantial number were recent arrivals from India".[12]

The Goan community formed a social elite not only through the privileges of the system of *prazos*, but also through the Hindu religious system to which they adhered in large part. It helped their promotion and their high position in the African context, a system that at the same time gradually lost its value in the process of miscegenation.

> "Perhaps the more dramatic changes may have occurred in the midst of the *prazeiros* of Hindu descent, who gradually went on ignoring the system of castes which had historically determined their form of social organization. When the first Indians, mainly from Goa, arrived at the Zambeze Valley, they adhered religiously to the system of castes (. . . .) and all the social relations were defined by the position of caste".[13]

We come across a variety of Goan persons and families, Portuguese as well as Indians, who lived in a process of growing acculturation in the African setting, as is shown by the example of the Pereira family who migrated from Goa around the middle of the 18th century and involved itself quickly into a flourishing commerce of ivory and slaves, to the north of the river Zambeze. (. . . .) The Pereira family adopted also the Chewa faith in witchcraft and sorcery (. . .) The Pereiras were incorporated in the local Malunga clan and practised polygamy, recognized the primacy of the older wife, and adopted the system of military inheritance, in place of retaining the Indian system of co-ownership.[14]

This type of acculturation was current in the contacts between the Portuguese, Indians and Africans and created the type of "across-borderer", which on one side had as a consequence the generalized acceptance of beliefs and local customs, but on the other hand, led the individuals to a social and cultural isolation.[15]

This acculturation not always increased the legitimacy of families[16] but in its origin, was always an attempt at maximum approximation to cultures of the area for assuring a social superiority.

Despite the miscegenation of races and cultures, there existed a hierarchy, a social vision, based on one's origin, on religion, on the colour of one's skin, but above all on one's social and economic position.

Rita-Ferreira makes a distinction between the Goan Hindus, Indo-Muslim Goans, and Catholic Goans:

> "The creation of the company of Mazanes of Diu, of the vania caste, allowed the Hindu importers and exporters settled on the island of Mozambique, to dominate completely the economy of Mozambique, thanks to their unbeatable competence and organization. This was mercantile capitalism with its particular interests, and the strict rules even of Hinduism, and with the central policy of economic subordination of Mozambique to Portuguese India".
>
> "The Indian Muslims, more inclined to the fixing and crossings, specialized in long-distance commerce. The Goan Catholics, benefiting from the rights similar to those of the Europeans, dominated in the clergy, the army, public administration, and in the private activities, particularly in the society of the *prazos* of the Crown".[17]

The part played by Goans and Indians of other territories determined Portuguese colonization:

> "The colonization by these three groups of people of Portuguese India and their respective descendants, led in large part, to the maintenance of Portuguese sovereignty and the penetration of the interior that laid the outlines of frontiers as they exist today".[18]

Each section of this group of Indians had and has till today its own reputation: a social function in the post-colonial society. In a study of Lourenço Marques (Maputo) the author describes the Indian ward of Rua da Gávea as seen through the eyes of an African, of the Goan community that is different for him, in the following manner:

> "The whites were not just the few metropolitans, but the Europeans of the province too, all more or less already slightly mixed, the Goans and the very *mulattos* of the land. The one who established the social system was the Negro population, that considered the *monhés* (Arab or Negro *mestiço*) apart by their self-isolation. Rua da Gávea was not for this reason an imposed ghetto, but a resultant ghetto, and the division was based on religion, that differentiated the systems of thinking and living. By this criterion, the Christian Goans were considered white by the Negroes, and the Muslims and the Hindus were considered Indians as these were merely the *monhés*".[19]

The Centre, Epicentre, Periphery in the Luso-African-Asiatic World

Portugal, the European colonizing power in the 16th century, started and continued a process of colonization in Africa and in India, a process that already has its origins in the preceding centuries. The Indians like the colonizers and the colonized perform in this period an ambiguous function. Goa, Daman and Diu serve as centres inside the colonial Portuguese world, forming centres of formation and models of civilization. In spite of the great facility of acculturation of the Indians and the integration in the African societies and cultures, they never left their socio-economic and cultural superiority. Independently of religion and of the political status given to India by Portugal, the Indians always got to defend their trade in the African context and defined themselves before the native African cultures. Thus Rita-Ferreira puts a question, "How did India underdevelop East Africa? in an allusion to the book of Walter Rodney, *How Europe underdeveloped Africa* (London, 1972). In fact, the link with the cultures and power-brokers in Africa was relative, the socio-economic superiority of the Indians was never placed in question.

The African country was a land of riches, and of commerce, the vital centre was India. In a typical Indo-Portuguese poem, the *mando*, which is a song peculiar to the Catholics of Goa, we come across this allusion to Africa which shows us the representation of the African continent and of its people in the Indian imagination, land of exile and a refuge inhabited by persons of a socially inferior status. Here is the dream of an adulterous Indian woman infatuated for an African servant:

> Aurora Sobina é o meu nome,
> e sou muito popular no bairro de Calangute;
> tendo resolvido ir para Africa,
> no barco senti-me atraída por um dos criados.
> Mas por amor de Deus
> Mojya potik samgum naka,
> não digam nada ao meu marido.[20]
>
> (Aurora Sobina is my name
> and I am very popular in my ward of Calangute.
> Having decided to go to Africa
> In the boat I felt myself attracted to one of the servants
> But for God's sake,
> Don't tell my husband
> Don't tell my husband anything).

The presence of the Viceroy in Goa and the monopoly of the Indo-African market by India marked a relative independence before Portugal which opted in many attempts for a free market, observing an important exodus of Europeans from Mozambique and from Zambezia, the two Portuguese commercial centres in Eastern Africa,[21] this exodus being due to the monopoly of commerce. Only with the reforms of Marquis of Pombal in 1752, this polarization neutralized itself by a centralization of commercial activities in Portugal. Here are some of the principles on which the political reforms of Pombal were based:

1. The colony, in its dependence on the power of the colonizer, had to expect the protection from this one.
2. Commerce and agriculture of the colony ought to be guided

exclusively by the necessities of Portugal.

3. As a result the produce of agriculture, trade and navigation of the colony became property of Portugal.
4. The profit of the colony by Portugal was frustrated since the time in which that could substitute for itself.
5. As a result whatever traffic of the colony with foreigners and whatever consumption of foreign articles in the colony constituted a theft to the property of Portugal and a fact punishable by this government.[22]

Fritz Hoppe gives the following view regarding the colonial politics of Pombal:

> "It is not possible in more decisive terms than in fundamental rules of the whole colonial expansion (. . .) a commercial system extremely mercantile as a principal element of a public economy self-sufficient and oriented in the sense of centralization by necessities of Portugal according to the model of the colonial pact decided by Colbert".[23]

The self-image and self-interpretation of Portugal corresponded to a centralist vision of Portugal refuting the whole form of concurrence and of a parallel market. In fact in spite of political declarations, Portugal never managed to establish a market in Mozambique and in reality there existed and continued an incontestable dependence of East Africa on India, as much in the commercial relations as in the effective presence of Indians in Africa:

> "The role of Portuguese possessions on the East African coast during this whole period (17th—18th centuries) was yet more insignificant. By the end of the 17th century, there was in Mozambique not more than 15 furnaces of white Portuguese, which in truth would mean only 15 male white persons and 16 of Indian Goans, without counting the clerics who were very few and the soldiers of the garrison. Spread out in all the territory of mainland Mozambique, less than a hundred whites controlled the few public offices that flew the Portuguese flag. Mozambique continued to depend on India as much economically as administratively. Much more commerce and

navigation existed between those two possessions than between Mozambique and Lisbon. From 1686 till 1777, an Indian company of Diu obtained the monopoly of trade between Diu and Mozambique which showed itself quite lucrative".[24]

The Role of Indians in Literature/Honwana: Nós matamos o cão-tinhoso

Until our own days the role of Indians/Goans in Mozambique is central, from the point of view of the implantation and real presence more effective than that of the Portuguese. The presence of Indians/ Goans in literature is not frequent, authors like Campos Oliveira (1847-1911) who studied law in Goa and lived there, or Rui Nogar whose parents were born in Goa, almost do not make a case in their texts of the experience of India. Nogar only attests to one event that shows once more the privileged position and the positive hetero-stereotype that Goans occupy in the view of the Portuguese.

The following incident happens to the young student Rui Nogar after a programme of cultural activities at the African Association:

> "It was one of these activities that took me to my prison by Pide. They wanted to know why it is that we had organized the feast, for what purpose was the money. Why did the feast end at dawn and why did I remain with the box? Why is it I was confided in, though a white? Well, two or three days later I went once again to be questioned and the inspector took me from the cell — it was a iron gate. They questioned me always about why it was that I was mixed up with the blacks and I responded: "I am not mixed up with the blacks, they are my friends. . . ", the old story. Afterwards, at the gate, before opening the gate, he asked me, "Where is it that your parents were born?" "In Goa". "Ah", said he, "Ah! look at that, till the next time take care". Then they opened the gate and I left at midnight from there. He left me just there".[25]

The closeness of an Indian to a Portuguese in contrast to an African is evident, and it justifies itself by the concurrence that exists between the Portuguese centre and the Indian centre. This closeness, however, remains always threatened by a discrimination, the Indian continuing to be of lesser right than an European. The hierarchy established between a Portuguese and a Goan on one hand, and the solidarity in discrimination of the African on the other hand, shows itself in a short story of Luis Bernardo Honwana (*Nos matamos o cão-tinhoso*, 1972). The story is a parable of a colonial situation, the sick dog is a symbol of an African, in its role of a victim: innocent but condemned to death for having insulted the Administrator by his stare, the dog in its shocking and repugnant appearance is a figure of a scapegoat, a true role of the unhappy animal. The configuration of persons forms itself around the dog according to the hierarchy established by the colonial system: the Africans Toucinho and Isaura, *forasteiros*, like the dog, the European Quim encounters himself by the side of the Administrator as the Goan Gulamo, the representatives of the Muslim and Chinese population being less prominent and subordinate.

> "The society of dogs like that of students structures itself in terms of a rigid scale. The dominant figure is a white boy, Quim, whose racial attitudes are well defined in his frequent disparaging of natives, and that in the final moments of the story, show also strong murderous tendencies. The other important person is a young boy of Goan descent, Gulamo."[26]
> "Toucinho does not behave as the other youths think that he had to carry himself and it is because at times he does not understand Portuguese well. For him not to offend himself with the physical appearance of a dog, the others say, that is black and enough. To be black and enough, is a notion that defines clearly the character of inter-racial relations in the story of Honwana, for their more marked facet is the racism".
> "His condition of being black according to the boys, is what explains the hesitation of Toucinho when he does not want to shoot the dog. *Preto de merda* and *Preto capado* as well as *negros cabrões* and *cabroada escura* are examples of racist curses shouted by the group."[27]

Gulamo, the Goan boy likewise insults Toucinho with expressions like *preto do merda* and he has the same racist attitude but Quim retorts with the same treating him as *monhé* or *filho de corno*.[28]

Mozambique and Goa: Socio-linguistic Peripheries

The view of speaking and understanding Portuguese well appears in colonial and post-colonial African literature constantly as a criterion of distinction and discrimination of the participants, akin to the peripheral situation of the African countries. It is evident for Goa as well as Mozambique that Portuguese is a language spoken by a minority in a multi-lingual context, that is, in a context of many local languages, spoken by a majority of the population as mother tongues. The socio-linguistic situation is characterized by a dominant role of a foreign language and a non-acknowledgement of mother-tongues. The official language being Portuguese in Mozambique and in Goa before 1961, and after the liberation by India, Hindi being the official language and English the associate language, the local languages regionally in majority till now look forward for an importance through a consistent linguistic and educational policy. In this situation, both Mozambique and Goa represent peripheral countries under the linguistic domination of a exterior centre. This situation constitutes a prolongation of the colonial period. In Goa till the 1980s there never existed an importance for Konkani, the language of the majority, the social linguistic description which Vimala Devi and Manuel de Seabra give of the past centuries with regard to Konkani, is valid for today:

> "Konkani was condemned to disappear totally and to be substituted by Portuguese (today English or Hindi). The anxiety to make Goa Portuguese reached such great extremes that in 1728 it was recommended to the government that a whole part of the population might be exterminated if it did not convert soon".[29]

Today the situation may appear less brutal but it is a fact that education in Goa has not yet given a proper place to the mother-tongue of children, that is Konkani.

> "In the public teaching, for example, it administered in 1960 joint Portuguese-Marathi education in 4 schools and Portuguese-Urdu in 12 schools. With regard to private schools in 1960 the state subsidized 174 Marathi schools and only 47 in

Portuguese. Even the number of schools teaching in English and subsidized by the government was more than those teaching in Portuguese for these went up to 74 beside the 6 in Urdu. There was not one school in Konkani which is the language of almost all the population.[30] And this in spite of the written codification and a rich literature in Konkani."[31]

The situation only changed in 1987. At present Konkani has been introduced from the beginning of 1987 at the primary level. Again Goa shows itself within India like a centre and as a proper recognized system of reference.

In the same way in Mozambique, neither the colonial government nor the post-colonial one gave an adequate place to African languages promoting only the official Portuguese language in the public sphere as in schools and in writing, although works were done in the field of orthography of the African languages in the 1980s but without consequences for a real promotion of these languages. The entry of Mozambique into the Commonwealth since 1995 because of its proximity with English-speaking countries and because of reasons mainly economic, marred once more a linguistic situation in the sense of getting away the social linguistic reality of the population. In the matter of a reasonable and democratic policy respecting the mother-tongue, Goa and Mozambique find themselves in a marginal and peripheral position, under a foreign and neo-colonial domination. As for the African countries so also the other multi-lingual countries solutions exist for a linguistic policy, respecting multi-linguism. For Goa a sequence could be recommended for the teaching, "the ideal to teach vernaculars and English during the course of 8 years", following the example of Kenya, starting in the first 4 years in the mother-tongue and introducing English as the second language in the second year before proceeding to English as medium of teaching 4 years later.[32]

Besides the lack of acknowledgement of the local languages a proper value still does not exist for Portuguese in its practical variety in the Indian or African contexts; it is evident that Portuguese like other multi-centric languages evolved local varieties, even authentic creoles. The Portuguese of Brazil received, meanwhile, more importance than the Portuguese of Portugal with the knowledge and codification of differences and particularities. One observes the same phenomenon in the ambit of the French-speaking or in the English-speaking world with a multiplicity of differences which characterize the multi-centric languages.

Although characteristics of African-Mozambique and Portuguese-Indian Portuguese exist the only norms taught and imitated are those of Portugal: noting at the same time a disdain of the proper manner of speech by speakers of one of these varieties which the authors of *Literatura Indo-Portuguesa*, sum up, explaining the phenomenon of purity by a double standard, one made by the Portuguese, the other by Goans themselves:

> "The purity of the Portuguese language always had in Goa many stout defenders (. . .) Despising the local forms of Portuguese and finding faults with the imitation and the lack of proper originality of the middle classes, these champions of Lisbon, contributed perhaps much to the fact that the Portuguese language did not evolve naturally, nor acquire in its local variety the prestige to which it had right within the sectors of the population that speak it".
> "In this way conditioned to despise their own linguistic expression, the Goan writers lost the opportunity to create a literature of genuine Goan usage, harming its own proper cultural identity".[33]

The authors of *Literatura Indo-Portuguesa* cite as exception to this rule the Goan author Gip (Francisco João da Costa). In Mozambique and in the African countries of the official Portuguese language, many authors who can be identified have freed themselves of the obligation to be "small Camões". In this matter of the authentic expression of Portuguese the Africans seem to bypass the Goans by a different history and independence.

Goa, earlier a capital by the side of Lisbon exercising a power almost parallel in the colonial rule of the East, has at the same time characteristics of more dependence on this empire. Goa, perhaps, neither centre nor periphery, continues existing in innumerable descendents in diverse nations and cultures, constituting substantial elements outside itself in the cultures and societies of Eastern Africa. The Goan identity is a part invisible of other identities placing thus in question the very concept of identity.

I have presented some remains of a disappeared cultural

element but which in fact are finally transformed in a whole that we may call universal culture.

NOTES AND REFERENCES

1. Vimala Devi & Manuel de Seabra, *A Literatura Indo-Portuguesa*, Lisbon, Junta de Investigações do Ultramar, 1971, pp. 12-13.
2. Gilberto Freire, *O Luso e o Tropico*, Lisbon, Comemorações do Quinto Centenário da Morte do Infante D. Henrique, 1961, p. 15.
3. Allen e Barbara Isaacman, "Os Prazeiros como Trans-Raianos: Um Estudo sobre Transforma Social e Cultural", *Boletim do Arquivo Historico de Mozambique: "Tete"*, no. 19 (Special), October 1991, pp. 5-6.
4. António Carlos Pereira Cabral, *Pequeno Dicionário de Mozambique*, Lourenço Marques, 1972, p. 94.
5. *Guia do Terceiro Mundo 93*, Lisbon, Tricontinental Editora, 1993, p. 560
6. Isaacman, pp. 12-13.
7. Rita-Ferreira A, "Mozambique e os naturais da India Portuguesa", *II Seminário Internacional História Indo-Portuguesa*, (Actas), Lisbon, 1985, p. 618.
8. Fritz Hoppe, *A Africa Oriental Portuguesa no tempo do Marques de Pombal (1750-1777)*, Lisbon, Agencia Geral do Ultramar, 1970, pp. 25ff.
9. Astrid Sauerwein, *Mission und Kolonialismus in Simbabwe 1840-1940. Kollisionenm, Konflikt Kooperation*, Geeben, Focus, 1990, p. 32.
10. Isaacman, p. 13.
11. *Ibid.*, p. 12
12. *Ibid.*, p. 14.
13. *Ibid.*, p. 27.
14. *Ibid.*, pp. 20-22.
15. *Ibid.*, p. 30.
16. *Ibid.*, p. 20.
17. Rita-Ferreira, *op. cit.*, p. 645
18. *Ibid.*, p. 644.
19. Alexandre Lobato, *Lourenço Marques, Xilunguine. Biografia da cidade*, Lisbon, Agencia Geral Ultramar, 1970, p. 198.
20. Devi & Seabra, *op. cit.*, p. 27.
21. Hoppe, p. 28.
22. *Ibid.*, p. 281.
23. *Ibid.*, p. 283.
24. A. H. de Oliveira Marques, *História de Portugal: Das origens as revoluções liberais*, vol. I, Lisbon, Palas Editores, 1974, pp. 636-637.
25. Patrick Chabal, *Vozes Moçambicanas. Literatura e Nacionalidade*, Lisbon, Vega, 1994, p. 166.
26. Gregory McNab, "Porque mataram o Cão-Tinhoso", in *Africa*, no. 14,

1977, p. 62.

27. *Ibid.*, p. 64.
28. Luís Bernardo Honwana, *Nós matamos o cão-tinhoso*, Porto, Edições Afrontamento, 1971, p. 29.
29. Devi & de Seabra, p. 46.
30. *Ibid.*, p. 48.
31. *Ibid.*, pp. 48-49.
32. *Ibid.*, p. 64.
33. *Ibid.*, p. 61.

PART III

ART, ARCHITECTURE, MUSIC AND NUMISMATICS

NINE

CONNECTING HISTORIES
Portuguese Music in Renaissance Goa

VICTOR ANAND COELHO

> In that city [of Goa] I enjoyed many times listening to very beautiful music for the feast days, especially that of St. Ignatius Loyola, which was celebrated with seven choirs and the sweetest *sinfonie* [instrumental pieces or sections] in the Professed House of the Fathers of the Society, where lies the body of St. Francis Xavier; and when I said that it was like being in Rome, I was told that I was not mistaken, because the composition was that of the famous Carissimi that was brought to that place. I cannot believe how musically proficient are the Canarini, and with what ease they perform.
> There is no town or village of the Christians which does not have in its church an organ, harp, and a viola, and a good choir of musicians who sing for festivities, and for holy days, Vespers, masses and litanies, and with much cooperation and devotion. . .[1]

The influence of Portuguese artistic and cultural traditions in Goa between the landing of Vasco da Gama and the middle of the 17th century has been studied chiefly in terms of the craft, architectural and painting industries.[2] This has been valuable (though incomprehensive) in tracing some of the cross-cultural exports of Portuguese cultures and aesthetic tastes to India, identifying systems of patronage, and following certain Portuguese cultural traditions as they evolved through contacts with indigenous Goan culture, like the mando. The spread of Portuguese courtly and liturgical musical traditions to Goa have, on the other hand, never been examined, despite the richness of Portuguese polyphony as represented by the Coimbra and Evora schools from about the middle of the 16th century,[3] and what would appear to have been an essential need for music, singers, and other musicians for use in the cathedrals, churches and secular events of Renaissance Goa. To expect the presence, then, of a Portuguese, or at least European, musical tradition in Goa between 1550 and 1650 is entirely justified within the context of the intensity of Portuguese religious activities and ceremonies in Goa, the rapid and systematic construction of churches and convents, the cultural impact of Portuguese nobility and *Padroado* during the Goan Renaissance and early Goan Baroque and Portugal's emergence during the 16th century as an active, if peripheral, centre of music.

Musicological neglect of this area until now is not difficult to understand. Despite the richness of Portuguese and Spanish Renaissance music, scholars of Iberian music have worked in a vacuum for years due to the general Anglo-Franco and Italo-centric canons that have persisted in musicology. Portuguese musicology has not instigated this kind of work until recently, and Indian music historians have generally not focussed their attention to music outside the Indian classical tradition; western music history in India is still largely dependent on the academic work of the British. But a study of Renaissance music in Goa faces even more daunting obstacles than simply historiographical ones. Reconstructing the musical tradition of a city as well documented as Renaissance Ferrara is already difficult, let alone researching the culture of a city whose Renaissance culture was virtually abandoned when the capital was moved to Panaji. More importantly, there has been no discovery yet of any primary 16th or 17th century musical sources whose provenance or repertory can be traced specifically to Goa.[4] That manuscripts and printed books of music were used in Goa is clear, but if they were prepared in Portugal and then brought over by the Portuguese fleet, there is unfortunately no trace of them anymore in Goa. If this music was returned to Portugal, as is very possible, much of it may have perished in the Lisbon earthquake of 1755 which destroyed most of the contents of King João IV's library[5]. It is certain that not all music sung in Goan churches or colleges was imported from Portugal; some of it must have been copied and composed in Goa, as it was in other colonial outposts in the New World. But we are still in the dark about music scriptoria and scribes in 16th century Goa, and there is no evidence of any music published in Goa during this period either. In short, until actual sources of music are discovered the task of studying this musical culture is like trying to reconstruct the ground plan, size, architecture, influences, and decorations of a church that was razed to the ground, and on whose site has seen some four centuries of subsequent buildings.

The reconstruction of the Portuguese Renaissance musical culture as it took hold on Goan soil must therefore rely at this stage on archival work and other documentary evidence taken from the usual sources we are familiar with in this field: 16th and 17th century travelogues; eyewitness accounts by travelers and other observers; dispatches from viceroys and other diplomatic correspondence; the voluminous Jesuit documentation; and the annual letters of the Province of India. Fortunately, this information is abundant and revealing enough to make this a worthwhile occasion for me to present some of the findings I have made with this material over the past few years, and form some tentative conclusions. In this contribution I shall provide a sketch of Portuguese music in Goa until about the end of the 16th century as revealed by documentary evidence, as well as discuss why this material is important and how it can be enhanced through its relationship with the parallel fields of cultural and political history, liturgical history, patronage, and the newer modes of discourse in the area of post-colonialism.

Although archival work had traditionally served as the foundation for studies on Renaissance musical cultures, as recently as a decade ago it was limited to the major cities and composers of the European tradition. Musical traditions beyond this perimeter, such as in Asia, the ancient New World, and even parts of Eastern Europe, were considered to be the territory of ethno-musicologists—oral traditions that are, for the most part, still alive. But the gradual erosion of the western canon that has been taking place in western scholarship has exposed both a strong interest in the cultures of so-called "others", and a global awareness of how the European cultural hegemony is tied up with its colonial strategies. The Columbus anniversary, too, focused attention on those cultures that evolved in confrontation and assimilation with the manifest destiny of European discovererers.

Consequently, several scholars in recent years have embarked on or completed projects similar to mine, which show the extent to which Renaissance European musical traditions were transmitted thousands of miles away along the routes of exploration. Alfred

Lemmon, drawing on Jesuit correspondence and New World documents, has examined the use of music among the Aztecs following the Jesuit arrival there in 1572,[6] though one must be careful about accepting his statements about how willfully the Aztecs accepted the music brought from Europe. Robert Snow and Paul Borg have found a large cache of manuscripts copied in Guatemala containing mainstream Renaissance polyphony by such composers as the Spanish Morales, the Portuguese Pedro Escobar and Gaspar Fernandes, as well as works by Josquin des Prés, Jean Mouton and others.[7] It is extraordinary to think that the same music might have been sung simultaneously in Evora, Guatemala Cathedral and the Sé in Goa, but this could have been the case. Fernandes, who was the composer at Evora Cathedral, emigrated like other Spanish and Portuguese composers, to the New World sometime in the 1590s, which suggests that it is also likely that Portuguese composers themselves may have ended up in Goa, not just their music. It should be remembered that it is due to the existence of musical sources that the extent of Guatemala's importance as a musical centre can be so precisely documented. This is not the case with Ian Woodfield's recent study of music and musicians on the English maritime campaigns.[8] Woodfield focuses not on sources of music (since the English were not missionaries, their musical needs were different from the Portuguese) but on more sociological topics that include the role of music aboard ships, the use of musicians as ambassadors, the presentation of instruments as gifts of goodwill to indigenous peoples, and the functional musical repertories—signaling, cadences, the changing of a watch on a ship — that were used for essential activities. In many ways, these roles run parallel to the use of music by the earliest Portuguese explorers in India, and the categories of music-making he describes are applicable to other cultures, like Goa, in which musical sources themselves are lacking. In summarizing the Portuguese musical culture in Goa before 1650, three categories of music-making emerge that will be useful for which to organize the information that survives:

1. *Functional music*: Largely improvised and probably standardized music used for processions, marching, signaling, ceremonies and occasionally dancing. In general this music was played by loud instruments (Renaissance instruments were usually divided into two categories,

"loud" [reeds, brass, percussion] and "soft" [strings, keyboard]). References to this sort of music appear in documents throughout the period here being studied. This music generally would have been played from memory, rather than from written sources.

2. *Sacred music*: Music used for church services, the celebration of feast days and for the daily office. Two types of music are cited: (1) *Canto-Chão*, or chant (monophony), which is cited regularly in documents before around 1540, and (2) *Canto d'orgão* (polyphony), cited more frequently after about 1540. This music was sung and played from either manuscripts or prints, and books containing both plain chant and polyphony are mentioned often in the documents.
3. *The musical activities at the College of St. Paul*: This must be regarded as a tentative third category, since the music taught and performed here was not patronized specifically by the Portuguese but the Society of Jesus, which had its own aesthetic and pedagogical programme involving music. Nevertheless, the college was supported by Portuguese funding, and as such can be considered as a direct beneficiary of the Portuguese presence in Goa. The music at the college consisted of occasional music for specific events, as well as more elaborate music to accompany plays and ceremonies.

As on the English ships of almost a century later, Vasco da Gama's boats included trumpeters for signaling duties, marches and certain ceremonies. This continues a practice that was already used by the Portuguese explorers in Africa in the mid-fifteenth century, as we known from Ramusio's account of these voyages.[9] He describes one of Alvise da Cadomosto's soldiers playing the bagpipe for Senagalese natives in 1455, which they apparently found enchanting. Consequently, on da Gama's trip around the Cape of Good Hope on his way to India forty years later, the practice of playing music for the newly encountered natives was apparently quite well known. Greeted by the natives playing flutes, da Gama instructed his own trumpeters to participate, and dancing ensued between the natives and the Portuguese.[10] Such musical practices fall into the category of ambassadorial protocol and gift-giving. Da Gama's boats also included an organist, Frei Maffrue and a singer Frei Neto.[11] Related to this are instances of an actual exchange of goods which was well-known practice of Portuguese diplomacy. During de Souza's expedition to the Congo in 1490, the missionaries in his entourage carried portable organs, which were often used as presentation gifts, and the first organ in India probably arrived around 1500 as a result of this practice.[12] Organs seem to have been the gift of choice. They represent, after all a brilliant example of Western science and engineering which is a symbol of power. The practice of Renaissance Europeans in the age of Leonardo giving portable organs to the "natives" of places like Mozambique is no different than Westerners who come to India wearing pocket calculators and beeping quartz watches to give as gifts. Technological superiority has always been used as a weapon of cultural dominance — a point that was not lost on the Communists during the recent elections in India.

During the expedition of 1520 from Goa to Vijayanagar made by the Portuguese ambassador Cristovão de Figueiredo he bore a number of gifts including an organ and both organs and harpsichords were taken on Portuguese expeditions from Goa to Ethiopia as well. In 1550 Francis Xavier brought musical instruments as gifts to Japan which has been variously described as a *monacordio*, *vihuelas de arco* and a *clavicordio*.[13] Organs, then, can be considered the most common instruments during the early settlements and they were used in the new churches in the service of the liturgy. This is confirmed by a letter from Albuquerque to the king of Portugal in 1512 in which he specifically mentions that in his opinion organs should be placed in the Indian churches.[14]

The earliest references to a specific type of music begin appearing around 1512 though not all of the references are from Goa. While instruments and books were brought over on the ships many essential music books had to be ordered. The purchase of "three large books of chant" in Cochin in 1512 and the *livro grande de canto* for the early Goan church of St. Catherine refers specifically to the very large book of chants that were commonly used in churches in Europe so that one book could serve for a small choir.[15] The acquisition of the necessary liturgical books for the celebrations of the church calendar was an obvious priority according to the documents of the first two decades of the 16th century.[16] Da Gama's brother D. Ayres da Gama mentions specifically in connection with a church in Cannanore that while the building is beautifully decorated "it is necessary to have the books to sing the offices" of which there were none.[17] This music would have been for the use of priests and clergy for the celebration of the daily office as well as for the mass, possibly accompanied by organs. A letter from Fr. Domingo de Souza to the king in December 1514, mentions specifically that ten clerks were used to sing masses and the office from the books "in the best manner as they could"[18] which does suggest that the essential celebration of the mass and office was not compromised but that the clerks were unaccustomed to singing them. Large books for singing psalms are also documented.[19] Thus in Goa as well as in Cochin and in Cannanore an infrastructure was established very early of celebrating the office and mass in chant. Unfortunately these chant books have not survived; the chant books at the Sé and elsewhere in Goa date mostly from the 18th century. This is unfortunate since chant books are essential sources for which to determine the liturgy in use in Goa during the early 16th century which would have governed the celebration of feast days as well as the organization of the yearly liturgical calendar.

Documents in general about the training of musicians and musical practice in Goa are rather scarce in the early 1540s, perhaps due to the outbreak of plague, but by 1546, musical practice in the Goan churches is once again a topic of some interest. At the end of a long letter from António Criminalis to Ignatius of Loyola of 1545, there is a discussion regarding the appropriateness of either chanting or intoning the parts (as in psalms) of the mass or the office. Since the language used is both archaic and unconventional for speaking about music, it is possible that the distinction is not between singing and speaking (or intoning), but rather between the use of chant (which is more like intoning — *entoar*) and the employment of polyphony.[20] At any rate, by the 1540s, the practice of polyphony was being cultivated in Goan churches, though by which composers and in what style remains impossible to know for sure. The emotional and spiritual benefits of having a sung mass rather than a spoken one is emphasized in a revealing letter written by Father Master Belchior from Cochin in 1561. He writes that people were satisfied only with sung masses which became necessary for the increased devotion of the Portuguese as well as the native population (*gente da terra*) and for the veneration of the divine mysteries. For the same reason, he concludes, the Feast of the Nativity is celebrated with many instruments, as well as many *prosas e jubilos*.[21] This is the same theme that is emphasized in Barreto's letter to Ignatius Loyola regarding the celebration of the divine office in Japan: that both chant and polyphony should be used for the principal feasts *porque la jente con estros exteriores se mueve en gran manera*.[22]

The use of polyphony in Goan churches and colleges was an extremely important development, but it required an intensive musical training for the boys, demanding increased time to learn counterpoint and to read measured music. Valignano, who is perhaps the most articulate commentator about music among the Jesuit correspondents, describes the difficulty of teaching "foreigners", and especially children to sing because of the amount of assistance and personnel that is needed — not so much in Goa, but in Cochin and Bassein.[23] The music-making at Goa earns high praise from Valignano, who mentions that every Sunday and feast day features Mass said by the priest, deacon and sub-deacon and the voices are sung by the boys who live at the College, assisted by some foreigners.[24] In Bassein, however, even though polyphony is used, it is done so with great labour and inconvenience because "the foreigners do not have the ability of the Portuguese boys in Goa". Valignano continues,

> "and because India had neither choirmasters nor singing teachers, but only those who learned their art in Portugal, to keep up this type of singing here it is always necessary to beg this or that Portuguese [teacher] to come, and flatter him a thousand times, as well as give to him a meal at the College".[25]

Much of this training was supplied at the new College of St. Paul from its inception in 1542. Given the opulence and frequency of musical events there over the next few decades, it appears that the high reputation the college gained throughout the East is entirely justified. As a Jesuit school, the education was rigorous and modeled on the curriculum in the Jesuit schools in Rome. Many of the feast days were celebrated at the college with unusual extravagance, involving not only singing, but plays, processions and the playing of the instruments. This *Spielfreude* encouraged at the college, however, became increasingly subject to some criticism, as occurs whenever music is taught within a varied curriculum particularly a scholastic one as in the Jesuit colleges. In Goa, both chant (*canto llano*) and polyphony (*canto d'órgano*) were taught along with grammar, arts and theology towards instilling in the students a character of virtue and morality. Musical training was also seen as effective in evangelization. But musical practice can quickly lead to subversion, as it has in virtually all periods, and by the late 1570s, following a few decades of a rapidly developing musical culture, the Tridentine reforms began to reach Goa and musical practice became subject to various reforms, to which I will return later on.

Polyphony in Goa was not an everyday practice but used for the mass on Sundays and particular feast days (*todos os dominguos e festas ... se fere missa cantada*[26]) often with instruments; chant was used otherwise.[27] The feast days cited most frequently in the documents are the Assumption of the Virgin (15 August), Corpus Christi (29 May), the feast of the Circumcision (1 January) — sometimes known as the "Feast of Fools" or the traditional "boys' night out" in Medieval Europe), the Feast of the Conversion of St. Paul (25 January), Holy Week, and the Feast of 11,000 Virgins or the Feast of St. Ursula (21 October), which called for the most elaborate music and decorations of any of the feasts. In one of the many descriptions of this particular feast, António da Costa writes in 1558 that there were many processions, along with the participation at Mass of instruments such as shawms, trumpets, flutes, viols and harpsichord;[28] a few years later a document describing the same feast day mentions the presence of *muitos instrumentos de musica como trombetas e charamelas, frautas e violas d'arcos, etc.*[29]. Instruments were used for other religious ceremonies as well. For a baptism in 1567 Fr. Gomes Vaz mentions "trumpets and other instruments with a gathering outside of a procession of singers."[30]

The genres of polyphony specified in the documents give us little clue to their style or composers. Music for the Mass is often mentioned though never specified. Such pieces might have been drawn from works by Portuguese composers which would have been readily available from when music printing began in Portugal in 1535. The excellent Coimbra school of composers might also have furnished works for use in Goa. As for other genres, Sebastian Fernandes (1569) among others, mentions motets which used sacred, though not always scriptural texts, and could have been sung at Mass, and *cantigas*, which were probably strophic songs with a sacred theme, more popular in origin.[31] Some of the performances employed double choirs, probably spaced on different sides of the church, which was a trend developing in Venice already by the middle of the 16th century. Or, this could represent an older *alternatim* style of practice common during the 15th century, in which, odd-verses of a strophic chant (as in a hymn text) alternate with even-verses of polyphony or vice-versa. The singing of the twilight office of Vespers is always mentioned in the documents, the requirements of which involved five psalms, the *Magnificat* and the *Benedicamus Domino*. For this office, one might expect a conservative style of polyphony for the setting of the psalms — homophonic, rather than contrapuntal — with greater complexity given to the *Magnificat*. Frequently, Indian instruments were used along with the voices and organ. The political and evangelical subtext — indeed, purpose, of such extravagant and pluralistic music is made very clear in the documents. Pasio writes from Goa in 1578 that:

> "the divine office is celebrated in this church (of the college of St. Paul) with as much solemnity and perfection as there can be, because to make the gentiles dismiss their own ceremonies and to make them seize the important meaning and affection of our Christianity and divine cult, the Fathers celebrate the offices very solemnly, singing the mass of the principal feasts with a deacon and sub deacon, and vespers with five Fathers with copes, employing very good music (performed by) orphans and new converts, who remain in one part of the college, and number a little less that one hundred and playing the organ and other instruments of the land".[32]

Despite the empowerment given to the missionary campaign by polyphony, multi-choral performance, and the participation of instruments, the cold climate of the Tridentine reforms began to blow through Goa in the early 1570s. Among the abuses cited by the Council of Trent in their discussions about music were the participation of instruments in church (besides the organ), the incomprehensibility of the Latin text when set within a dense contrapuntal framework, the use of secular techniques (such as virtuosic rapid notes, or word painting) in sacred composition, and the incorrect setting of Latin text. Although we have retained only the descriptions of Goan polyphony and not the actual music, it is clear that the Council could surely have found much to reform in Goa. The important tradition of processions and celebrations that is mentioned by every visitor to 16th century Goa began to have an impact on sacred music. The increasing use of "loud" wind instruments, along with flutes, trumpets, indigenous instruments, and drums were eventually thought of as being distracting and disrespectful to the Mass or other services. In Travancore for the feast of the Assumption in 1577, dances such as the *folias* were performed, which had erotic connotations in Spain.[33] A Counter-Reformation austerity was encouraged for music in the churches, though such radical reforms, were met with some resistance.

But there is another reason for the musical reforms that were suggested in Goa after 1570. By this time it had become clear to the Jesuits that the successes they had hoped for in converting Indians to Christianity were falling short of their goal. Where music was traditionally used by missionaries as an evangelical technique — the students at St. Paul's would frequently walk through the streets singing the Credo — the extravagance of music at the Jesuit College was becoming a profession into itself, rather than being an activity in the service of missionary training. Implicit in the reforms, then, was the conviction that music was becoming subversive. This was, and would not be, an original thought. Throughout history, music has always been seen as a double-edged sword, as a source of edification as well as contributing to the ills of youth. Now, mounting financial debts and sustained disappointments in the missionary campaigns made music the scapegoat. In assessing this period purely from a documentary standpoint, three figures emerge as the most outspoken concerning the issue of music at the college. Francisco Cabral and Claudio Acquaviva, the Provincial and the General of the Society, respectively, were strongly convinced that reforms were needed and that many facets of music-making should be discontinued. On the other hand, there is Alessandro Valignano, who was supportive of the need for musical training, and persuasive in his attempts to keep music alive for the sake of proper education. He saw musical training as one of the most valuable activities of the colleges, and he was convinced of the power of music, to aid in the Christianization of India, and particularly Japan, the country that held his strongest interest. Given the difficulty in training native boys, to sing measured music in Latin, he admitted Portuguese boys to the part of St. Paul's that was for natives only, for the reason of helping out with the choir. This was challenged by Acquaviva, who included music among his general reforms of abuses at the College and wanted to reduce the number of boys who were contracted to furnish liturgical music, with the eventual aim to abolish completely the practice. Wicki felt that this was "a wise decision".[34] Valignano insisted that liturgical music could not be suppressed in an area like India, in which music had a very strong effect; therefore the number of boys at the College could not be reduced. In support of the reforms, the lack of finances was often cited. Francisco Fernandez wrote to Acquaviva in 1589 that it was unnecessary to have so many *ministriles* — a word that suggests the playing of secular songs rather than singing liturgical polyphony — at the college, as well as *moços* or servants. The grouping of young musicians and servants in the same breath as elements to be purged from the college reveals much about Fernandez's cultural and aesthetic orientation and the inferiority he felt existed among the music played by the boys, probably heavily influenced by "local" musical traditions and the native population.

Acquaviva himself did not permit even organ music in the new Professed House, but more often he was on the receiving end of complaints. Fr. Nuno Rodrigues wrote to him in 1591 about the "scandal" that occurred when instrumental music and *cantigas* (probably Portuguese secular songs) were performed at the 5.00 am Saturday service at the College. Also included "were other vulgarities, which in Portuguese is called *chacota*, and instruments appropriate to these, such as guitars, citterns and the like. This was not for any absence of organs, because in our choir there are many good ones".[35] For all of his displeasure at what he heard, Rodrigues succeeded in leaving us with one of the most revealing documents we have in all of the Jesuit correspondence. For a conservative priest like him, this was all that he needed to see to suggest the imposition of strict musical reforms; but for a musicologist like myself, the "scandal" offers a tantalizing view of cross-cultural music-making, and the strong influence of Portuguese popular culture in India and on Indian youth in the 16th century.

Wicki writes that by the 1590s, "singing and instrumental music were not in favour in the Society of Jesus at this time".[36] If the letters Acquaviva received from Fernandez and Rodrigues were not enough, he was no doubt pushed to take action following his correspondence with Francisco Cabral, a veritable crusader against excesses in the church and something of a racist who opposed the admission of Japanese to the Society and, by extension, even the use of silk for the Jesuit robes.[37] Before Cabral was thankfully kicked out from office he strongly urged Acquaviva in a letter 1594 to end the practice of singing mass and the office in the college for three reasons: (1) that in order to sustain the tradition, a Father or a brother of the Society is always needed as choirmaster and to teach singing, but these are not always dependable or available, nor is it economical; (2) while singing was originally permitted and cultivated in order to assist in conversion by singing the office, the end result is that few new-converts actually come to church, and therefore the singing of the office might not have the impact for which it was intended; and (3) singing was originally introduced to attract faithful and honourable people to church, but this has not been the case.

What Cabral points out has little to do, of course, with music *per se*. By using music in such a specific context of missionary interests, it was inevitable that it would be blamed for the larger problems that occurred in the missionary campaigns and successes. What is interesting about the letter is that in having to justify the specific use and expense of music, Cabral reveals information about the Society's mission that is often not said as explicitly. Here, the value of documents about music is quite clear, for it allows the sounding of a different voice, a multi-vocality, to emerge from the author.

These reforms were only temporary. Even as the Portuguese empire in India began to collapse, St. Paul's became increasingly active in its use of the arts as a powerful source of identity and self-aggrandizement, commensurate with the close relationships, the Jesuits were forging with the popes in Rome. The weeks of festivities in Rome following the canonization of St. Francis Xavier and Ignatius Loyola in 1622 (which included a Jesuit "opera" by Kapsberger in which India is one of the characters)[38] were echoed a few years later in Goa, which Pietro della Valle describes in detail.[39] From his description of chariots, music, processions and drama, it is clear that the musical austerity envisaged by Cabral and others was very much a passing phenomenon. The archives in Goa (*Jesuitas*) show regular payments for viol and harp strings, as well as an organist and this combination forms the basis for any of the mainstream genres current in Europe in the early 17th century such as cantata, accompanied song, villancico and even opera. Sebastiani's letter of 1663 (published in 1683) quoted at the beginning of this essay leaves no doubt as to the musical proficiency in Goa by the end of the 17th century and of the mainstream music that was being performed there.

Of what significance are these documents and in a larger sense what can the history of Portuguese music in Goa tell us about the Portuguese in India? Despite our lack of the actual sources of this music it is clear that a strong musical infrastructure similar to that of a small city in Europe was established in Goa within a few years of the Portuguese settlements in the early 16th century. This included the use of music for signaling and ceremonial purposes, the employment of liturgical chant for celebration of the Mass, the daily office and the feast days and music for processions and other civic events. Organs, trumpets and shawms were brought over on the first ships and occasionally these instruments were supplemented with indigenous instruments. Large books of chant also came over on the ships.

The introduction of polyphony after about 1540 required more intensive training for the singers and greater expense all around for teachers, books and maintaining of a choir. Since music had already been used successfully by the Portuguese as a way to find a common ground with native people, the added expense and training required could be justified. It proved to be an effective evangelical tool despite the difficulties in training native singers, and polyphony added special significance to the major feast days and ceremonies during the year. Consequently music ceased to be seen as purely functional and the documents now raise questions about the aesthetics, purpose and finances. But the Portuguese, concerned mainly with building an empire, proved to be poor patrons of music. Their interests were directed not on developing the choirs and repertory of the musical institutions, but on the more public displays of processions and celebrations.

With the Jesuits becoming the major patrons of music after the 1550s music was placed under the microscope. Discussions about music from this time on invariably focus on the Aristotelian concerns of music's function, the appropriateness of its use within the education of youths, and its moral value. One would be hard-pressed to find letters that confront issues of sense, style, or aesthetics. There is no document from this period that even remotely touches on the auditory experience of the listener. The very strictly defined roles for music as seen by the Jesuits resulted in various reforms that took place in the 1580s and 1590s, the discussions of which are some of the most interesting documents in the entire corpus of letters. In debating the purpose of music within Jesuit education, the cultural and missionary imperatives implicit in musical training come into focus. Music in the eyes of the Jesuits is very much linked up with the Platonic concept of Republic, as well as a concept of Nation. Music is thus both a cultural product as well as a political vocabulary, and the nature of the reforms the Jesuits pressed for tell us much about colonialist and missionary strategies. Their discussions about music open up a new vocality in Jesuit (and Portuguese) discourse, revealing information about cultural priorities, nationalism and the success of the missions. They also reveal their own cultural biases in their reactions to Indian music. While a strictly analytical perspective on music in Portuguese Goa cannot be offered at this time because of the lack of sources, and the fact that itemized account books do not exist for religious institutions prior to the 17th century, it is along the lines of seeing how cultural and nationalistic policies are embedded within the discourse of discussing music that seems to be the main direction this research could take. Music was seen as a powerful political medium in Renaissance Goa, and it was very much part of the cultural and political imperatives of both the Portuguese and the Jesuits. Because this music was imposed on a culture which had its own much older traditions and because it was used as both an ambassadorial and evangelical tool, Goa is one of the most interesting laboratories for studying the political role of the arts, and how hierarchies of culture and cultural exclusion are formed. I am sure that many would agree that this could represent a promising line of inquiry in Indo-Portuguese historiography.[40]

NOTES AND REFERENCES

1. Joseph di Santa Maria (Giuseppe Sebastiani) *Seconda speditione all'Indie Orientali*, Venice, 1683, iii, p. 105.
2. José Pereira, *Boroque Goa: The Architecture of Portuguese India*, New Delhi, Books & Books, 1995 and the articles published in *Purabhilekh-Puratatva* (Panaji). For a brilliant study of western reactions to Indian art, see Partha Mitter, *Much Maligned Monsters: A History of European*

Reactions to Indian Art, 2nd ed., Chicago, Univ. of Chicago Press, 1992, which includes some discussion of Goa.

3. Owen Rees, *Polyphony in Portugal, c.1530-c.1620: Sources from the Monastery of Santa Cruz*, Coimbra, New York, Garland, 1995.
4. Mira Mascarenhas, citing Pereira writes that "Private collectors and Goan churches possess a host of masses, *motets*, litanies and hymns composed by Goan masters", though no further details are given. "Impact of the West on Goan Music" in *Goa: Cultural Trends*, ed. P. P. Shirodkar, Panaji, Casa Packmaster, 1988, pp. 189-204. My own search through the Sé archives produced nothing from before the 18th century.
5. A study of the contents of this library is in Rui Vieira Nery, "The Music Manuscripts in the Library of King D. João IV of Portugal (1604-1656): A Study of Iberian Music in the Sixteenth and Seventeenth Centuries", Ph. D. diss. Univ. of Texas, Austin, 1990.
6. Alfred E. Lemmon, "Jesuits and Music in Mexico", *Archivum Historicum Societatis Iesu*, 46, 1977, pp. 191-198.
7. Robert Snow, *Gaspar Fernandes: Obras Sacres. Portugaliae Musica 49*, Lisbon, Fundação Calouste Gulbenkian, 1990; Paul Borg, "The Polyphonic Music in the Guatemalan Music Manuscripts of the Lilly Library", Ph.D. diss., Indiana Univ., 1985; Robert Snow, "Music by Francisco Guerrero in Guatemala", *Nassarre Revista Aragonesa de Musicologia 3*, 1987, pp. 153-202.
8. Ian Woodfield, *English Musicians in the Age of Exploration*, Stuyvesant, Pendragon Press, 1995.
9. G. B. Ramusio, *Della navigazione e viaggi*, Venice, 1550, quoted in Woodfield, p. 96.
10. Woodfield, p. 96.
11. *Ibid.*, p. 182.
12. *Ibid.*
13. *Ibid.*, pp. 183-84.
14. *Documentação para a historia das missões do Padroado Português do Oriente*, ed. António da Silva Rego, 12. vols., Lisbon, Atica, SARL, 1947, (hereinafter *DMP*), I, p. 149.
15. *DMP* I, pp. 127, 431.
16. *DMP* I, pp. 395, 411.
17. *DMP* I, p. 371.
18. *DMP* I, p. 250.
19. *DMP* I, p. 336.
20. *Documenta Indica: Missiones Orientales*, ed. Josef Wicki, Rome, 1948-, I, p. 20 (hereinafter *DI*).
21. *DMP* 8, pp. 464-465.
22. *DI* 3, pp. 125-126.
23. *DI* 10, p. 622.
24. *DI* 13, p. 17.
25. *Ibid.*, p. 24.
26. *DI* 8, p. 432.
27. Belchior's letter of 1561 from Cochin in *DMP* 8, pp. 464-465.

28. *DI* 3, p. 189.
29. *Ibid.*, p. 735.
30. *DI* 7, document no. 90.
31. *DI* 8, pp. 87-89.
32. *DI* 11, pp. 358-359
33. *DMP* 12, p. 390.
34. *DMP* 15, p. 25.
35. *Ibid.*, pp. 721-722.
36. *DI* 16, p. 7.
37. David Mitchell, *The Jesuits: A History*, New York, Franklim Watts, 1981, p. 145.
38. Victor Coelho, "The Apotheosis ... of Francis Xavier and the conquering of India" in *The Work of Opera: Gender, Nation, Genre* (forthcoming). Also Victor Coelho, "Kapsberger, Giovanni Girolamo" in *The New Grove Dictionary of Opera*, ed. S. Sadie, London, MacMillan, 1992, ii, pp. 949-950.
39. *The Travels of Pietro della Valle in India*, 2 vols., ed. Edward Grey. London: Hakluyt Society, 1892/rpt. New Delhi, Asian Educational Services, 1991, II, pp. 402-413.
40. I follow Teotónio de Souza in his attempts to move documentary work into the areas of critical historiography. See his "The Voiceless in Goan Historiography: A Case for the source value of Church Records in Goa", in *Indo-Portuguese History: Sources and Problems*, ed. John Correia-Afonso, Mumbai, OUP, 1981, pp. 114-131.

TEN

GOAN AND CHRISTIAN ARCHITECTURE OF THE 16TH CENTURY

ANTÓNIO NUNES PEREIRA

Vasco da Gama arrived at Calicut in 1498 but was unable to settle there. After facing similar circumstances, Pedro Alvares Cabral in 1500 settled at Cochin, which in 1505 became the first seat of the Portuguese government in the East.

The conquest of Goa took place in 1510. Afonso de Albuquerque built some chapels there, most of them in fulfilment of vows. He built in 1510 the chapel of St. Catherine (Goa having been conquered on her feast day), in 1513 the chapels of Our Lady of Serra and Our Lady of the Mount respectively. In his will, he left money for a chapel to be built in honour of St. Anthony of Lisbon. None of these has remained in their earlier forms. They were very modest structures, built quickly to satisfy immediate religious needs. They were later rebuilt, some of them several times over, so that there is nothing left of the 16th century in them.

The only exception is the church of Our Lady of the Rosary, said to be built in 1529. Completely rebuilt during 1549-50, it is the oldest church in Goa and belongs to the late Manueline period.

But the foundation of a real Christian architectural tradition did not exist till the arrival of several religious Orders from Portugal (Franciscans in 1517, Jesuits in 1542, Dominicans in 1548 and Augustinians in 1572). These religious first settled in Goa and built their monasteries. The Cathedral was the first and most important church of the time ever built in this part of the world. With the exception of the first church of the Franciscans, built as early as 1521 in the Manueline style, all the other churches were designed in the new style, which was current in Europe and which was definitely adopted in Portugal after 1521, the year king D. Manuel I died. Unfortunately, some of these churches were either destroyed or collapsed, after the suppression of religious orders in 1833.

The church of the Dominicans, built between 1550 and 1564 (and demolished in 1841) was probably the first of the great churches in classical design. It had three aisles separated by columns, side-chapels, transepts and a choir. The choir alone was vaulted, the church itself had a wooden roof. The front facade was structured by pilasters, which separated three vertical rows of doors and windows (bays). It had two complete stores, the middle bay had one additional store. Stores were separated by cornices. This facade had no towers. An engraving published in 1886 shows a tower by the choir, as was usual with Jesuit churches.[1]

The church of St. Paul of the Arches replaced the first one at the Holy Faith (Santa Fé), begun between 1541 and 1543. This college was given to the Jesuits in 1546, who rebuilt it during the 16th century. Between 1560 and 1572 they erected the new church, St. Paul of the Arches (demolished definitely in 1829), one of the first Jesuit churches outside Europe. Today only a fragment of the facade of the church, the central portal frame, remains. This portal was restored in the 1950s. The church had also a classical design, three aisles separated by columns, one main choir and two lateral ones. The whole building was barrel-vaulted. It had no towers at the front facade, but only one by the choir, as was the case with the Dominican church.

The Cathedral of Old Goa, begun after 1562 and still standing, is contemporaneous with three other cathedrals built in Portugal: the cathedral of Miranda do Douro in the north-east of Portugal (begun in 1552); of Portalegre in the south-east (begun in 1556); and of Leiria in the centre of the country (begun in 1559). There are certain similarities among all these four churches: they have three aisles separated by cruciform pillars, a Latin cross plan and transept with a detached crossing.

Unlike the Portuguese cathedrals, which are all hall churches (*Hallenkirchen*) with groin vaultings, a late medieval typology,[2] the Goa cathedral is a false basilica (no clerestory) with barrel vaultings above each aisle. There are side chapels all along both side aisles, as at Portalegre, but unlike the cathedrals of Miranda and Leiria. The facade of the Goa cathedral has flanking towers, like the ones at

Miranda and Portalegre and unlike the one at Leiria.

One of the most differing features in all these churches is the front facade. The one of Miranda, all in stone, is surprisingly stripped off any structural element, basis, pilaster or cornice - only the classical portal and window decoration allows one to date the building as 16th century. At the one at Leiria, there are three colossal pilasters, which divide the facade into three vertical bays. The same is the case at Portalegre, but here is also a horizontal element: a cornice separates the two lower floors and an attic. At Goa the structure has been carried out even more consistently: pilasters and cornices build an orthogonal frame, which divide the facade in stores and bays of one window or door.

Different as these facades may be, they are similar in one point. They reflect the interior of the building behind. The bays correspond in number and width to the aisles inside. In the case of Leiria e.g. the pilasters in the facade are buttresses, i.e. they have a structural function and belong together with the pillars which divide the interior in aisles.

After the start of the Cathedral there was a three decade break before another big church was begun. The Franciscans and Dominicans were busy building there monasteries and churches and had no interest in other enterprises in Goa (except for parish churches). So were the Jesuits, who did not really have a monastery, but nevertheless were occupied in building the Seminary of Holy Faith, where they were living since 1544. But it was precisely their wish to build a monastery that led them in 1585 to begin one in the centre of the town. The church of the new complex, the Bom Jesus Basilica[3] was begun in 1594 and was consecrated in 1605. It is probably the first great church in Goa with only one aisle,[4] which should not surprise us, as it were the Jesuits who disseminated this typology over Portugal, in opposition to the traditional hall-churches. The latter became rare in the last third of the 16th century, being replaced by the one aisle-churches. The model was St. Francis at Evora (1495-1508) and it was taken over by the Jesuits for two of the earliest and most important monastery churches in Portugal: the Holy Spirit (1566-1574) also at Evora and St. Roque (1567-1586, consecrated in 1573) at Lisbon, the leading institution of all Jesuit monasteries in the kingdom. All these churches have a longitudinal, rectangular space, into which the side chapels and the choir open. Two bigger side chapels, close to the choir and opposite each other, replace the transept.

St. Roque at Lisbon was initially planned as a three-aisled church. Later it was decided to build it with only one aisle, so that the community could not only listen to the preacher, but also see him. Although new foundations were laid, the width of the church was such, that the original idea to vault it had to be given up and, instead of this, a timber roof was constructed.[5] Both these facts are very interesting: architects in the middle of the 16th century were still vacillating between both typologies and that a single aisle church was not yet a must for Jesuit churches; and if it was not for the technical difficulties, St. Roque would have been vaulted, that means that the church was intended to be very similar to Holy Spirit at Evora.

Bom Jesus in Goa shows all these influences from Portugal. But Goa was very far away and journeys took very long. The architects there had to take the local churches as models to resolve practical problems. One good example is given by comparison between the Cathedral and Bom Jesus. In the first, the side chapels are organized in two rows behind the towers. Bom Jesus has no towers, as it was usual with Jesuit churches in Portugal and unlike churches of other Orders, and so there are also no side-chapels. The three central bays of the facade of the Cathedral reappear in the facade of the Jesuit church. In the interior, however, there are two bigger side-chapels, close to the choir and opposite each other, replacing the trancept[6], just as is the case with the church of St. Francis and the Jesuit church of the Holy Spirit, both at Evora.

There is also another difference between both buildings, which shows evolution in the architectural design from the middle of the 16th century till the end. There is less correspondence between facade and interior in Bom Jesus than in the Cathedral. The three bays, common to both facade correspond in the Cathedral to three aisles inside, which is not the case with Bom Jesus, as this church has only one aisle. The upper floor in the facade of Bom Jesus, with the round windows (*oeils de boef*), does not correspond to any floor in the interior, as it is the case with the first floor in the facade of both churches, with the rectangular windows, which corresponds to a gallery inside. This evolution, although late in time, can be seen as similar to the evolution in Europe from Renaissance to Mannerism and later to Baroque. The similarity of evolution exists not in terms of form but in design concepts: facades become more scenic and correspond less to the interior.

The last big church of the 16th century was the church of Our Lady of Graça (1597-1602), in the monastery of the Augustinians who were the last Portuguese friars to arrive in Goa. This church (today in ruins as is its monastery) seems to make a resumé of the architectural evolution in the 1st century of Portuguese rule. Like the Cathedral it has two towers flanking the front facade, and side chapels behind them. Like Bom Jesus it was a church with one rectangular, longitudinal space and two bigger side-chapels, close to the choir and opposite each other, replacing the transept.

Unlike Bom Jesus, it was possible to vault Graça. For such a wide vault side buttresses were needed, whose function was served by the walls between the side-chapels. Since side-chapels were avoided for Bom Jesus, a vaulting had also to be given up. The Cathedral with its side-chapels and thick walls between them, was vaulted. Here, however as the central space was divided into three aisles, the pillars between them also carried a part of the weight of the vaultings. Moreover, two vaultings lean on each other above the pillars at the point they come together. The whole weight is taken by several supporting points on the sides and between them. There is nothing similar in the Augustinian church. An enormous vaulting, covering the one aisled space lay on the walls between the side-chapels.

One main problem while comparing these churches is to know which building served as a model for the other. Bom Jesus and Graça are contemporaneous. The first was begun three years before the other (in 1594), which in turn finished three years before the Jesuit church (1602). The front facade usually being the last part of a church to be built, it is probable that the Augustinian facade was already three years old as the Jesuit one was just being finished. And yet the designs of both churches were surely fixed before the buildings were begun. It is almost inconceivable that the architects of both churches did not have knowledge of each others' design. This is confirmed by many similarities of both churches. It might even be the fact that a single architect was responsible for both buildings. All these building enterprises were under royal responsibility, which in Goa was laid by the Viceroy. He might have sent an architect of his confidence (the state chief engineer?) to both Orders, to build their churches. The theory can only be proved if any documents could be found to confirm it.

The Cathedral is a bigger problem. It was begun three decades before both churches mentioned above (shortly after 1562), but it was finished three decades after they were completed (in 1631). Such a long building period means that several generations of architects worked on it. The Cathedral is quite a homogeneous building, yet it would not be surprising if there had been some alterations to the original design in the course of its building. If there has been any, we do not know how the original design looked like, how it possibly influenced the churches which were begun later, and, last but not least, how it was influenced by the same churches which were finished before it. In other words, it is very difficult to know exactly in what church certain design solutions were first carried out. This problem concerns particularly the facades. The one of the Cathedral was in fact built in the 17th century. Does it follow the original design of 1563? Was it then a model for Bom Jesus and Graça? Or is it a later alteration of the 17th century and therefore a simpler solution to the model represented by the two other churches?

In the 17th century the arrival of Orders directly from Italy brought new architectural traditions to Goa. The Carmelites arrived in 1607 and the Theatines in 1639. Both their churches and monasteries, of which only the Theatine church has survived, were Italian in design. They remained isolated, for they were not widely used as models for new buildings. There were not other models coming from Portugal either. With the competition of the British and the Dutch, Goa was losing its economic importance since the end of the 16th century. The Portuguese were now investing in the American continent, rich in gold. The Portuguese Baroque knew a very creative continuation in Brazil, but only very few examples were built in Goa.

The Franciscan church of the Holy Spirit (begun in 1661), which replaced the Manueline church of 1521, follows the Portuguese tradition as it had developed in Goa over the last hundred years. The structure is similar to the one of Graça and yet there are some major transformations: the side-chapels, scarcely deep, become niches with altars. Two bigger niches on the sides of the choir replace a transept. The proportions of the front facade are quite different to those that were usual. But as this church is a rebuilding of an older one, this might have been due to the medieval structure which was not completely destroyed but integrated into the new building.[7]

Conclusion

The main stream of the development of religious architecture in Goa has its origins in Portuguese models of the 16th century. This development was mainly local, where the existing Indian traditions played a more important role as the influence of Portugal began to fade. The synthesis of both traditions led to the Indian Baroque studied mainly by Dr. José Pereira. Only the study of the 16th century will enlighten us about the transfer of European architecture to the East and thus the origins of the Goan architectural tradition, which, in spite of its development over five centuries, remains remarkably homogeneous.

NOTES AND REFERENCES

1. The reconstruction of this church and of some others is possible due to descriptions of travellers to engravings and in fewer cases, to old photographs. (António Lopes Mendes, *A India Portuguesa. Breve descripção das Possessões Portuguezas na Asia*, Lisbon, 1886, vol. 1, p. 130).
2. George Kubler, *A Arquitectura Portuguesa Chã. Entre as Especiarias e os diamantes 1521-1706*. Trans. Jorge Henrique Pais da Silva, Lisbon, (original English edition 1972), p. 30.
3. The word "Basilica" does not refer to its architectural classification, but .o its status as a Minor Basilica since 1946 on account of its historical and religious role in Goa.
4. The "Priorado do Rosário" church has also only one aisle, but this was the normal case for a parish church in the late medieval period, whereas the three-aisle-typology was reserved for bigger and more important churches (as churches of big monasteries and cathedrals).
5. M. Balthasar Telles, *Chronica da Companhia de Iesu, da Provincia de Portugal*, vol. 2, Lisbon, 1645-47, p. 109.
6. In Goa this solution was not entirely new. The "Priorado do Rosário" church, built at least a half of a century before, already had such opposite chapels near the choir, as a replacement of the transept.
7. José Manuel Fernandes, "Vestígios do Manuelino na Arquitectura Religiosa de Influência Portuguesa na India", *Oceanos*, No. 19-20, Sept.-Dec. 1994, p. 149.

ELEVEN

OLD GOA IN THE CONTEXT OF INDIAN HERITAGE

PERCIVAL NORONHA

To project Old Goa in the context of Indian heritage is a subject matter enormously vast. With a continuous history of more than five thousand years, India has inherited a rich cultural heritage, splendid in expression, illuminating in thought and fantastic in imagination.

The scope of this presentation, however, is restricted to the architectural heritage of India in relation to religious monuments, sometimes with slant reference to civil structures also. Yet, the sweep is enormous from Harappa to the 17th century monuments, i.e. contemporary of the religious monuments in Old Goa which are reckoned as outstandingly fine examples of Iberian architecture in India.[1]

The architectural tradition of India can be traced back to the times of the dawn of Indian history around third millennium B.C. a civilization developed in the Valley of the Indus with its chief centres at Mohenjo-Daro and Harappa. Here, civilized communities lived in planned cities with adequate arrangements for sanitation, etc. They also built houses of burnt bricks. "No Indian city" writes D.D. Kosambi, "possessed anything of the sort until modern times; far too many still lack these amenities".[2]

The outstanding quality of Indian architecture is essentially its spiritual content.[3] It has an important place in the history of that civilization, for it is a part of India's religious, as well as aesthetic expression. Every architectural work is infused with symbolism, bound up with a conception of the universe and with the hallowed traditions. Hence, the most characteristic architecture which can be seen in India is that of Hindu temples. Large or small, they are easily recognized by the typical prismatic or pyramidal towers with spires.

They dominate the countryside with their presence particularly in the South. Even the temples of Goa do not deviate from this trend and most of them exhibit interesting towers generally prismatic in shape.

The great Indian temples were built in centres of pilgrimage near a river, a lake or a man-made tank because water was needed by the worshippers for abolutions and, at the same time, it was invested with an inner meaning, becoming symbolically the stream of time, crossing which, the enlightened worshipper reached the farther shore of eternity. This vein of rich symbolic meaning runs through the architecture of the temple itself: its three parts namely, the base, the walls and the spire, corresponding to Earth, the Intervening Space and Heaven, or, in other words, the Feet, the Body and the Head of the Cosmic Man. The temple is conceived as a model of Universe, a microcosm, a house of God, an altar at which the devotee makes his offering to the Presence enshrined within. This is the fundamental meaning of the temple building and it has always remained constant.[4] Even the humblest shrine carries the symbolism.

Even more ancient than the temples are the Buddhist stupas. The *stupa* (reliquary) is based on the Vedic funeral mound, that symbolizes the cosmic mountain, the pivot of the world. It enshrines the relics either of the Buddha or of a great figure of the Buddhist church and it is identified with the subtle body of the Buddha. Hence, like a temple, it is a place of worship. As Buddhism spread from the North to the South, the deep impact of the new faith is evident from the remnants of the great stupas of Amravati and Nagarjunakonda.

The Buddhist constructor, who had to build sanctuaries intended for communal prayer, was faced with a quite different problem from that of the Hindu counterpart. The Hindus tried to convey the idea of the mysterious and the divine; the sanctuary housed the sacred image, and was served by a single priest. The Buddhist sanctuary (chaitya), on the other hand, was spacious, airy and sufficiently lit to enable one to admire the painted and carved decorations. The finest example is the great stupa at Sanchi, dating back to the third century B.C.[5] The other contributions to the architecture of Buddha period, besides stupas are: (1) series of edicts inscribed on the rocks, (2) certain monolithic pillars, (3) several monolithic accessories to shrines, (4) vast sanctuaries, and (5) a group of rock-cut chambers.[6]

Most of the houses in India were originally built of mud, timber, bamboo, unfired or burnt bricks and thatched roofs. Such types of civil construction can be seen even now in rural India. Against this background, around 350 A.D., Buddhists and even Hindus turned gradually towards stone masonry, as the most suitable dwelling place for sacred purposes. The earliest structural temple, a small shrine, not cut into rock, but built up stone by stone, was discovered at Aihole next to Huchimalliguddi temple in Karnataka.

There is evidence that stone masonry and stone carvings were imported during Mauryan period, in the emperor Ashoka's days (*c.* 272-232 B.C.) from Achaemenids (dynasty in Persia 553-330 B.C.).[7] In fact, the earliest remains, outside the proto-historic finds of the Indus Valley culture, discovered at Rupar and Lothal near Ahmedabad, are of that period. Mauryan stone sculpture, the best specimens of which are to be seen in the country's many museums, had a rare feeling of monumental form and majestic power. Among Mauryan sculptures is the lion capital in the Sarnath Museum which has been adopted as the State seal of India.

Here, it is worth referring to the rock-cut architecture of India. Caves are not usually included in the history of architecture but Indian cave temples and monasteries are considered because they are masterpieces of "organizing space" with beauty in view as well as convenience.[8] Cave architecture, which received the greatest elaboration in India, also developed during the Buddhist period (fourth century B.C.). The caves, mostly in groups, were self-contained monastic establishments with rooms for the monks to live in and temples for the worship of Buddha.

The Jain caves cut into the hillside of Barabar constitute the most ancient sanctuary (third century B.C.) that has come down to us. Situated near Bodhgaya in Bihar, some of the caves bear inscriptions dating back from Maurya period. The plan combines rectangles and circles which is quite unusual but the best specimens of caves are also to be found in the hills of the western coast, where the nature of the rock made them suitable for excavation. The great cave at Karle is probably the finest of the cave temples. Imposing in size, its interior illuminated by soft light from a great window, the Karle cave induces in the visitor the feeling of benevolence and peace.[9]

The cave architecture was developed further by the Hindus at a later period and the great cave temples at Badami, Elephanta and above all, Ellora are remarkable monuments to their creative activity.

The great Buddhist, Hindu and Jain rock temples of Ellora vie with one another in splendour and size, the most staggering achievement being the Kailasa shrine (eighth century). Entirely hewn out of a rock it has the appearance of a small man-made mountain, imitating the heavenly mountain-abode of God Siva.[10]

The Gupta period (*c*. A.D. 320-540) is considered as the 'Golden Age' of art. Yet, the temple architecture did not show much development. However, the outline of the stupas, changed considerably during this period. The dome became bell-shaped or bulbous and merged into its circular base. It was this type of building of the Gupta period that was to be perpetuated throughout South-East Asia. Another significant development was the use for the first time of dressed stone masonry, a pronounced step in the technique of building construction. The Gupta period with its prolongations, gradually leads Indian art towards a medieval period (9th-16th centuries). It is marked by temples with a pyramidal roof especially seen in North Indian temples and others of curvilinear roof.[11] A wave of architectural activity swept the country during the 10th and 11th centuries, and great temples were built at Khajuraho in Madhya Pradesh (10th-11th centuries) and Bhubaneshwar in Orissa (8th-11th centuries).

Most of the temples of the period of 11th-13th centuries are lavishly decorated with sculptures that are to be viewed not as individual pieces but as forming a part of the elaborate texture of the walls of the temples. The marble Jain temples at Dilwara (11th-13th centuries) represent the final Baroque phase when the exuberance of ornamentation begins to obscure the plasticity of architectural design.[12] The last masterpiece in North India is probably the Konark temple (13th century). Conceived in the form of the chariot of the Sun God, it is a most remarkable example of Hindu architecture.

In South India also there was an upsurge of building activity from the 7th century onwards. The foundations of a vital movement of sacred architecture was already laid during the Pallava period with the construction of rock-cut temples at Mamallapuram (7th-8th centuries). For the Pallavas goes the credit of having kept burning the torch kindled by the Buddhists in the early centuries of Christian era.[13]

The Chola architecture is conceived in much more grandiose proportions. The Brihadisvara temple at Tanjore is probably the largest Indian temple surviving from this period. It was constructed by the Chola king Rajaraja I towards the end of the 10th century. Another colossal temple was built at Gangaikondacholapuram by Rajaraja's son, Rajendra around 11th century.

The created impulse in the South lasted much longer than in the North. This achievement was made possible by the comparative security from invasion, which was achieved during the reign of the valiant rulers of Vijayanagar (*c.* 1336-1565) whose deserted capital at Hampi is a monument to their lavish patronage of art and architecture. Vijayanagar was a powerful bulwark against Islamic expansion that could hold until the battle of Talikota in 1565.[14] In fact, the remains of extensive buildings and system of terraces that have escaped the destruction wrought by the Muslim conquerors of the city of Hampi after the fateful battle, are yet so beautiful which causes admiration to any visitor and student of art. Even in the dismantled condition, these elevated and orderly pile of masonry finely moulded, retain some glamour and romance of that brilliant period when Vijayanagar — the city of victory was one of the most famous capitals of the East like Old Goa, its counterpart. It is worth mentioning here, the relationship between the court of Vijayanagar's greatest ruler Krishnadeva Raya (1509-30) who cultivated good ties of friendship with Old Goa as a trade outlet and source of military supplies.[15] Several carvings on the walls of the *adhishtana* (lower part) of Vithala temple at Hampi depicting the Portuguese horse sellers, were found sometime back after the excavations of the site by the Archaeological Survey of India (ASI) team. The panels depict the Portuguese in their typical trousers, coats and caps leading the horses to a seated chieftain. One of the carvings shows a man training horses. The Vijayanagar style also arose in other parts of the southern empire, as for instance in Vellore, Kumbakonam, Conjeeveram, Tadpatri, Virinjipuram and Srirangam.[16]

The last great builders in South India were the Nayaks of Madurai who continued to rule till the 17th century. To this period belong many of the great gateways (gopurams) of South Indian temples.[17] Several South Indian temples as they exist today, are not single units built at a particular period of time. In fact, they are complex structures representing the growth of centuries. The original temple was in course of time, surrounded by subsidiary shrines and these were considered too holy to be tampered with, the devotion of subsequent generations found expression in the great gateways in the walls. Some of them were as high as 70 meters and covered with a proliferation of sculptural forms. Here, everything appears to be an excuse for carving and for multiplication of lavish decorations.[18] This was possible because the nature of the stone of the ornate medieval temples in Halebid, Belur, and Somnathpur is soft and can easily be carved when freshly quarried but hardens with exposure. Hence, it was possible for arriving at an advanced stage of ornamentation i.e. Baroque towards an ever richer profusion that could be aptly termed as Indian Rococo.[19]

Several chieftains of Deccan and Konkan also introduced temples of typical Chalukyan or Hoysala styles in those areas. The small temple of Mahadev at Tambdi Surla in Sanguem taluka of Goa shows some affinities with the medieval temples of the Deccan because the Kadambas of Goa were the feudatories of Chalukyas of Kalyani and Yadavas of Devagiri. There is no inscriptional evidence to date the temple. However, on the basis of art, architectural style, ornamental and decorative motifs the temple can be dated to the 13th century A.D.

The architectural scenario takes a different turn with the entry of Islamic hordes in India. Islam's conquering armies arrived in Punjab as early as 775 and gradually reached each of the states in turn. Their first invasion did not immediately make a great impression. Indeed it is important to understand that up to the 15th century, the Muslims lived here as outsiders, conquerors having subdued more or less successfully the Hindu princes and people, but fighting went on all the time well into the days of Aurangzeb, and the Muslims felt that they were living in the midst of a sea of Hindus, many of them hostile. All Islamic cities or capital cities were, hence, fortified. None felt secure, as Hindu rajas did, by living in a palace in the middle of his town and his people. Islamic palaces are all walled-in fortifications: the Fort at Agra, the Delhi Red Fort or the Lahore Fort, although much less formidable than the older Lodhi and Tughlaq forts, are still surrounded by battlemented walls once guarded by armed men.[20] It is for these reasons that the early Muslim period is not marked by any architectural progress. In fact, the magnitude of the destruction wrought by invasions in the North can be inferred from the fact that Varanasi (Benares), the holiest city of the Hindus, has hardly a monument that can lay claim to antiquity. The great temples that have survived are in such out-of-the-way places as Khajuraho in Madhya Pradesh and Bhubaneshwar and Konark in Orissa, where they escaped the fury of the invading hordes. It is said, not without reason that the period up to the 16th century has been termed by an eminent art historian as a period of "architectural asceticism".

It is only after the 15th century that Islamic architectural activity started. Developing that style they had created in Persia, the Muslims provided India with a large number of magnificent buildings, both religious and civil: mosques, tombs, citadels, palaces and monumental gateways.

Many fine early Islamic monuments are to be found in Delhi, the most famous being the Jama Masjid, built by Qutb-ud-din Aibak, near the notable Qutb Minar (early 13th century). The rise of the Sultanates of Gujarat, Malwa and Jaunpur, during the 15th-16th centuries, marks the emergence of provincial styles of great beauty, that of Gujarat being remarkable for a successful assimilation of Hindu architectural and decorative motifs.[21]

The most splendid phase of Muslim architecture in India, however, was the one initiated by the Mughals under the emperor Akbar who is recognized as the greatest and most capable of the Mughal rulers. It was during his reign that indigenous Indian elements both Hindu and Muslim, were incorporated consciously into Mughal structures.

The Agra Fort and the deserted capital city of Fatehpur Sikri near Agra (16th century) bear testimony to greatness of his vision and the catholicity of his taste. Also, near Agra is the splendid mausoleum of Akbar, known as Sikandara, conceived by the emperor but completed in the reign of his son Jahangir. The principal attraction of Agra, however, is the Taj Mahal, tribute of emperor Shah Jahan (1627-1658) to his beloved wife, Mumtaz Mahal. Of chaste proportions, built entirely of marble, it never fails to please in its charming setting of fountains in a lovely garden. Shah Jahan, whose first passion was architecture, also built the magnificent Red Fort, and the famous Jama Masjid at Delhi. Mughal architecture is the product of innovative genius that borrowed from Indian, Timurid and even European sources. The Mughal architects interpreted these borrowed forms, both in terms of symbolism and style, for their own purpose.[22]

Fine buildings were also erected in the Deccan, where Islamic architectural tradition had already grown up in the time of the Bahamani sultans. Rulers of the Adil Shahi sultanate of Bijapur built several excellent buildings in the capital city of which Ibrahim Rauza, the tomb of Ibrahim Adil Shah II (1580), and Gol Gumbaz, the tomb of his successor Muhammad, are easily the most outstanding.

On 20 May 1498, the Portuguese navigator, Vasco da Gama, approached the west coast of India and made landfall at a point near Calicut. The search for the sea route to India was complete. The political and religious map of India was by now experiencing a process of great transformation. In the north, following the invasion of Tamerlane (Timur) and his Tartar enemies an Afghan dynasty was ruling the Islamic state. Babur had not yet conquered the Lodhis to establish the Mughal empire. In central India there were Muslim kingdoms as well as Hindu realms. The Bahamani kingdom of the Deccan had resolved itself into the five sultanates of Berar, Ahmednagar, Bidar, Golconda and Bijapur while to the south of the Deccan sultanates, stretched the mighty Hindu kingdom of Vijayanagar.[23]

The town of Goa[24] on the Konkan coast, in the tiny island of Goa (Tisvarhi) was an important centre for trade and commerce under Yusuf Adil Shah, king of Bijapur. Duarte Barbosa in his work writes: "This town is very large, with goodly edifices and handsome streets and squares surrounded by walls and towers. There is a very good fortress in it, and in the environs many gardens and orchards of fine trees and fruits and many pools of good water. There are many mosques and houses of worship of the Hindus. The country all round is fruitful and well cultivated and enjoys much produce both from sea and land".[25] Another Portuguese chronicler referring to planning of the Moorish town, says: "It had good arrangement of streets with storeyed houses of stone and lime, surrounded by low walls; a good fort and huge warehouses and some palaces of Sabayo".[26] A sketch plan of the town dating back to 1509 i.e. one year prior to its conquest by the Portuguese, is available.[27]

The town prior to its occupation by Mohammedans, was a Hindu hamlet which became a great religious centre. Here God Shiva was worshipped under the name of Goveshwar at a site known as Brahmapuri. Few copper laminates dating back to 1107, of the time of king Tribhuvana-Malla, refer to the foundation of Brahmapuri (colony of Brahmins).[28] The other centre of devotion was the old temple of Shiva where later the Portuguese constructed the chapel of Santissima Trindade. The huge temple had an underground hall which was built below a hill. The entry to this hall was through a subterranean staircase. At its centre, there was a huge square-shaped tank with steps of basalt stone. At a certain height of the walls of the tank there were niches where images of deities were installed. Innumerable pilgrims used to come for their ablutions especially in the month of August to purify themselves of their sins in the waters of this tank leaving on their return a considerable sum of money in the city. In the neighbourhood of this temple there existed the Tirtha, a sacred tank, where still the followers of Shiva come to bathe.[29] The Hindu temples of this town that were destroyed either by the Mohammedans or by the Portuguese, must have obeyed the architectural lines of the temples of the later Chalukyan or Hoysala style (1050-1300 A.D.).

The Portuguese would eventually conquer Goa on the 25 November 1510, turning it and the areas around into a strange socio-religious experiment. Here, the alliance between the sword and the cross was very close. In fact, the religious policy of the new state was a forward one, and it placed at the disposal of the ecclesiastical authorities all the resources. The process of evangelization represented the ideals of the new policy. For this purpose, several religious orders started flocking in the city for the propagation of the Catholic religion.

Though the Dominicans were the forerunners in the field, the glory of sowing the seeds of Christianity in Goa belonged, however, to the Franciscans, the hardy pioneers of the Eastern missions who were the first to set up their Mother House in Old Goa in 1517. The Jesuits followed. Among them, the first to arrive on the shores of India in 1542, was Fr. Francis Xavier who would later become the great Apostle of the East. He had in him the fire of "hidalgo", the learning of the scholar, the perseverance of the Jesuit and the zeal of the seraph. The Dominicans were the first missionaries to come to Goa, but they settled as a community only in 1548. The Augustinians arrived in Goa in 1572 and in the same year they laid the foundation of their convent. The order of the monastery of St. Monica was founded in 1606 by archbishop Dom Fr. Aleixo de Menezes. It followed the rules of the Order of St. Augustine. The Carmelites established themselves in 1607. The Theatines reached Goa in 1640 but were allowed to have their house only in 1655. Still latter, in 1681, arrived the Hospitalers of St. John of God and other minor orders like the Philippians or Congregationists (1683), etc.

Also, the city, soon assumed great commercial importance. The natural advantage which the geographical situation gave to Old Goa, combined with a stable and strong form of government, provided a tremendous impetus to its trade and commerce. Portugal had by now established the nucleus of her extensive colonial undertaking in the east. Indian princes began to send their ambassadors, and many treaties were entered into within its gates. It rapidly spread out and new and beautiful buildings patterned on Portuguese models totally changed the face of this Moorish town. In fact, the riverine city came to acquire a unique appearance, a wonderful blending of the western architecture and oriental exoticism.[30] The aspect of the city at this time, is described by several travelers. Pyrard writes:

> "It is about a hundred and ten years since the Portuguese made themselves masters of this island of Goa, and I have often wondered at the rapidity with which the Portuguese have been able to rear stately edifices, so many churches, convents, palaces, fortresses and other buildings, after the European fashion; at the internal order, regulations, and government which they have established, and at the power to which they have attained, everything being managed as in Lisbon itself".[31]

With the establishment of religious orders, an intensive drive for conversions started. At the same time, an increasing number of religious buildings being raised. Soon, the Portuguese rule in Goa, strongly influenced the art and architecture which in this part of India, blossomed like a summer without a spring. The extent to which Portuguese architecture flourished in Goa during the course of 16th and 17th centuries is surprising. Till the last decade of the 17th century, there were in Old Goa, around 31 churches, 38 convents and monasteries and a large number of chapels and oratories. This circumstance led many travelers and writers to name it as "The Rome of the East". By 1580, the old city attained the zenith of its splendour. However, at the turn of the 16th century the devastating epidemics which started plaguing the city right from 1570, had reduced the population and severely crippled her manpower. Wars followed the incursion by Ali Adil Shah, fifth king of Bijapur and the invasion of the Marathas. The Dutch which had already made their way into the Indian Ocean, also challenged the supremacy of the Portuguese in the East. War, disease and vice dealt a blow to the city's pride, when finally, the Jesuits and later on, other religious orders were suppressed, a finishing stroke was dealt to what was no more than the shadow of the once proud capital of an empire.

Of Goa, the "Golden" there still remain some monumental buildings which testify in a harmonious succession, to the various stages of evolution of its architecture, a gradual transition from the rigid Portuguese Gothic (Manueline) of the early days, through its style of the Italian Renaissance, down to the admirable outline of the great gilded Baroque. However, according to art critic D. Carlos de Azavedo, the churches in Goa, belong to the Mannerist period - late 16th and early 17th centuries — and although at a later date it is possible to see Baroque influence, the flowering Baroque in its full blossom did not make its appearance in Goa.

The early 16th century Portuguese architecture did not differ much from that of Spain. But the continued success of the Portuguese navigators in distant seas inspired a small band of Portuguese master architects to adopt a peculiar Portuguese Gothic style latter known as 'Manueline'. Outstanding specimen of such style is the doorway of the church of the Holy Spirit attached to the old Convent of St. Francis of Assisi built in 1521-29, and the facade of the church of Our Lady of the Rosary raised before 1543, both in Old Goa. The main decorative elements of this style are inspired in various navigational accessories and equipment used in Portuguese sailing ships — caravels — which sailed across the oceans and opened the sea route to India. The trifoliated portal of the church of the Holy Spirit wrought in basalt stone is framed by a thick twist resembling rope which was an essential accessory in the sailing ships. This portal was retained in the present church which was rebuilt in 1661.

In an epoch that was seeking stability and security, the early Portuguese architecture responded with static firmness in its buildings. It extolled the values of robustness, consistency and weight. There was now a sense of the volumetric mass of the construction. The Sé Cathedral (1565-1631) dedicated to St. Catherine is a typical example of such architecture. The temple has a simple frontispiece of mixed Tuscan and Doric architecture, in contrast with the architectonic style of the facades of other churches. It is a church with three portals and three choir windows with granite frames among colonnades of Doric-Corinthian style. It is divided into three naves which communicate with each other under Mosaico-Corinthian arcades with large pillars supporting the ornated dome. The whole composition sets off beautifully with the refulgence of gilded carvings and the painting of the chapels. The temples offers for the contemplation of the visitor, a sight of majesty and grandeur comparable, according to Msgr. Zaleski, former Apostolic Nuncio in India, to the cathedrals of Cracow and Nurenberg.[32]

Another monument close to the Cathedral bearing the name of St. Catherine, was built soon after the conquest of Goa to mark the entry of Portuguese in the Moorish fortification, on 25 November 1510. The chapel was rebuilt in 1550 and restored in 1950. It bears tinges of the Renaissance.

The massive nunnery of Santa Monica (1606-27) on the Holy Mount, hillock on the western side of the old city, so called because of the cluster of religious buildings standing in close proximity is another piece of architecture of this period. The facade of its church has two doors with basalt frames. Three solid arched buttresses, a later addition, support the facade and through the arches runs the road that leads to the tip of the Holy Mount. The church of the nunnery is of Doric style. The three-storeyed building of the nunnery is divided into a great number of apartments. The whole structure is impressive due to its solidity and massiveness.

Close to the nunnery of Santa Monica lie the ruins of the large complex of the Augustinian friars. The remnants of the facade of the church of Our Lady of Grace attached to the convent of St. Augustine is a landmark of the grandeur of the once imposing church.

Another landmark on the Holy Mount, is the chapel of St. Anthony (1543). It lies to the northwest of the ruins of the church of Our Lady of Grace (Augustinian complex). The facade of the chapel bears imprints of Portuguese Gothic style (Manueline). It was extensively restored in 1961.

Also, on the foot of the Holy Mount, towards the east, is the restored church of Our Lady of Good Success and the convent of the order of St. John of God built in 1685. The multiple pyramidal roofs of the complex are typical of the monuments exhibited in the 18th century drawings of Old Goa, while the facade is simple with manneristic trends in its architecture.

At the end of the 16th century, the Jesuits built the Basilica of Bom Jesus, a monument of characteristic art of the Society of Jesus which introduced the classical forms with combined effect of the five orders of architecture, viz., Ionic, Doric, Corinthian, Tuscan and Composite styles. According to Albert Mendelslo, it is "one of the most stately buildings that were raised in Asia by the Jesuits".[33]

A reference is to be made here to the ruins of the church of St. Paul built by the Jesuits in Old Goa in 1543. Today, only the facade of the famous monument remains. Yet, through those ruins, the rigour of classic makeup of forms of architecture can still be visualized.

The church of Our Lady of Divine Providence attached to the old convent of St. Cajetan built by Italian friars of the Order of Theatines, is a classical architectural achievement on the lines of St. Peter's Basilica in Rome. It reveals strong influence of Italian Renaissance in Goa, very much visible in the framing of the facade and in the majestic cupola topping the monument.

The chapel of Our Lady of the Mount is another historic landmark in Old Goa. It is located on the summit of a hillock with access through a long flight of steps. It was built prior to 1557 on the spot where the Mohammedans had placed cannons to pound the Portuguese forces during their first attempt to occupy the old city in March 1510. The chapel is vaulted and presents a facade of early Renaissance character.

Upto the end of the 17th century, outside the confines of Old Goa, there were in the old state of Goa more than 200 religious buildings. Besides Goa, Daman and Diu, which were held by the Portuguese till 1961, they had also occupied for almost one and half centuries, large stretches on the west coast of India where religious shrines were built and can still be seen, especially on the Malabar coast.

Old Goa represents an important architectural landmark of the 16th and 17th centuries in Goa where the classical canons of Portuguese art — unity, coherence and harmony are reproduced in every specimen transcending the bounds of idealism and delights of extravagance of the bygone period, leaving to the posterity a dream of grandeur of the past.

During four and half centuries, Goa was cut off from greater India. During this long period, it was always considered as a separate entity till 19 December 1961, when it was integrated into India. Today, it being rightfully a part of Indian cultural environment, Old Goa's importance was duly recognized by UNESCO which already included its main churches and sites in the list of Monuments of World Heritage in India (1977). This list so far consists of 13 cultural sites and 4 natural ones.[34] Recently, there is a move to add two more cultural sites (Sanchi Stupa at M.P. and the Humayun's Tomb, New Delhi).

The isolation of India has never been absolute. Few passes through Himalayan ranges and the large coastal stretches along the Arabian Sea and the Bay of Bengal, have been open routes from all directions. The circumstance turned the great Indian subcontinent into a cauldron of different cultures and civilizations.

History has taught us of several incursions, invasions and trade contacts right from the period of the highly advanced urban Harappan cities till the decline of the Roman Empire. During the second millennium B.C. the Aryans came to India laying the foundation of Vedic civilization. From then onwards, continuous exchange due to trade and culture, brought closer the links with the Greeks, Romans, Celts, Germans, Slavs, Turks, Arabs and people from North Africa, Central Asia and others. However, with the discovery of the direct sea-routes between India and Europe in 1498, Western culture crept faster into India. Influences due to these approaches have greatly enriched Indian art and cultural heritage especially in the field of architecture in a wonderful fusion, a symbiosis of the East and West, best exemplified in Old Goa.

NOTES AND REFERENCES

1. Charles Fabri, *An Introduction to Indian Architecture*, Mumbai, Asian Publishing House, p. 50.
2. D.D. Kosambi, *The Culture and Civilization of Ancient India in Historical Outline*, London, 1965.
3. Percy Brown, *Indian Architecture (Buddhist and Hindu Periods)*, Mumbai, D.B. Taraporevala, p. 1.
4. Jeannine Auboyer, *Landmarks of the World Art (The Oriental World)*, London, Paul Hamlyn, p. 10.
5. Gina Pischel, *The Golden History of Art*, London, Paul Hamlyn, p. 184.
6. Brown, *op. cit.*, p. 7.
7. Fabri, *op. cit.*, p. 8.
8. *Ibid.*
9. Auboyer, *op. cit.*, p. 37.
10. Francis Watson, *India — A Concise History*, New York, Thames & Hudson, 1979, p. 98.
11. Auboyer, p. 66.
12. Banister Fletcher, *A History of Architecture*, 18th ed., Athlone.
13. Brown, p. 83.
14. Watson, p. 85.

15. *Ibid.*, p. 1C8.
16. Brown, p. 94.
17. *Ibid.*, p. 95.
18. Fabri, p. 8.
19. *Ibid.*, p. 34.
20. *Ibid.*, p. 36.
21. Catherine B. Asher, *The New Cambridge History of India*, Cambridge Univ. Press, p. 10.
22. *Ibid.*, p. 1.
23. Watson, p. 105.
24. Originally known as Ella, and later as Cidade de Goa (City of Goa). When Nova Goa (Panaji) became capital of Goa (1843), it was being called Velha Goa (Old Goa).
25. *A Description of the Coast of East Africa and Malabar in the beginning of the 16th century*, trans. H.E.J. Stanley, London, 1866, p. 74.
26. Fernão Lopes Castanheda, *História de Descobrimentos e Conquista da India pelos Portugueses*, Book 3, Chapter 8, Coimbra, 1833, p. 24.
27. Luis Silveira, *Ensaio de Iconografia das Cidades Portuguesas do Ultramar*, III, p. 361.
28. Rui Gomes Pereira, *Goa — Hindu Temples and Deities*, Panaji, Printwell Press, 1978, p. 53.
29. *Ibid.*, p. 53.
30. Pacheco de Figueiredo, "Goa Pre-Portuguesa", *Studia* (OEHU), nos. 13-14, p. 225.
31. *Voyage*, Part 2, p. 16.
32. *Velha Goa — Guia Historico*, Repartição Central de Estatistica e Informação, p. 20.
33. José Nicolau da Fonseca, *An Historical and Archaeological Sketch of the City of Goa*, New Delhi, Asian Educational Services, 1986, p. 283.
34. Monuments of World Heritage in India, Archaeological Survey of India, New Delhi.

TWELVE

EVOLUTION OF BAZARUCOS OF PORTUGUESE INDIA

Their Classifications, and an Unpublished Value in 1748

FENELON REBELLO

It was around the mid-19th century that some began to get interested in Portuguese coins of India and the Far East. They tried to sort known samples, thus establishing the foundation for future advancement in the studies of one of the most important and variegated colonial series.

As more and more specimens were discovered, the accepted views had to reviewed and errors, including certain assumptions arrived at due to missing specimens which subsequently surfaced, had to be rectified. Even now, the value attributed to some pieces of copper and tin alloys of the 17th century, is in doubt both due to their varied weight as well as to the uncertainty about the periods during which they were minted. The existence of spurious coins at different times further complicates the study. Most doubts were, and continue to be, usually about the lower coinage, the *bazaruco*.

Most of the facts about coinage of India are known but doubts arise in a few cases both where the coins and their records do not tally and due to the availability of documents without actual coins to support them. Could the coins have been minted according to decisions taken at the time, and if so, could these have then, disappeared? Recently, coins of values hitherto unknown have been discovered and even of an undocumented series with designs of an unknown type.

Let us briefly go through the actual facts and a few assumptions, so that we may be able to follow the changes of the lower denomination coins and ultimately arrive at a realistic reclassified evaluation of a *Diu series* in view of the new find.

On the reconquest of Goa in November 1510[1] new types of coinage that were a novelty to the local public, were put into circulation. Besides the already abundant copper coins the *leal, dinheiro* and *cepaica* emerged, displaying the cross, the sphere and the Greek *A* (perhaps standing for Albuquerque?). These signaled the beginning of a monetary system, the first colonial one for India and the Far East. The issuing of new denominations and their equivalents, alien to a people long accustomed to established commercial transactions, would soon bring about recurrent difficulties which would linger on, even up to the 18th century.

Newer issues both with regard to their equivalent values as well as to composition of the metals used (introduced by subsequent governors) gradually aggravated the situation rather than brought about any monetary stability. Commerce was well established in India and was based on gold and silver coins going back to Roman times when merchants from the Middle East used to effect transactions with Aureii, Venetian and Arab coinage whose specimens can be found in India even to date, among the occasional finds.

The then current coinage in India whether in gold, silver or copper, had its own intrinsic metallic value proportionate to its face value, which guaranteed the people at least its metal worth, however fluctuating it was from time to time.

The *leal* was minted during the reign of D. Manuel I and even during that of D. João III (1521-1557), but it is not known when exactly its issues ceased.[2] It had an average weight of 15-16 gms. A half *leal* had that of 8.5 gms and soon continued as a *bazaruco*, then regarded as the unit of lower value coinage. In fact, the *bazaruco* denomination was mostly used in the Portuguese territories of India and among the known specimens there were coins of one of the issues in Sri Lanka, ascribed to the reign D. Filipe III (IV of Spain).

There are various interpretations regarding the origin of the word *bazaruco*, but the fact is that this was the coin that was used the most in daily dealings and for the general public usage. But it was the *bazarucos* that caused many problems.

With fluctuations in prices of metals, the weight of the coin would also be altered to maintain to a certain extent its intrinsic value; however, some governments arbitrarily altered the *bazarucos* resulting not only in harm to the public but also in difficulties and unforeseen consequences to the administration of their own territories. But with changes in copper prices, the *bazaruco* was minted at the rate of 16 *pardaos* per quintal (58.752 kgs.) and came to weigh 7.1 gms. for the period 1532-33 and yet, it was favourably accepted by the public and yet again by them, when the weight per unit was brought down slightly, around 1738-42, due to a rise in the price of copper.

The real problem arose during the rule of Martim Afonso de Sousa who reached India in 1542 (coincidentally in the same fleet where St. Francis Xavier traveled). He had the *bazarucos* minted at the rate of 36 *pardaos* per quintal[3] which equaled less than half of its metallic value and as a result the *bazaruco* was to weigh 4-5 gms. He did not stop at this and ordered that the earlier coins which weighed more be exchanged for the new ones, not weight-wise but unit-wise. Thus, besides devaluation, more copper than was given out to the public would be collected back in exchange! In protest, the market closed since with a coin worth so little it was not possible to buy everyday items which came from abroad.

Soon after, D. João de Castro, aware of the injustice done, promptly minted *bazarucos* of 5.7 gms. value. In fact, there are many more instances of the generosity and honesty of this Viceroy, that set him apart along with a few others as those who ruled conscientiously the Portuguese territories in the East. So we see that the *bazaruco* fluctuated from 8.5 gms., falling to 7.1 and even to 4-5, but soon rising to 5.7 gms.

No other basis for minting the *bazaruco* is known till the beginning of the reign of D. Sebastião I (1557-58), during which it is evident from the known samples that they fluctuated during various years. We have a sample of 2.5-3.0 gms. that would have been minted when Viceroy D. Constantino de Braganza devalued the *bazaruco* in 1559,[4] although there were also copper coins which varied in weight from 4.7 to 5.9 gms.

The last increase in 1562 was effected as it was thought that the people in the Indian territories would lose, since the *bazaruco* did not have the same value assigned to it by the Portuguese government.

At this time, *bazarucos* were also minted at Cochin at the rate of 5.5 gms. per unit. Thus, it is possible to identify specimen of 1, 2 and

4 *bazarucos*. The government of D. Sebastião was rich in this variety of *bazarucos* minted in Goa, but usually badly finished pieces and of inconsistent type, indicating a degree of inexperience which leads us to believe that some of these could be products of the workshops of Diu.[5]

Till date, besides alterations in weight, it is to be noted that among the known samples, more than twenty minted varieties can be differentiated, and it would be necessary to clarify at this point the system of connecting the pieces to various governments and of classifying their values. Among the documents issued, only the changes in the decrees are known but nothing about the amount of coins minted or the type of structuring carried out. Besides, the expression "mint *bazarucos*" does not indicate the denominations being put into circulation. Could the issues consist of single value coins or those of different denominations? Therefore, this is the only way (at times doubtful) of differentiation: assigning the dyes and value classification by weight.

During the reign of D. João II, the *bazaruco* weighed initially 7-8 gms. on the basis of which those of 4.3 gms. have been classified as half *bazarucos* and those of 1.9-2.4 gms. as quarter *bazarucos*. However, these latter ones could well be a *bazaruco*, and half a *bazaruco* of the time of Martim Afonso de Souza, but in the absence of data about either the values minted or even about the design structure, a more accurate identification is not possible. As copper pieces were minted on different basis during the time of D. Sebastião, those weighing between 2.4-4.8 gms. are classified as *bazarucos* precisely due to the alteration in their weight and are assigned to this period by their relevant dyes.

As we come to the Philippine period (1580-1640) we have to take into account that the increase in prices of gold and silver during 1581-84,[6] affected the poor *bazaruco* and the prices of the day-to-day requirements rose by 150 per cent! In 1592, during the government of Mathias de Albuquerque there are references to tin and tin alloys (*calaim bazarucos*) that are not known probably for having been withdrawn from circulation. There was also a drain of copper pieces as they were carried outside Portuguese territories, and this led the government to suspend the use of this metal and to revert to a tin alloy of which samples are not known.

During these times the overpowering might of the Inquisition was gradually changing it into an almost autonomous organization.

People who felt persecuted, feared the powers of the *Casa Grande* or *Odlem Ghor* (the Inquisition Palace), and as a result the people fled to Indian territories,[7] and a lot of coins got carried away on different occasions. This seems to be confirmed from the fact that some unknown samples have been discovered in Goa's neighbouring states and even in the water-tanks of abandoned temples.[8]

The copper *bazarucos* stamped with F-R on both its sides and sometimes with F and the Cross are connected with the government of D. Filipe I, and possibly continued during the following one. The monetary laws of this period are somewhat hard and diverse to allow us to classify the specimens fairly. With the monetary base of 3.5 gms. per *bazaruco*, there are pieces of 1 *bazaruco* with weights that vary between 2.5-3.2 gms. and those of 2 *bazarucos* that are between 7.0-9.2 gms. Besides, there were in circulation, tin alloy *bazarucos* which are not known to us today.

The first known tin alloy *bazaruco* was minted in Goa according to the *alvará* of 1600 where it is clearly mentioned "on one side a sphere and on the other the crown and royal arms".[9]

This piece should have weighed 6.1 gms. whereas the specimen discovered of late weighs half of it. There are others with the cross, the crowned court of arms and a monetary stamps, weighing 2.3 gms., all of tin alloy. From the same period, pieces of copper, with the sphere and crowned shield, too, can be found, seeming to point out that the types used for minting tin alloy were also reproduced in copper, with minor changes and a weight of 3.6 gms. according to the *alvará* of 20 August 1611.

Regarding the copper pieces just mentioned, Daman and Bassein were also granted licenses to produce these *bazarucos*. Coins of 1, 3, and 5 *bazarucos* having been classified as coming from Daman in spite of the doubts raised due to their minting. This was in an age when the Portuguese reeled under strong attacks from the Dutch and the British, and the government had once more to revise the existing copper tin alloy and tutenag minting.

In 1619, the use of tin alloy or tutenag *bazarucos* was prohibited in Goa and by May, Viceroy D. João Coutinho (1617-18) ordered that the exchange rate should be "three for two" and soon after allowed the use of "two for one" tutenag *bazarucos*. Subsequently, to avoid all the confusion that the exchanges used to bring about, he ordered pieces of 10, 20 and 30 *bazarucos* minted, which were for the first and last time made in silver.[10]

Thus we see that besides the variations in their weight, copper coins, tin alloy and those of tutenag were alternately introduced and occasionally all three types were current simultaneously. With the intent of profiting from the minting with one metal or the other, the one which was cheapest and easiest to obtain was always availed of. And we can imagine therefore the doubts arising in the investigator's mind as he finds variations in the weights of these pieces.

But the actual truth is that whereas in India the governors struggled with problems to balance the financial situation, with a limited budget at their disposal, in Europe there was rivalry among the big traders at the beginning of the 17th century. Patronized by the powers of the Iberian peninsula, trade in oriental spices, earned great profits in American *reales*. It is even recorded that the merchants who settled in Goa, would annually remit 5,00,000 silver *cruzados* to Macau, to be sold in China.[11]

A problem that emerges in the study of Indo-Portuguese coins is the uncertainty about the mintings having been executed in accordance with the *Assentos* or decisions of the *Conselho da Fazenda*, since there is evidence that the workshops were not necessarily following orders faithfully.[12] Besides the mintings done by rather primitive methods resulted in specimens of different weights, the variations being between 15 and 20 per cent. The metallic composition of tutenag melted by the money changers is highly unstable and seems to have been done by inexperienced craftsmen and without proper supervision, the obvious proof being their varying diameter and thickness.

It has not been possible to locate *bazarucos* that could have been minted on the basis of any new law during the government of D. Filipe III (1621-40) and it is not known if any samples were minted, as per the provision of 1623, passed in Cochin.[13] There are, however, tutenag *bazarucos* displaying the sphere and grill of St. Lawrence meant for circulation in Sri Lanka, weighing 3.0 gms. and 1.4 gms. respectively, and classified as a *bazaruco*, and half a *bazaruco*. We do not know for sure if these pieces were made in Sri Lanka or in Goa. There happens to be specimen, that are known to have been minted in Goa, for circulation in various other Portuguese territories as well as specimen with monetary pieces from places where they were issued but made with open dyes in the Goa workshop.

Some copper pieces discovered at Diu, dated 1626-27 and 1628 are not documented and it is not known if they resulted from an irregular issue especially since they have captions unrelated to the Portuguese series. The pieces were minted during the captaincy of António Telles at the Diu fort, with captions of + *Antonivs Teles DVX* and *Philipvs III Rex Portugaliae.*[14] In the Indo-Portuguese issues, legends on copper pieces are rarely seen.

Already during the government of D. João IV, copper *bazarucos* weighing a little above 4 gms. were brought out but it is not known when these were authorized. Due to the crowned court of arms and the stamp C - B (Chaul Bassein), and starred cross with the date 1-6-5-4, we tend to connect this minting to the mint at Goa for the style and perfect workmanship. Soon after, from 1670 to 1680, copper *bazarucos* from Diu with their respective dates and weighing 4.0-4.5 gms., were issued and again subsequently from 1686 to 1700, heavier ones of 5.5-6.5 gms., all displaying the crowned shield and their respective dates.

From the beginning of the 18th century the development of factional coins was rapid. Besides the *bazarucos*, the *réis*, the *rodas* and *atias*, also appeared. The *rodas* (St. Catherine's *roda*) perhaps came out to commemorate the second centenary of the reconquest of Goa, and were made of a tin alloy and tutenag, just like the other specimen with various combinations of metals as mentioned below.

During the government of Vasco Fernandes Cesar de Menezes (1712-17) *bazarucos* of a mixture of tutenag and tin alloy in the proportion of 4:1 were minted in June 1716. In July of the same year another directive ordered the minting of *bazarucos* of tutenag and a lead alloy, both to weigh 1.4-1.6 per piece.[15] It was later realized that an alloy of tutenag and lead was inappropriate as it resulted in coins of variable proportions due to excess of the latter which meant that coins could easily be bent.

The motive behind the government's wavering between the two different combinations of metals is not clear, and it failed. It was also, an occasion for the falsification of coins brought from outside. This resulted in an order for the withdrawal of these coins. We can well assess the consequences of this among the people and their daily transactions. In 1720, because of the administrative mismanagements in the Northern territories the weights of the tutenag *bazaruco* was increased to 1.98 gms.! And next, in 1722 a tutenag alloy was smelted for a new issue of *bazarucos* that should have weighed 1.4 gms. each.[16]

We mentioned "should have weighed" as the variations in weights became so common that hardly any coins corresponded to the decisions taken. We have undated specimen and some dated after 1722, both with similar dyes and in denominations of 15, 10, 7.5 and 5 *bazarucos*, besides which the undated series consisting of 2 and 1 *bazarucos*. In both these series the value is indicated in the dyes but in the former it can be noted that 10 *bazarucos* weigh 11.6 gms. whereas the 7.5 piece is 13.6 gms. The latter series had 10 *bazarucos* weighing 9.0-9.8 gms. and 7.5 *bazarucos* of only 8.9-9.2 gms.[17] Even the 10 *bazarucos rodas* minted in this reign and used at Daman and Chaul boast a weight above 21 gms. Whereas *rodas* of 15 *bazarucos* from Goa and Daman-Bassein vary in their weight between 17.5-19.8 gms. It is likely that these last ones could have been minted on different basis.

In the 1722 issue there is proof that the minting did not always conform with the *Assentos*. In this case the values of 10 and 2 *bazarucos* coins had not been authorized. As the tutenag was always of an uncertain or variable composition, we cite here the results of analysis published by certain researchers:

	Cu	Zn	Ni	Fe	Sn	Al	Pb	Mg	Si
Cunha[18]	40.4	25.4	31.6	2.6	—	—	—	—	—
T.D. Yi &	0.2	90.0	—	2.0	4.0	0.3	1.5	0.1	1.0
J. de Kreek[19]	0.1	70.0	—	0.5	—	0.2	0.6	24.0	6.0
Rebello	0.05	85.3	—	1.7	—	0.1	0.3	ND	ND

The results indicate the tutenag to be a zinc ore (zinc blend or sphalerite) processed to a certain extent to be supplied in sheets. As pure metal, zinc was known in Europe only in the 17th century, thus supporting the belief that the rulers of India had no knowledge of this metal at the time when they initiated its use in coins.

Since the tutenag was cheap and easily obtainable[20] there appears to have been a tendency to use this composition in coins of low value. However, during the government of D. Pedro Mascarenhas (1732-41) the Portuguese territories were passing through difficult times, due to problems created by the Arabs and the English. Besides the troops were being poorly provisioned and the influx of a large number of spurious coins, created a general unrest which worsened during the subsequent government of D. Luis de Menezes (1741-42). The principal reason was the low value that the *bazaruco* had, for the tutenag of which it was composed was worth intrinsically less than half of its face value, and affected even internal transactions.

We have to consider the exchange system which led the people to lose even more in dealings through *bazarucos*. The *sarrafagem* system of exchange existed since the arrival of the Portuguese in India and the exchanger or *sarrafo* continued to function initially and perhaps more at the time when the *bazaruco* had lost its value. In 1687 an attempt was made to end this system but in fact it appears to have continued till the time under consideration. All this produced a general uproar which led the competent authorities to unanimously admit the injustice caused and suggest, as a remedy to the evil, a reduction in the face value or an increase in the equivalent weight of the tutenag. This was decided in 1741.[21]

Finally in 1742 the value of the *bazarucos* minted was lower in relation to the *réis* and *rodas*. Thus, for example, 15 *bazarucos* is equal to 12 *réis* which is equal to 8 *rodas*.[22]

There exists examples of *bazarucos* of 1748 tutenag with marking from the Diu mint; however the estimated face value by weight corresponds to less than 1 gm. per *bazaruco*. Thus the denominations followed today appear doubtful being contrary to the decision earlier taken to reduce their value relative to their weight. Also the assigned value does not confirm to the earlier series, whether of *réis* or *bazarucos*, minted in Goa as well as those minted at Diu, which perhaps being more convenient for transactions, are seen in the denominations of 15, 7.5, 5 and 2.5 instead of 20, 10 and 5 as they are classified today.

Recently in a find from Diu, we discovered to our surprise, pieces of tutenag of the 1748 series weighing more than 30 gms.[23] In the Indo-Portuguese series excluding those of Malacca, there is no known piece of tutenag which goes beyond 22 gms. We obtained four specimen which have a mean diameter of 35 mm., thickness of 4-5 mm. and weight of 30.35, 31.13, 32.51 and 32.97 gms. respectively.

It appears that these specimen now discovered, should solve the problem, in the light of the decisions to raise the value of the *bazaruco* by increasing the weight of the unit, for it would be more accurate to assign 1.8-2.0 gms. to a *bazaruco*, maintaining the fractional value in use at this time. Thus with the variations normally observed in cast coins, we can arrive at a tentative classification based on the weight of the known specimen.

(1748)		Variations in weight
2.5	*bazarucos*	4.(- 4.8 gms (1.76)
5	*bazarucos*	8.0 - 9.6 gms (1.76)
7.5	*bazarucos*	16.0 - 16.7 gms (1.78)
15	*bazarucos*	30.0 - 32.9 gms (2.09) (our sample)

The *bazarucos* were slowly substituted by *tangas, réis, atias* and *dognis*. They continued to be issued in Goa till 1769, in Daman till 1776-77 and in Diu even during the government of D. Pedro IV, till 1828, this being the last known issue from Portuguese India.

With the discovery of dozens of specimen in these last decades and now of these made of tutenag, it can only be concluded that the study of the Indo-Portuguese series is not yet complete.

NOTES AND REFERENCES

1. J. C. Barreto Miranda, *Quadros Historicos de Goa*, Margao, 1864.
2. Fenelon Rebello, "Cruz de São Tomé no reinado de D. João III", *Moeda* (Lisbon), 15 (no. 2) 1990, p. 73. The first known example in copper with the cross of St. Thomas.
3. F. Neri Xavier, "Memória sobre as moedas cunhadas em Goa", *Boletim do Governo*, no. 7, 1866, p. 625.
4. A. C. Teixeira de Aragão, *Descripção geral e histórica das moedas cunhadas em nome dos réis*, vol. 3 (doc. 5), Lisbon, 1880.
5. F. Rebello, "Cunhagens de Diu antes e depois de 1684", *Actas — III Congresso Nacional de Numismatica*, Sintra, 1985, pp. 241-253.
6. Aragão, docs. 15-18.
7. A. K. Priolkar; *The Goa Inquisition*, Mumbai, 1961, pp. 179, 183.
8. Coins were collected from an abandoned temple in Verna.
9. Aragão, doc. 41: Livro de Alvaras e Provisões 1593-1781, fl. 8v;

Rebello, in *The Numismatist*, USA, 1973, pp. 2025-30.

10. Aragão, doc. 64, *alvará* of 26 August 1619; F. N. Xavier writes that this *alvará* is fairly explicit with respect to the value of each coin.
11. James C. Boyajian, "Portuguese Bankers at the Court of Spain (1626-1650)", USA, 1983, pp. 10ff, P. Grierson, *Numismatics*, London, 1975, p. 63. Since the time that the Portuguese established themselves at Macau, the *reales* that came were in the beginning into metal, but much later, in the 18th century were accepted as current coinage.
12. F. Neri Xavier, p. 629.
13. Aragão, p. 210.
14. F. Rebello, "Coinage of António Teles (1626-1628)", *Numis. Circ.*, June 1981, pp. 200-202; C. R. Boxer, "O General do Mar, António Teles", *Boletim do Instituto Vasco da Gama*, Panaji, 1938, no. 37, pp. 4-5.
15. *Assentos do Conselho de Fazenda*, 16 June 1716; Book 19, fl. 217; F. Rebello, "An unpublished issue of 1715", *Numis. Circ.*, London, 1976, p. 143.
16. Xavier, in *Assentos do Conselho de Fazenda*, 25 June 1722, Book 20, fl. 22v.
17. F. Ferraro Vaz & Alberto Gomes, *Catalogos*.
18. Gerson da Cunha, "Contributions to the Study of Indo-Portuguese Numismatics", IV, Mumbai, 1881; Francisco Magro, in *Boletim da Associação Numismatica*, 1978-82.
19. T. D. Yi & J. de Kreck, "Preliminary data on metallic composition", *Numis. Circ.*, London, February 1993, p. 7.
20. Charles Boxer, *Francisco Vieira de Figueiredo: A Portuguese Merchant-Adventurer in South East Asia, 1624-1667*.
21. Aragão, doc. 118.
22. Aragão, doc. 119.
23. J. M. do Carmo Nazareth, *Catálogo das moedas Portuguesas*, mentions two examples of tutenag with weights of 15.06 gms. and 30.6 gms. respectively (see nos. 628-9); M.J. Campos, *Numismatica Indo-Portuguesa*, Lisbon, 1901, p. 200.

PART IV

GOA-PORTUGAL TIES AS REFLECTED IN LITERATURE

THIRTEEN

THE PORTUGUESE IN THE GOAN FOLKLORE

TEOTÓNIO R. DE SOUZA

Some Preliminary Comments

I shall start by defining briefly the aims of this Chapter and its limitations. It will analyze some Konkani proverbs and a few folk songs which evoke some historical events and convey native reaction to those events and the native perception of the colonial attitudes implied by them. These folk expressions are here considered as genuine filters of the native sensibilities. There are certainly many other cultural and folkloric expressions that preserve the images of the many centuries of the Portuguese presence in Goa. I do not consider myself sufficiently qualified to handle all of them, neither a symposium like this would permit such an extensive and intensive exercise. I have spoken and written on other occasions about some aspects of Goan folklore as source of Goa's history[1], and some of these reflections have been taken up again here, along with some fresh considerations.

Most historians are accustomed to rely almost exclusively upon the archival sources for their research productions, and only exceptionally make concessions for oral sources, which they usually view with suspicion as methodologically weak and of doubtful value. The written texts tend to be accepted very often for the simple reason of being written, and this happens more often in the western tradition. In the introduction to his *The Portuguese Empire in Asia—1500-1700*[2], Sanjay Subrahmanyam focus the attention on the "mythical faces of Portuguese Asia". He analyses a Malay text of late 17th or early 18th century to illustrate the internal logic and the utility of such texts based on local native traditions as a source of historical evidence. He demonstrates how, despite the lack of chronological precision or even factual inaccuracies, it succeeds in conveying the native perspective on the Portuguese entry into Malacca. He goes further, and draws parallel with the myths accepted in Portugal as historical facts, and concludes with a note of caution: "Separating myth from reality is of course a task that any historian must approach with trepidation, for while history is the stuff from which myth is made, myth-making too is part of the historical process".

The folk traditions seem to have merited greater attention of the anthropologists, and also of some historians more recently, having taken greater interest in the daily life of the people and influenced by the trend of "new history", which was also responsible for the discovery of the "long duration". These innovations have helped to give credibility to the cyclical time concept of India. Fernand Braudel, a master "new historian" believes that half the life of mankind is made up of daily routine, which he defined as "little things one hardly notices in time and space. . . The everyday happening is repeated, and the more often it is repeated the more likely it is to become a generality or rather a structure. It pervades society at all levels, and characterizes ways of being and behaving which are perpetuated through endless ages".[3]

The problem with the oral sources, and with the folk traditions in particular, is that of determining their time of origin and of collating the variant versions. A useful utilization of folk evidence requires advanced linguistic abilities and understanding of the pertinent culture. Rarely is a foreigner likely to possess these two-fold requirements. Often, it is this lack of abilities, together with lack of interest or respect for the native view of events, that leads the foreign researchers to minimize the value of folk evidence as source of historical interpretation. It should not be forgotten that due to climatic and other problems connected with transmission of written documentation in India, the rules for oral transmission were all the more demanding, assuming even a sacred character that would reduce the chances of corruption. In spite of these traditional precautions the western orientalist research has not treated kindly the Indian concepts of time and history. It did not find in the classical Indian texts, like *Mahabharata, Dharmashastras*, or *Puranas* the linear chronology to which the western historical tradition is accustomed. Western scholars failed to comprehend the "cosmological time" scale of *yugas* and *kalpas* adopted by the above mentioned classics, from the *jyotishastra* literature dealing with mathematics and astronomy, and which took time calculation very seriously. Satisfied with a stereotyped Indian concept of time, western orientalists did not care till very recently to perceive diverse philosophical perceptions of time within the Indian tradition. The Indian cyclic time did not preclude other categories of time.[4]

James Mill (1773-1836) was one of the early western critics of the Indian concept of cyclic time, which he interpreted as expressive of a "primitive" phase of social development.[5] The biblical tradition of Christians passed through a chronology, from creation of the universe culminating with the creation of Adam and Eve, the phases of Jewish history, and with the Final Judgement to come. It did not find parallels in the Indian tradition. For Christian Europe the linear concept of history was part of its tradition, and Islam, despite its other unpleasant features, shared the same concept of time. The modern science objections to biblical chronology were yet to come. The "new historians" with their concept of "long duration" are even more recent. Until then every event was unique and irreversible. If Indians did not take time seriously as an expression of change, and if they had reduced all reality to mere illusion, they would not have bothered to create the tradition of horoscopes to determine an auspicious moment (*muhurta*) for the important decisions in one's personal life, economic activity, social events, or political actions.

Romila Thapar defends the Indian concept of cyclic time (initially consisting of five years or *yuga*, and later extended to longer periods) as not exclusive of other categories of time, including those that come close to the linear time of the modern historians. The *Dharmashastra* of Manu refers to various divisions of time, including the twinkle of an eye. It explains the possibility of various concepts of time co-existing, and rules out a necessary dichotomy between linear and cyclical concepts of time. The Indian tradition of cycles never excluded the influence of *karma* or of human actions in the process of *Samsara* (transmigrations) and of *moksha* (salvation). Each cycle represented a decline in moral standards (*dharma*) and consequently an historic change. The last cycle of *Kaliyuga* represented a total chaos in the moral order, and only the tenth incarnation of Vishnu as *Kalkin* could restore mankind back to its original state. Curiously, the classic Indian texts maintain a distinction between mythic and cosmogonic time that preceded the great deluge and the time that followed, namely the time of the great dynasties of *Kshatriyas*, the solar dynasty (*suryavamsa*) and the lunar one (*chandravamsa*). Two types of calendars were thus recognized. The term *vamsa*, used to designate a generation, means literally a bamboo, and each knot represented a generation. It was a linear conception of genealogical time, but always with the larger framework of *Yugas*. Instead of dates some important historical events were chosen for periodization markers, such as the *Mahabharata* war, or the exile of Rama. *Vishnu Purana* goes beyond and identifies the beginning of *Kaliyuga* with the appearance of a constellation. Astronomers have calculated the date of the phenomenon and placed it at the beginning of 3102-1 B.C. The end-part of *Vishnu Purana* provides dynastic lists. It utilizes a new concept of regnal time for the period that follows the *Mahabharata* war. It enters that way in the realm of real and historical time. That is how the various Indian eras are reckoned: *Vikrama* or *Samvatsa* (58-57 B.C.), *Saka* (78 A.D.), *Gupta* (319-20 A.D.), etc. which utilize more precise dates to determine events and kingships. The formation of states influenced this process of time-reckoning in India, not unlike the process of state and nation formation that accompanied the evolution of the European historiography. The Buddhist influence was quite decisive through the evolution of its *sanghas* and the importance they attributed to the chronology of the founder. Its commercial activities and many endowments that its monasteries received explain the Buddhist interest in a more precise and chronological documentation.[6]

The folkloric illustrations selected in this Chapter may share the quality of imprecisions which Braudel attributed to "everyday life", but we do have documentary evidence that can be utilized to locate many of the folk impressions on a more precise time-scale. We need to be aware of the geographic and social provenance of the folk traditions, including caste and religious provenance, to avoid generalizing the conclusions as applicable to all inhabitants of Goa. The sectorial provenance can help to identify also better the social difference of reactions to the Portuguese colonial presence in Goa. The illustrations will enable us also to identify the linguistic impact of the Portuguese upon the daily life of the Goan people.

The Portuguese in the Goan Folklore

The Indian Jesuit Anthony D'Costa describes in the preface to his *The Christianisation of the Goa Islands* a tradition that was current among several Christian families of Goa. According to that the Portuguese soldiers would fill wax dolls with wine and then chop off their heads to drink the wine. Many natives were scared by this practice, because they were under the impression that they really drank human blood, and this led many to adopt Christianity out of fear. The author concludes that if such a thing really happened, the tradition only suggests that some converts invented the story to justify their interest in changing their religion. The author then goes on to prove with historical evidence that this was what really happened to a great extent.[7]

The Portuguese missionary campaign in Goa was not seen by all sections of the population in the same fashion. For many Goans of higher castes, it was an opportunity to collaborate profitably with the new rulers, even though there were more conservative elements among them, and for whom a change of religion and tradition as demanded by the Church and Inquisition was not acceptable. There were naturally many Goans who preferred to go into exile to the neighbouring territories of Kanara and Malabar. A Jesuit visitor who travelled through Kanara in the second half of the 17th century calculated as 30,000 the number of Goans, chiefly Hindus, who had migrated to that region to escape the religious and other pressures in Goa.[8] It was among these communities of emigrants that appeared the proverbial saying *Goeam firongi na mhunno khoim*? (Who dare say that the Portuguese are not in Goa?).[9] It was a rhetorical question, which did not require an answer from the Goans who had experienced the heat of the conversion drive in Goa and had run away from there. The expression implied sarcasm and criticism aimed at those who stayed behind, hopeful of resisting Portuguese control and pressures.

To continue along the same lines, the Portuguese missionary efforts manifested an interest to learn the language of the territory, not only the Marathi language that was used for religious texts, but also the spoken language of the people, namely Konkani. This missionary effort was seen in the creation of a boys' school attached to the College of St. Paul that trained the Jesuit candidates in the East. The initiative of setting up that school came from none other than St. Francis Xavier, who saw the need of training native interpreters who could accompany and assist the Jesuit missionaries in the endeavours all over the East. He was so serious about this plan that he lost his temper and even dismissed from the Society of Jesus a senior Jesuit and Rector of the College for replacing the native boys with Portuguese kids and half-breeds during one of his many absences from Goa. In 1563 the boys' school had 645 inmates, and some years later the register showed 800 boys of various ethnic origins. It was a boy of this school that helped the Jesuits to prepare the first Konkani grammar, and also helped some Jesuits to learn that language. It was during this initial phase that some manuals were composed to aid the natives to prepare themselves and to make their confessions in Konkani.[10] Also several other books were composed and published in Konkani for training the missionaries, and also as manuals of devotion for the converts. However, this missionary zeal was no longer there in the latter half of the 17th century, and the trend had even reversed. There was missionary pressure upon the State administration to enact legislation that would force the natives to learn and speak Portuguese under penalty of not being allowed to celebrate their weddings in the Church, or of having their sons ordained as priests.[11] The attempts were fruitless, because the natives were already used to the liturgy in the local language and had no great interest in hearing the sermons in Portuguese. Hence a traditional saying attributed to an old Goan lady: *Sermanvak gel'lim axên, sermanv zalo firangi bhaxên* (I went to hear the sermon with great enthusiasm, but the sermon in Portuguese was a pain in the . . . .).[12]

The above saying did not necessarily imply any critique of the colonial language, but it conveyed well the reality of the Goan life. Practically till the end of the Portuguese colonial presence in Goa the total of those who could speak and understand Portuguese did not exceed 5 per cent, and this was the case at a time when primary education in Portuguese was made compulsory. The compulsory education did not raise the level of literacy, and as noted by the late Dr. Mariano Saldanha, it only succeeded in creating "a unique class of illiterates who could read and write, a strange breed in the history of education".[13] The need of migrating to British Indian and the dependence of Goans upon the remittances of the emigrants proved beyond doubt the futility of learning Portuguese with any degree of seriousness.

The colonial vicissitudes were not restricted to the vernacular language which had become increasingly corrupted, and even its use was discouraged. The natives who cared to use it in public were made to feel inferior social beings. The historian-administrator J. H. Cunha Rivara described this tragic state of the native language in his historical essay on Konkani, entitled *Ensaio Histórico da Lingua Concani*.[14] The socio-political relationship of dominance-subordination formed the essence of the colonial regime, and it is but natural that some sectors of the native population should have expressed their unhappiness about it from time to time. The more vocal elements were those who were more in touch with the people and had greater influence over them. They were the priests who experienced a sort of racist discrimination when it came to promotions. The white clergy dominated the scene with their ethnic and political links with the colonizers.[15] Even though the Portuguese colonialism was relatively less racist, racial discrimination was not entirely absent. In the initial period or centuries the racist feelings were less felt, because they were not necessary. But as the natives proved their competence or even superiority in comparison with the many Portuguese who served in the East, references to colour and to patriotism became increasingly necessary for the Portuguese from the 18th century onwards. This was noticeable in the attitude of the white friars and the *mestiços* (*descendentes*) who felt threatened in their careers, and invited nationalist reaction from the natives. The Franciscans resented and resisted the pressure of the native clerics who wanted to take over the control of their parishes in Bardez with the backing of the Archbishop Fr. Ignacio de Santa Thereza in 1724-28. One cannot help taking note of the overtly racist language utilized by the friars on that occasion against the native clerics: "All these black priests (with the exception of some by miracle) are by their very nature ill-natured and ill-behaved, lascivious, drunkards, etc. and therefore, most unworthy of receiving the charge of the churches". They continued their accusations: "It must be pointed out in the 4th place that these natives naturally hate the Portuguese and all "white-skinned", and their hate is directed more against the parish priests, because these live in their villages and watch keenly their behaviour. That is why white priests and religious are a burden to them".[16]

The motives that caused the *mestiços* to behave arrogantly and to manifest racist tendencies were not very different. As a part of administrative reforms of Pombal in Goa, the Viceroy issued an ordinance that put the finger on the wound: "The pride that dominates in this part of the world is the chief reason for the misery of these natives. . . By Portuguese I also mean *mestiços*, and these suffer more from the diabolic vice of pride than the Europeans proper".[17] The decree warned the whites against calling the natives "negros" (niggards) and *cachorros* (dogs). The *descendentes* held the control over the militia in Goa, and this gave them a privileged position of power, but with the military reforms and abolition of a standing military corps, they lost this position. In this context must have appeared the Konkani saying: *Sorop mhoncho nhoi dakhlo, firngi mhoncho nhoi aplo* (None dare say that a snake is small or that a Portuguese is one of us).

It is not necessary to depend upon the opinion of the colonized people to form a judgement of the weaknesses of the Portuguese administration. There are many recorded views of other Europeans about it, and also of the Portuguese themselves.[18] The Portuguese dailies dedicated lots of space to the incapacity of the Portuguese to manage anything there was to manage, and their great ability to interfere in other people's business. These were not new habits, because the 16th century Portuguese chronicler and humanist João de Barros says it in his *Decadas da Asia*: "A Portuguese is hurt more by his neighbour being praised than by his own deeds being forgotten". Nowadays, the Portuguese accompanying the preparations for Expo-98 are much entertained by the political decisions and counter-decisions of their leaders. However, all admit the Portuguese capacity to improvise, while they are most incapable of keeping a schedule. Probably, if all end up happy with the results, it is because the expectations are never high. The Goan population had not failed to observe this trait of the Portuguese. They coined a proverb for that: *Firngyachem kam' noveak vô Maiak* (The Portuguese do everything at the last moment. You will find them when the reaping season is on, or when the monsoons are about to start).

The Portuguese administration of justice was the butt of most criticism. It was considered the most corrupt department of the Portuguese administration. Diogo do Couto, the founder-curator of the Portuguese Historical Archives in India wrote in his *Soldado Prático*: "Here, he who has more power can have more justice, and this cobweb can only catch mosquitoes: a Gujarati is penalized for squatting to urinate; a Hindu is put in irons for quarrelling with another of his kind or abusing him, but if a favourite of the authorities or a wealthy person breaks open the safe of a Hindu and takes away his goods by force, that is a light matter and permissible".[19] Hence a Konkani proverb that does not find anything worse to wish for an enemy than the Portuguese justice: *Goynchi neai tea gorar poddum* (May he be a victim of Goan justice). The administration of justice in Goa had become a profitable business for a host of solicitors, and as described by the chronicler who succeeded Diogo do Couto, Goa had become a big academy of solicitors who made a good living by court-suing. António Bocarro states in the middle of the 17th century that Goans had developed a great penchant for court procedures and were pretty skilled in drafting the papers. He had calculated more than a thousand such solicitors who made their living in the city of Goa and the adjacent islands. He noticed that the Portuguese encouraged this business. There were more than 6,000 cases pending in the courts at this time.[20] The financial consequences of such an administration of justice are expressed in another Goan proverb: *Goynchi neai ani vaddhlelem cheddum sogleanchea ghorak nosai* (Goan justice and a grown up girl no family would want). Both situations had one element in common, namely the uncertain costs. The dowry for marrying a grown up girl, and the fees of justice were equally worrisome.

Not all the problems of the Goans were caused by the Portuguese. Many Goans felt the oppression of the caste structure or of the traditional class structure. Many had changed their religion to escape from these structures and with the hope of improving their life conditions. The conflict was not necessarily between the higher and lower castes, but it occurred also within the two upper castes, namely brahmins and chardos, fighting for pre-eminence. Instead of reducing the caste differences after conversion, confraternities were created on caste-basis and with distinguishing colours. Mass conversion were preferred and so also the preservation of the social structure to solve the problem of marriages. These considerations were responsible for the perpetuation of the caste system among the converts.[21] The caste exclusivism is beautifully illustrated with an incident that seems to have occurred in the Guirim parish of Bardez in Goa. The parish had a confraternity of Jesus and another of O. Lady of Rosary. An old woman was being helped with spiritual assistance on her death bed. She was instructed to call upon the name of Jesus. She was indignant and replied angrily: *Jezu? Jezu nam! Jezu tencho!* (Jesus? By no means, he belongs to them). Obviously, she was of the chardo caste, and the confraternity of Jesus was of the brahmins![22]

Another curious incident refers to two Goan historians, namely Felipe Nery Xavier e Miguel Vicente de Abreu. Their contribution to Goan history has been significant. The former was a first grade officer of the finance department, and he had already made a mark as historian before the arrival in Goa of the Portuguese historian-administrator Cunha Rivara in 1855. The latter was a low-grade employee of the Government Printing Press, and was a disciple of Cunha Rivara who trained him as historian. At some stage Abreu felt victimized by his country colleague who decided to reduce his pay by half. At the bottom of the quarrel was perhaps an academic rivalry between the two, even though both belonged to the same caste. Abreu presented a letter of protest to his patron Cunha Rivara, the then Chief Secretary of the State. He stated in that note: "If Your Excellency deems that the law is on my side, please do not leave its interpretation to the intelligence of Mr. Felipe Nery, because this native chief (sorry to use this expression) has no concern for his subjects as the Portuguese masters have for their people. Perhaps that is the reason why God has placed you over us. May God keep your Excellency for many years as my boss."[23] Such situations must have occurred often, and they help us to interpret another Konkani saying: *Firngeanchea paeam melolo hoi, punn Kanddeachea sangata jielolo nhoi* (It is better to die at the feet of a Portuguese than to live in the company of the Goan Christians). Goans may have preferred the Portuguese as a lesser evil in some ways, but there were other aspects of the Portuguese behaviour that left the Goans in a more doubtful attitude.

The British military camps had found a solution to the sexual needs of their men in the "red-light areas". The Portuguese had adopted a more Catholic policy. Instead of "divide and rule", they preferred to "multiply and dominate". Soon after the conquest of Goa, Afonso de Albuquerque chose some "fair and good looking" (*alvas e de bom parecer*) captive Muslim women and gave them to his soldiers in marriage.[24] But there were also some local Hindu women who seduced the Portuguese and entered in the class of the so-called *casados*, or married settlers.[25] However, the sexual appetites of the Portuguese were not always fulfilled within the bounds of Christian marriage. Albuquerque was once writing to his king: "Some of your men are tired of sleeping with the Christian women and are going to Hindu women".[26] They were the *kolvontam* of the Hindu temples, and others who lived as prostitutes. Fr. Gonçalo Martins, a Jesuit procurator of missions in Goa had the bright idea of purchasing the island of Kambarjua and making it a haven for prostitution after paying him a tax.[27] The minutes of the pastoral visitations of the Archbishops of Goa refer to the villages where there were Portuguese military bases, such as Rachol and Tivim. The documents reveal frequent cases of prostitution in the 18th and 19th centuries.[28] In 1858 the Secretary of the State was addressing a memo to the President of the Health Board and described the gravity of the problem of venereal disease among the Portuguese military personnel in Goa.[29] It is in this context of the sexual behaviour of the Portuguese soldiers that one should interpret the native reactions expressed in some folk songs that warn the women to watch out against bearded *pakle* that roam at late hours of the night (*Edê ratiché pakle bonvtai khaddache. . . .*", or try to peep through the key-holes. In the folk song *Modgovam Thoviager* (In the house of the carpenter of Margao) a Portuguese is told to stop peeping through the key-hole. He is informed that the lady inside is a widow, and not a young girl (*Teka ek paklo choita burkan ghalunu tonddu. . . . Arê paklea choinaka rê, cheddum tem bailu randdu*). The composers seem to have forgotten or did not know that the Portuguese had enacted legislation already in the 17th century inviting the poor Portuguese to marry local widows of means, despite the native tradition against it.

There are many folkloric composition of mando type that transmit the popular nationalist feelings against the Portuguese administration that sought to interfere in elections in favour of white candidates in Divar and Margao. The Divar incident took place in 1854 and is registered in the mandos *Luizinha, mojea Luizinha*, which laments the tragic end of Capitão Joaquim Garcez who sought to interfere in the elections. The village inhabitants pretended to hear calmly the anxious queries of his wife, who wanted to know what had happened to her husband. The villagers pretended to sympathize with her and described how badly the husband was treated (*foddleai pole*, *keleai vantte*). There are at least four other folk songs of this type referring to the incident of firing in Margao in the wake of the elections of 1890, and resulting in 23 deaths and exile of many (*Setembrache ekviseri / Camarachem foddlem re darui, Corneti vazoun soldad re aile, Povak marle faru, Rogtache zale vallu, Niti na re Goeantu / Justis na re Saxttintu, Inocenticheam rogtanu/Vasco Guedin kelem re eleisanvu*).[30]

To conclude, here are just a few more proverbs that convey popular impressions about the Portuguese in Goa. *Pão* or bread is an important Portuguese contribution to the Asian staple food. Even some years back the Goans were called *poder-pão* (bakers) in Mumbai, and the Portuguese bread-making art was considered inimitable. Hence the saying: *Te firngi mele, te undde kabar zale* (The Portuguese have gone and the bread is no more). It is also possible that the reference to "those" Portuguese sought to compare them with poor quality of their latter day counterparts.

Goans have also retained the memory of the Portuguese ceremonials and pompous ways of behaviour. There is a current saying in Konkani: *kumpriment kori naka* (do not make fuss). There is also the proverb: *Chodd firngi bhas, haddank urta mas* (Too many Portuguese speeches leave the bones with meat). Initially it may have meant the need to use hands, rather than knife and fork to eat chicken, but it tries to convey to someone the need to get down to the point and leave the long-winded discourses. The Portuguese have the habit of making long speeches or using many words to say little or nothing. This same tendency is also recorded in the Konkani proverb: *Faz favor, kortten dhunvor* (Too many speeches, but no action). We could cite dozens of sayings in which the Portuguese linguistic influence is noticeable, but have no other historical content. For instance: *Girest pielear alegre mhonttat, dubllo pielear bebdo mhonttat* (When a rich man drinks he is in happy mood, when a poor man drinks he is a drunkard) to indicate the different criteria adopted to judge the rich and the poor; *Amcho Juze Mari dekor kantar kori* (Our José Maria sings by heart) to say that he talks without evidence or a good foundation.

Conclusion

The few folkloric-linguistic expressions that we have analyzed constitute the sedimentation of the folk memory with references to the Portuguese colonial presence in Goa. These expressions have survived the dulling effect of time, and one wonders how much longer they will retain their hold upon the memories and the usage of the Goans. The new generation of post-1961 Goans do not utilize many of these sayings, and when they hear or use them, they no longer comprehend their background. Only a resumption of contacts between the people of Portugal and Goa could help to sustain and reinforce the cultural legacy left by the Portuguese in the soul of the Goan people and their language. If many Portuguese visit Goa today and fail to find the Portuguese soul there, that happens because they are looking for the Portuguese soul in the ruins of old monuments, or because they go looking for the Goans who can speak Portuguese. They fail to understand that the Goan soul is expressed in the Goan language, just as the Portuguese consider their language as an expression of their soul. Five hundred years after the arrival of the first Portuguese in India, the Portuguese are yet to discover the Goan soul. The Portuguese are proud of the *universalism* of their Discoveries and of their national identity, but in reality they seem to run all over the place in search of themselves. The Discoveries do not seem to have been an encounter with the *other* as *other*.

We cannot forget that popular culture is an expression of the historic identity of a people and as such it is a process in constant evolution. If our present analysis revealed some negative images of the Portuguese, it is due to the fact that they relate to the colonial past. The new relationship that is evolving is a new challenge to create different images that could be more positive. For the first time in the history of Goa, its people have their own political identity as a State within the Indian Union, and have financial support to develop their language as never happened in the past. It is a privileged situation to enrich the language of the Goans, and it is to be seen how this process integrates the colonial past and seeks new links for its future growth.

NOTES AND REFERENCES

1. "O Mar no Quotidiano Popular Goês", *Estudos da Academia de Marinha*, Lisbon, 1993. "As expressões folcloricas e religiosas do quotidiano popular na India portuguesa" (seminar on "O Quotidiano na História Portuguesa", Lisbon, 1993).
2. London, Longman, 1993, p. 8.
3. F. Braudel, *The Structures of Everyday Life: Civilization and Capitalism,*

15th-18th Century, vol. I, New York, Harper & Row, 1981, p. 27.

4. Romila Thapar, *Time as Metaphor of History: Early India*, Delhi, Oxford India Paperbacks, 1996.
5. *The History of British India*, vol. I, London, 1858 (5th ed.), Bk. II, Ch.I, p. 107.
6. Thapar, *op. cit.* pp. 39-40. Cf. D.D. Kosambi, *An Introduction to the Study of Indian History*, Mumbai, Popular Prakashan, 2nd. ed., 1975, pp. 162ff.
7. Mumbai, 1965, p. v.
8. Teotónio R. de Souza, *Medieval Goa*, New Delhi, Concept Publishing Company, 1979, p. 54.
9. António Pereira, *Konknni Oparinchem Bhanddar*, Panaji, 1985, p. 153.
10. T. R. de Souza, "Uns confessionários inéditos: Instrumentos de missionação e fontes para a história de Goa", *Amar, Sentir e Viver a História: Estudos de Homenagem a Joaquim Verissimo Serrão*, ed. Colibri, Lisbon, 1995.
11. de Souza, *Goa Medieval*, p. 92.
12. *Firangi* was a generic designation for the Europeans in the East. Probably the term was derived from the first contacts of the East with the French crusades. The Portuguese were called *pakle* (pl.) in Konkani, derived from *pak* or feathers which the early Portuguese displayed on their caps. The English were called *topikar* in the Maratha literature of the 17th century. Hence, there is some similarity in the choice of the two terms.
13. *Boletim do Instituto Vasco da Gama*, Bastora, 1953. Translation is mine.
14. Panaji, Imprensa Nacional, 1858, ch. 43. *Cf.* also the comments of J. Gerson da Cunha in his *The Konkani Language and Literature*, Mumbai, Govt. Central Press, 1881, pp. 41-42.
15. T. R. de Souza, "Christianisation and cultural conflict in Goa: 16th -19th centuries", *Congresso internacional de história: Missionação portuguesa e encontro de culturas — Actas*, vol. 4, Braga, 1993.
16. Biblioteca Nacional (Lisbon), Cod. no. 179: *Memórias e documentos para a história eclesiastica na Asia, 1728-1729*, fls. 11-13v.
17. Arquivo Histórico Ultramarino (Lisbon), Cod. no. 446, fls. 75-75v.
18. George D. Winius, *The Black Legend of Portuguese India*, New Delhi, Concept Publ. Co., 1985.
19. Souza, *Medieval Goa*, p. 92.
20. A. B. de Bragança Pereira (ed.), *Arquivo Português Oriental*, Tomo 4, vol. 2, Part I, Bastora, 1937, p. 262.
21. Leopoldo da Rocha, *As Confrarias de Goa*, Lisbon, 1973, p. 320.
22. *Ibid.*, p. 338, n. 812.
23. Drawn from the private correspondence of Cunha Rivara in the Municipal Library of Evora in Portugal.
24. Charles R. Boxer, *Relações raciais no império colonial português 1415-1825*, Porto, Ed. Afrontamento, 1988, pp. 66ff.
25. Rafael Moreira, "Goa em 1535: Uma cidade manuelina", *Revista da Faculdade de Ciências Sociais e Humanas*, II, 8 (1995), pp. 177-221.

26. R. A. de Bulhão Pato (ed.), *Cartas de Afonso de Albuquerque*, vol. I, Lisbon, 1884, p. 40.
27. T. R. de Souza, "Gonçalo Martins: A Jesuit procurator, businessman and diplomat in the Estado da India", *Mare Liberum*, no. 5, Lisbon, 1993, pp. 119-128.
28. T. R. de Souza, "The voiceless in Goan historiography: A case for the source-value of the Church records in Goa", *Indo-Portuguese History: Sources and Problems*, ed. John Correia-Afonso, Mumbai, 1981, pp. 114-131.
29. *Historical Archives of Goa*: *Cartas, Ordens, Portarias*, no. 125, fls. 134v-135.
30. Pratima Kamat, "Political life of 19th century Goa as reflected in its folksongs", *Goa: Cultural Trends*, ed. P.P. Shirodkar, Panaji, 1988, pp. 229-241.

FOURTEEN

DESASSOSSEGO IN LUSO-INDIAN GOAN POETRY*

GEORGE V. COELHO

Introduction

Goa Bela; lar e liberdade; musica e dança; amor e amizade; nostalgia e saudade. These are the dominant themes of Goan poetry written in Portuguese in this century. They define complex interacting elements in the Indo-Portuguese cultural crucible that moulded the Goan poetic temper. This essay delineates salient aesthetic features of Goan sensibility that was influenced by the village *comunidades* and Portuguese education. Goan poets tell their people's story as lived and owned by Goans themselves. They rejoice in the beauty and bounty of their land, river, hill, lake and stream, close to each other, church towers glistening and palm trees casting a spell over the endless seashores of the islands of Goa.

The Indo-Portuguese encounter of ideas and inventions expanded the Goan poet's consciousness. Goan creative arts flowed in the wake of the cross-currents of Lusitanization and Christianization.[1] Conquered in 1510, Goa captured the imagination of Portugal's Renaissance poet of the new world, Luís de Camões. Many young Goans had pressed to their heart, during their Portuguese Liceu days, his immortal lyric:[2]

> Alma minha gentil que te partiste
> tão cedo desta vida, descontente,
> repousa lá no Céu eternamenta,
> e viva eu cá na terra sempre triste.

* This Essay is dedicated to the Late Dr. Joseph de Barros.

(Gentle soul of mine, who parted
So soon from this life, unfulfilled.
Heaven holds you now in eternal calm,
And here on earth I live in sorrow,
For evermore. . .)

But the Goan who learned the language of the marvelous epic, *Os Lusíadas*, also listened to an unfinished story of the sap in the family tree struggling through its ancient roots, longing for the free air and voices of the song of Goa. This is the poet's *desassossego*, the cross-cultural crux in the Goan poetic temper. In the five themes presented here, the Goan poet tells of his contentment with the visible soil of the land. Here is nature's unadorned beauty; warmth in the bonds of the extended family; freedom to enjoy the laric pieties of life in the comunidade.

Music and song, secular and sacred, European and Indian tell of friendship and love, sensual and romantic, domestic and spiritual. Village history dances in the Konkani folk songs of Goa, telling of union and separation, joy and sorrow, yearning and lamentation, and the seductive arts of the *bailadeira* in the village temple. Here is also the poet's anguished cry of uprootedness, and the emigrant's plaint as he explores newer fortunes on the farther shore. So while celebrating the bounty of the earth and its visible soil, the Goan poet also hears the struggle of the entangled roots in the subsoil that are straining to catch the fertilizing sun and the nurturant rains. As ancestral voices resonate through the dilapidated rooms of his imagined home, the poet realizes the predicament of the *desterrado*. The poet's experience of the Indo-Portuguese cultural experience evokes a lacerating sense of exile, even at home, his lyrics tell of his wandering lost in the pages of an ancient history that he has not learned to read because he was long ago estranged from the vocables of Vedic India. The Goan *desterrado* says the rosary in faith without much hope. In the Goan grammar of personal attachments, nostalgia is the imperative mood: it summons the *angst* of pieties betrayed. The *desassossego* in Goan poets represents a swirl of turbulent memories: joy in the beauty of their Goa, love of music and song, respect for friendship and family relations, and at the same time, distress and despair over their people's ignorance.

Theme I: Goa Bela (Beautiful Goa)

The poet exclaims with zest and reverence, *Goa Bela*! My own voyage in Portuguese began at home with my parents in Mumbai where they had migrated from Goa about 100 years ago. Going down to Goa in May meant a long voyage of sea-sickness with my mother, 24 hours along the Konkan coast line, about 300 nautical miles; today you can fly from Mumbai to Goa in 45 minutes! Summer holidays in the family home in Porvorim meant a new language of festivals and fairs, and the exhilarating sensations of drawing water and bathing from the household well in the compound that overlooked our rice fields. Calangute beach was the beat for holidaying Goan students from Mumbai. But other quieter seashores also promised Portuguese serenades and Konkani and English songs that mingled with the star-sparkling ocean that splashed along the shores of Tiracol, Arambol, Morgim, Chapora, Anjuna, Baga, Candolim, Aguada, Majorda, Colva, Benaulim, Carmona, Cavelossim, Betul and Cabo.

The Goan poet B. B. Borkar,[3] invokes three natural features of Goa's islands. Goa is small (80 km. × 60 km.) with a small population — less than a million persons, mostly Christians and Hindus. Goa also offers, at one glance, a view of hills, river and sea-conversing gently in quiet colours. Moreover, the Goan landscape is modulated to small proportions. Adeodato Barreto[4] writing from Coimbra in 1931, extols the beauty of the land, and in the same breath exclaims his *desassossego*:

A Terra!
A nossa Terra!

Jardim florido
estendido
do mar a Serra. . .
Jardim plantado por Brahma,
com a propria mão,
. . . .Jardim tão pequenino
e delicado
— fruto divino—
gerado
da monção—

que, por tudo o mundo infindo,
(já o corri por meu mal),
eu nunca vi outro igual;
E lindo, muito mais lindo
do que o lindo Portugal.

(My Land!
Our beautiful land!

Garden in bloom
reaching out from the sea
to the mountain range. . .
Garden planted by Brahma
with His own hands. . .
A garden so small
and gentle
— divine fruit —
born of the monsoon
showers —

Wandering through the
whole wide world —

(and how I wandered far and away
all to my own sorrow, alas!) —
I never saw anything to rival
such beauty — so much more beautiful
than Portugal the beautiful).

Mariano Gracias,[5] (the sweet poet of nostalgia, hope and love) hymns the glory of Goa in a robust and mellow Portuguese, resonant with large and open vowels, and in the metaphor of a beautiful garlanded bride:

Sob a benção do sol, a Natureza, commovida e ridente, canta e reza a velha prece ardente e misteriosa!. . . . Ha beleza, frescura, encanto, en toda a redondez

Ha grande paz, sagrada e religiosa..Toda perfume, e um encanto a Goa!

Florida de mil lotus a lagoa, e uma linda noiva engrinalada..

Theme II: Lar e Liberdade (Home and Liberty)

Goa Bela evokes not only sensory pleasures but *pietas* — the ritual obligations to the memory of ancestors, and duties to the extended family and the comunidade as underlined by Mariano Gracias:

> "Hindus, Cristãos e moiros tem um fogo sacrado a que acendem os seus desegos, os seus votos, os seus sonhos do futuro"... na porta d'um lar goese — servatis servandis — podiam inscrever-se num azulejo, estas palavras do ultimo concilio: "a familia é como uma escola de valorização humana".
> ("Hindus, Christians and Muslims carry a sacred fire which receives the burned offerings of their desires, their vows, their dreams of the future"... on the door of the Goan household, these words of the last Council might well be inscribed, — all things considered, — as on the *azulejo* (azure painted tile) : "The family is like a school of human values").

Paulino Dias[6] who died at the age of 45 in 1919, translates his *desassossego*, by adopting a Sanskrit heteronym, Privi Das (slave of love). Invoking the Muses the Science and Poetry, and Renaissance ideals, he mourns the decadence of his people:

Deusa de peito d'aço, O Musa da Ciencia
que estranhos ideais, que enormes impossiveis
põe o teu lábio austero ante a minha inocencia,
paria na flor da vida, orfão da iniqua sorte,
posso eu assimilar essa alvorada imensa,
posso eu saudar a Vida, eu que saudo a Morte?
A terra do meu berço é um antro de geenas,
o céu da minha pátria é um palio de rancores
pode a ovelha soltar o grito das hienas,
pode a andorinha erguer o voo dos condores?

(Goddess of steely heart.
O muse of knowledge!
What strange ideas.
What vast visions do you place

with your austere face before my innocent eyes!

An outcaste am I in the flower
of life, an ill-fated orphan,
how can I embrace
the immensity of this dawn.

How can I welcome Life, I who welcome death?
The land which was my cradle
is now a cavern of ghosts.

My motherland is no heaven
but a seedbed of hate.
Can the lamb scream like a hyena?
Can the swallow rise
to the height of the eagle's flight?)

In a similar mood of *desassossego*, Adeodato Barreto[7] recalls the loss of ancient virtue:

O Goa Bela! Acorda!
Esqueçe-te e recorda!
Esqueçe-te os longos anos de desdita
de miséria infinita,
de revolta, de luto, de oppresão

Esqueçe a Inquisição
e o Jesuita
que te torceu a alma
que te deixou por arma a hipocrasia
cavou mil abismos penetrantes
fé, costumes, lingua, tradição

(O beautiful Goa! Awake!
Forget and remember!
Forget the long years of misfortune
and endless misery,
of revolt and struggle and oppression!

Forget the Inquisition and the Jesuits

who twisted your mind
and left you armed with hyprocrisy
and dug many a deep wound
into your faith and your customs. . .
language and tradition).

Continuing in the same mood in *Redenção* (1940), the poet feels dispossessed and lonely as an outcaste in a land without a name:

O meu dias azuis, meu sonho primitivo
das conceições na selva e tamarindo em flor?
E que tristeza eu sinto as aflições d'um monge
vendo a bater as grades dum mosteiro,
e logo me regressa a visão solitaria
de meus pais sem nome e a minha alma de paria. . .

(Oh my blue days, my primitive dream
of births in the forest and tamarind in flower?
And what sadness I feel the afflictions of a monge
coming and battering the steps of a monastery,
and as soon as I return to the solitary vision
of my country without name and my soul of a pariah..)

Now the poet's voice breaks into agitated tones, irregular in metre and rhyme, as if unable to control his indignation, over his people's emptiness and pettiness: mindless indolence:

Hoje na tua vida
tudo é monotonia;
sem ciencia, nem cultura
sem genio, nem poetas
vegetas. . .

pobre minha exaurida. . ..

Eis a lição
"a exploração"
que te legou a Europa, tua senhora:
ela explorou-te outrora,

tu exploras agora
os filhos do teu próprio coração!
Pobre, Goa, tão pobre. . .
O Goa Bela! Acorda!
Esqueçe-te e recorda!. . .

(Today is your life
all you have is monotony
without science, or culture
without any genius or poets
your are vegetating.

Poor exhausted mine!. . .

The "Explorations"
which linked you to Europe
your mistress,
She exploited you long ago
but now you are exploiting
the children of your heart!
O poor Goa! how very poor . . .

O beautiful Goa! Wake up!
Forget and remember . . .!)

Tão pobre! So very poor indeed!. These poets worked in turbulent times when Goan intellectuals launched new journals and wrote about Goa's role in the anti-colonial movements of the day. Their mournful refrain of cultural impoverishment was echoed, after Goa's independence in 1961, during the revolution of fallen expectations, in the novel, *Sorrowing Lies my Land*, by Lambert Mascarenhas.[8] Here again the visionary deplores the mentality of his people who drink at the bar of political rhetoric and slumber in indolence.

Theme III: Musica e dança (Music and Dance)

Composers of Goan song carry the burden of *desassossego* in a light-hearted manner, telling the tales of the Goan soil and soul in the people's language. These Konkani folk songs evoke scenes of village life, in a melodic idiom that blends Portuguese and Christian and Sanskrit vocables, especially in the three main genres of Konkani dance songs, namely, the *mando* (the song of love), *dulpod* (the song of joy), and *dakni* (the song of *bailadeira*).[9] In the Goan poet's social environment, the *mando* was danced on festive occasions in elegant and graceful measures, and mainly in Portuguese-speaking homes. Today the melodies of yearning and lamentation, union and separation, are heard in Goan communities around the world.[10] Susana Sardo describes the *mando*[11], in her ethno-musicological field-study carried out in Goa, beautiful illustrating dance attitudes, period costumes, furniture and related choreographic features. The *dulpod*, typically following the *mando*, is accompanied by a violin and drum (*rebec* and *gumot*); it is sung with gusto and danced in quick tempo. The Goan poet is inspired by the figure in the *dakni* (or *dekkni*) which tells of the Hindu temple dancer (*bailadeira*; *kolvont* in Konkani; *devadasi*, servant of the temple deity, in Sanskrit). *A Sheaf of Deknnis* and *A Treasury of Dulpods* (containing over 200 songs), systematically organized with historical notes, by José Pereira[12] suggests the exuberant and exciting melodic environment in which the Goan poet thrived in those days. The Konkani lyrics are redolent of a tender nostalgia for a simpler village life, and a disquieting sense of changes for the worse.

Portugal also brought home to Goa the sacred music of the Renaissance. As part of their Christian faith and observances, these poets of well-to-do families in Goa absorbed the traditions of western classical music, and especially of the Catholic liturgy that was universally intoned in Latin and accompanied by organ and choral music on feast days. Included in this musical legacy are the Gregorian chants, the madrigals of the Elizabethan age, (that were accompanied with the lutes and violas common on the Shakespeare stage), the *motets* and the polyphonic music which became part of an autonomous Goan musical tradition, as explained by Victor Coelho[13] in his pioneering archival study of Renaissance music in Old Goa of the late 16th century.

The Goan Christian poet was fascinated with the image of the *bailadeira*, the ritual temple dancer accomplished in the arts of classical singing and dancing in the ancient Hindu tradition of aesthetics and worship. The *bailadeira* was the *devadasi* figure and the dance in Indian art history has a historic and mythic significance in Indian cosmogony. The *devadasi's* ritual role and musical tradition were preserved in India till the early part of this century. The complex policy issues and dilemmas posed for Church and *Estado de India* at the time are well-documented in Charles Boxer's "Os Fidalgos Portugueses e as Bailadeiras Indianas (séculos xvi e xvii)".[14] Within this swirl of musical traditions, Indian and European, the Goan poet uttered a nostalgia for an ancient myth, a paradise lost. The *bailadeira* figure cast a spell of erotic turbulence into the vale of tears; she spelt a profound *desassossego* in his poetic imagination.

The *bailadeira* figure is an aesthetic phenomenon for Floriano Barreto[15] whose poem flows with her voluptuous body swaying in tune with the hypnotic tones of the Indian classical instrument, the *sarangi*.

Chora o sarangui. Bate os guizos, feiticeira,
e lança para a turba um olhar cintilante
que se apinha ao redor para vér-te o semblante
e a curva musical dos seios, bailadeira..

Tchin, Tchin! ondeia o busto em curvas de serpente
e desenrola o crasso olhar languidamente
e esbelta sedução do colo escultural!

(The sarangui moans. Cast your spells, sorceress,
with tinkling bells
and play those sparkling eyes on
the crowd gathered around to watch your figure close.
And the harmonious curve of
your breasts, o bailadeira. . .

Tchin! Tchin!
Let your bust undulate
sinuous like a snake
and let your large gaze languorously unwrap the
sculpture of your bosom
endowed with seductive grace).

In contrast to this erotic appeal of the seductive temple dancer, Floriano Pinto's *bailadeira*[16] bites into the conscience of the people watching her dance:

Não me desprezes, poeta, se gentil
me vés bailando, em voltas donairosa,
enchendo o ar de sandalio e de rosa
num ambiente rubido e febril.
Se ao calor da murdanga um coro vil
morde numa volupia amaviosa
do meu contorno a curva languorosa,
reprime e afasta o teu sarcasmo hostil!

Mais reprobo que o meu é o erro, o crime
de quem me aponta a senda da desgraça
e cedo o estigma a minha sorte imprimé. . .
Corro para o bordel numa vertigem?
Meu corpo em lama é vitima da raça,
escravidão fatal duma alma virgem.

(Don't look down on me, o poet, when you watch,
my gentle gestures, my bountiful curves,
folding the air with sandalwood aroma and roses
kindling the surround with a feverish glow.
When the sounds of the murdanga fanned by a choir
of voices vile inflame and pierce my body
into amorous languorous voluptuousness,
for heaven's sake, be kind: keep your sarcasm to yourself!

Alright! I'm to blame, the fault is mine;
mine is the error that leads to the trail of the crime;
quite early was stigma stamped on my fate..
don't I run giddily to the brothel, in a daze?
If my body is sullied with slime I am the victim of my people,
ill-starred slavery of a virgin soul).

In a reproachful mood, Mariano Gracias[17] visualizes the *bailadeira* as a narcissistic figure and loveless siren:

Fatal mulher que a si adora
mulher que ri, mulher que nunca chora
Bailadeira, mulher que nunca ama.
(Woman damned who loves only herself
Woman who laughs, woman who never weeps,
Bailadeira, woman who never loves).

In many a Goan poet inspired by the *bailadeira* of those days, *desassossego* recurs as a theme of philosophical and social dilemmas. Nascimento Mendonça, Floriano Barreto, Paulino Dias, Lino Abreu, Mariano Gracias, Eucaristo da Costa, all these poets recognize that tantalizing power of the *bailadeira*'s figure and ritual dance.[18] But in various metaphors, they also emphasize the power of the gender and caste conventions prevailing when Tomas Ribeiro visiting Goa, in the late 19th century was mortified by the degraded status of the *bailadeira*. The figure of the ritual Hindu temple dancer has gone into Indian history but the *bailadeira* seen a personality with her own story sharpens the *desassossego* of the Goan poet.

Theme 4: Amor e Amizade (Love and Friendship)

Goan folk songs in Konkani as noted above, are matched in the poetry of lover's joy in union and fulfilment, and more often in sorrows of separation, trust betrayed, unrequited love, romantic and reckless love and arranged marriages escaped or borne in despair. Vimala Devi's *Tentação*[19] conveys a woman's passion in hesitant but compelling tenderness:

Não ponhas as tuas mãos duras
No meu corpo de petalas,
Como o deus mudo e fundo
Filho de dois sois ardentes,
Não, meu deus, não toques
Esta pele macia e pura!
Esconde a tua ansia.

(Do not put your rough hands
on the petals of my body
Like a silent god
unfathomed
offspring of two blazing suns,
no, my god, do not touch
this skin, smooth and pure
Conceal your longing).

She pleads for time to grasp the unpredictable mutual moment:

Cala a tua furia impotente,
Pois a minha carne estremeçe de fraqueza
Ao contemplar o teu sorriso vasto.
Sinto aromas de sedução
Pela noite implacavel,
E bem dentro de mim
Oiço bailadeiras a cantar,
No templo ornado de lotus,
Como as minhas promessas ocultas.
Amanha, se as tuas mãos
Ansiarem repouso na morte,
Na palidez dos dias sombrios
Serei eu
Quem buscara as tuas mãos!

(Silence your impotent passion
for my flesh trembles
vulnerable in the contemplation
of the immensity of your smile.
I sense the aroma of seduction
through the inexorable night,
and deep within me
I hear the bailadeiras singing,
in a temple adorned with lotus blossoms,
like may secret promises.
Tomorrow if your hands
yearn for the quiet of death,
in the pallor of darkened days,
I will be the one,
who will come looking for your hands!)

In sharp contrast José Rangel's "Village Belle" (*Um Sonho*)[20] confronts and overcomes the male lover's offensive with her redemptive grace:

Os bicos dos teus seis
hirtos
(como a baioneta da sentinela vigilante
envoltos no sari do teu pudor)
me provocam

o assalto ao reduto.

Tumidez da vida
a rebentar de esperança
aviva a brasa do meu sangue
que nenhuma agua de prudencia
pode apagar

(The tips of your breasts
erect
(like the bayonet of a vigilant sentinel
wrapped in the sari of your modesty)
incite me
for the assault on the fort.

Turgid with life
nearly bursting with expectation
my hot blood is aflame
which the water of prudence
cannot extinguish).

The following last three lines are quintessentially Goan in taste. "The high tide of Her presence", — changes the metaphor from solid to liquid state, from the fortress to a heaving tide that casts a spray of salt to enliven dead flesh and fertilize the dreamer's barren soil:

Ao redor o mundo se inunda
de amargor
boiando carne morta.

Mas a maré-cheia da tua presença
salga e preserva
a semente do meu ser.

(The world about me is engulfed
with bitterness
floating dead flesh.

But the high-tide of your presence

savours and preserves
the seed of my being).

(Translated by Frederick G. Williams)

The dominant tone and message of these Goan poets is philosophical, Eros and Psyche are allegorized in the two faces of Eve, the sensual and the spiritual. The earthiest of Goan poets, Nascimento Mendonça[21] deepens the mood of his *desassossego*, by dramatizing the seductive power of the *bailadeira*, Vatsala, and her futile entreaties, as she dances in front of the rishi, who is silent, sitting in meditation, ritually half naked on a tiger skin, in a forest near her temple:

O fluida sombra azul das arvores gigantes,
és um veludo a arder na minha carne linda!
Que delirio me abrasa os seios palpitantes?
Rompeste como um sol na noite que não finda,
lubrica visão mostruosa e divina.
Mas que importa! Sou moça e sou formosa ainda.

(O floating shades of blue in the great gigantic trees
What madness sets ablaze my throbbing breasts
You come bursting, like the sun, into my endless night
O tantalizing vision monstrous and divine
But it does not matter! For I am young and beautiful).

Vatsala revels in her voluptuous dance in front of the rishi and in vain, offers him her beauty and the warmth of a festive home in Goa bela:

Bem séi que tu és casto e não vés que sou bela?
mas que importa! Sou moça e sou formosa ainda
Mas so per ti deixei,
como as ranins vencidas
meu leito de rubis
e de astros cravejado.

(Don't I know you are chaste;
But don't you see I am beautiful?
For you, only for you I renounced,
as a vanquished queen,
my bed resplendent with rubies
and star-strewn carnations).

Then in her lasting fling of total passion, she confronts his cold silence with her sublime sense of the deity in her beauty:

Tu és casto, mas não sou linda?
(Chaste you are, but am I not beautiful?)

Finally, as the rishi lies dying from the poisoned milk offering she has prepared and given him, she throws her body on his, joining him once and for all, on the blazing funeral pyre. Is this the way to salvation? To deny love on earth as unreal? Or to touch the beloved flesh and sing the love of a human face divine? This is the question at the crux of the Goan poet's *desassossego*.

Theme V: Nostalgia e saudades (Yearning and Nostalgia)

Resonant with the theme, Goa Bela, is the theme of *pietas*, the freedom to enjoy the laric intimacies in the extended family and the *socegado* quality of life that was possible for the well-to-do in early industrial Goa. Here again we hear the counterpoint theme, the *susto* that comes with partings of family members from Goa. A persistent *desassossego* haunts Goan nostalgia.[22] Separation-anxiety hovers ghost-like over the emigrant's wanderings. Goan *saudades* are redolent of home longings, but are not the same as the *saudade Portuguesa* which is tuned to a peculiarly Lusitanian key. Dislocated in space and time, Goan poets speak to their ancestral roots and their own feelings of uprootedness. The seashores of their mind are emblematic of the joining and severing of bonds with their villages and their childhood songs. Leaving behind his Goa with all her loveliness, Joseph Furtado[23] realizes, too late, his loneliness and loss:

Como, receiando mil revezes, danos,

Eu não chorei, quando há quarenta anos
A minha terra eu deixei!
Porém, em tais e tantos disenganos
Nunca Pensei! Nunca Pensei!

(Dreading many a misfortune
and many a loss;
I did not weep, when at forty
I left behind my land!
And so, disillusioned in many ways,
I never once thought! not once!)

Nostalgia for a mythic tradition seeps through the earthiness of Goan poetry. Adeodato Barreto and Paulino Dias anguish over their felt loss of a Vedic past and deplore the decadent Goan mentality of their times. They sigh despairingly for the wisdom of the Upanishads, while they are grounded in the vale of tears of their Christian faith. The unquiet grave of their dreams is the seedbed of their *desassossego*.

However, in *Lonjura* (translated into English by F.G. Williams), José Rangel [24] reconciles the near and the far. Reseeding the soil of Goan exile, he proudly praises another modern Goan poet who has transplanted his art and life to Lisbon:

Lonjura

Ser, e não ser
é a vivencia do Goes?
Raizes cá,
alma lá,
Será vida de entremez?
Não há
Dilema

Nem traição,
para os que
tem como a lema
A ascenção
Do Povo

Aqui, acolá
Um mundo novo!
Alma peregrina.
Em ti
Confia e espera
A tua terra
Pequenina.

(Distance

To be and yet not to be —
Is the Goan's way of life?
Roots here,
Soul there,
Charade of life perhaps?
There's no
dilemma
nor betrayal
For those who have
as their motto
the ascension
of the masses,
Here, there, everywhere —
A new world!

Pilgrim soul:
In your repose
the confidence and the hope
of your small
Earth. . .)

This poet's promising vision of Goan compatriots here and there is not shared by modern Goan writers in Indo-Anglian literature. For Peter Nazareth[25] director of the International Writers' Programme at Iowa University who suffered bitter exile when he left Uganda during General Idi Amin's regime, the end of exile is not "going down to Goa" (notice the Goan longing in that phrase) to stay. We cannot insult history. We have something to say to everybody, but somewhere along the line, we have to say things to ourselves". Another modern writer, Eusebio Rodrigues[26], professor of English at Georgetown University, born of Goan parents in Aden, speaks of a special form of exile in the Christian Goans' sensibility. "The Goan is, as it were, an exile in his own land; paradoxically in his own home, a stranger in a strange land. An exile need not leave home in order to suffer from the pain of not belonging."

In the last two decades, Goan poets at Mumbai University have amplified the existential issues of intellectual disquiet and literary *angst*. They raise angry voices crying over the split milk of their faith, which they feel no longer nourishes their spiritual thirst.[27] The *desassossego* in the earlier Goan poets, illustrated above, cries out with a vengeance in these post-modern Goan writers in Indo-Anglian literature.

After all, is there not a lesson to be learned by the Goan writer abroad caught in the crux of a nostalgia that is not appeased? For the Goan poet's *saudade* is a mirage in the desert of his exile. He longs for the *socegado* state of the mind, while his ancestral home is dilapidated and practically empty except for ghosts discarding the broken toys of childhood dreams. Can the poet then take up the challenge of the 21st century and reach out as the Goan has always done, to explore new worlds and affiliations. Will he listen to the various songs and music of the world? Perhaps he may discover his own voice, intrinsic and intimate, within an extended family choir. A great poet of Goa, Manohar Sardessai[28] hails in his lovely lyric "We are the World Wanderers" (1971), the freedom to discover new friends and Goan communities settled in all the continents, and to revisit to enjoy the bountiful fruits of his providential coconut tree:

> We are the world wanderers and squanderers of love,
> We have gathered shells and pearls from the seven seas
> and cast them on the shores for children to play.
> We have built our huts on the crests of waves
> and uncaged songs from our hearts for the blue winds of freedom,
> We have carried on our shoulders the weight of exile,
> and in our flesh the thorn of thought against this ceaseless wandering
> and the unseen unbroken thread that runs through our history.
> We are the sons of the land, . . .where church bells keep time to the temple chants.
> We are the world wanderers and squanderers of life

come home to rebuild the promised dream
in the heart of peace
under the coconut tree.

Here at last, the ancient ghosts of unquiet graves are laid to rest. Here the restless sap of the ancestral tree has climbed up into the suns' expanse and the fruitful rains. Singing of the promise of world wanderers who seek a wider community, old roots sprout new saplings that re-vitalize the songs of *lar e liberdade, musica e dança, amor e amizade, nostalgia e saudades* of *Goa Bela*.

Conclusion

The Goan poetic temper is in my perspective, molded in the crucibles of his Luso-Indian cultural experience. The five themes illustrate the poetic expression of the Goan sensibility. The surface structure of Luso-Indian Goan poetry reveals pious content and idyllic calm, simple joy in the natural beauty of the land and the many moods of love in their folk songs, romantic, maternal, spiritual and sensual. Nevertheless, the subsoil of the heart of the their poetry is rife with a deep spiritual disquiet, where ancestral demons ceaselessly contend with angels of their faith, and where restless roots seek sustenance from ancient wisdom of Vedic India. Now, as we approach the end of this millennium and the quincentennial of the Indo-Portuguese encounter and embrace in Goa, strong new voices sing, not only of the Goan exile's intellectual deformations and *desassossego* but also the transformation of his wanderlust into new bonds of friendship and ultimate *socego*.

NOTES AND REFERENCES

1. Anthony D'Costa, *The Christianisation of the Goa Islands (1510-1567)*, Mumbai, St. Xavier's College, 1965.
2. Luis de Camões, *Lírica*, ed. Nassaud Moises, São Paulo, Cultrix, 1981.
3. B. B. Borkar, "The Secret and Significance of Goa's Scenic Beauty", *Boletim do Instituto Menezes Braganza (BIMB)* (Panaji), no. 112, 1976, pp. 151-154.
4. A. Barreto, "Aposteose" and "Redenção" in *Livro da Vida (Fala Ishwara)*, Panaji, Swatwa, 1940.
5. M. Gracias, in *Colectanea de Escritos do Doutor António Colaço*, Margao, 1988.

6. P. Dias, "A Lira de Ciencia" in *A Literatura Indo-Portuguesa: Antologia*, eds. Vimala Devi & Manuel de Seabra, Lisbon, Junta de Investigações do Ultramar, pp. 137-139.
7. A. Barreto, "Redenção", *op. cit*.
8. L. Mascarenhas, Mumbai, Hind Kitabs, 1955. Also *The Greater Tragedy or the Death of a Nationalist*, Dona Paula, Lamas Publications.
9. L. Rodrigues, "Mando — the Song of Love; Dulpod — the Song of Joy; Dakni — the Song of the Dancing God", in *Folklore*, 4 (no. 11), November 1963, pp. 361-368. Also "Indo-Portuguese Konkani Folk Song Recordings", in *Archives of Traditional Music* (Univ. of Indiana).
10. J. Pereira, "Some Mandos of yearning", in *Proceedings of the 1st International Goan Convention*, (Toronto, August 1988), p. 28; "A Treasury of Dulpods" (forthcoming); "A Sheaf of Deknnis", in *Konkani Folk Songs*, Mumbai, Konkan Cultural Association, 1967.
11. S. Sardo, "Sons e Silencios", in *Oceanos* (Lisbon), nos. 19-20, September-December 1994, pp. 246-256.
12. Pereira, *op. cit*.
13. V. A. Coelho, "Connecting Histories: Portuguese Music in Renaissance Goa", *Goa and Portugal: Their Cultural Links*, eds. Charles J. Borges & Helmut Feldmann, New Delhi, Concept Publishing Co., 1997; "Cross-Cultural Repertories and the Politics of Music in Renaissance Goa" in *Encomium Musicae: A Festschrift for Robert Snow*. ed. D. Crawford, New York, Stuyvesant, 1977; "Kapsberger's Apotheosis . . . of Francis Xavier and the Conquering of India", in *The Work of Opera: Gender, Nation and Genre* (forthcoming).
14. C. Boxer, *Revista da História*, 22 (no. 45), January-March 1961, pp. 83-105.
15. F. Barreto, "A Bailadeira da India", in *Phalenas: com uma parte sobre assuntos Indianos*, Bastora, T. Rangel, 1898.
16. F. Pinto, "Bailadeira", in *Brisas do Mandovi*, Bastora, T. Rangel, 1931.
17. M. Gracias, "Bailadeira", in V. Devi & M. de Seabra, *op. cit*.
18. G. V. Coelho, "Images of Woman in Goan Portuguese Poetry: The Bailadeira theme and variations", in *Actas II Congresso Internacional: Rosto Feminino da Expansão Portuguesa*, Lisbon, Comissão para a Igualdade e para os Direitos das Mulheres, pp. 365-379.
19. In *Suria*, Lisbon, Agencia Geral do Ultramar, 1962.
20. *Toada da Vida* (Life's Refrain).
21. N. Mendonça, Bastora, T. Rangel, 1939.
22. G.V. Coelho, "Nostalgia in Seven Goan Poets", *BIMB*, no. 171, 1994, pp. 79-112; Teixeira de Pascoaes, *A Saudade e o saudosismo*, Lisbon, Assirio e Alvin, 1988; Carolini Michaelis da Vasconcelos, *A Saudade Portuguesa*, Lisbon, Guimaraes, 1996.
23. J. Furtado, "Nunca Pensei", in *Primeiros Versos*, Bastora, T. Rangel, 1927.
24. J. Rangel, *op. cit*.
25. P. Nazareth, "The end of exile, or why should Goans read Goan literature", in *Goa: Continuity and Change*, eds. Narendra K, Wagle &

George V. Coelho, Toronto, Centre for South Asian Studies, 1995, pp. 25, 35-50.

26. E. Rodrigues, "Stray Thoughts on Goan Exile, in *Goa: Continuity and Change*, pp. 51-58.
27. Rochelle Almeida, "Breaking the fetters: Convention, tradition and propriety in contemporary Goan poets" (mimeographed).
28. M. Sardessai, "Poemas", *BIMB*, no. 96, 1971; F. Barreto, "Coqueiro" in *Colecção de Versos*, Bastora, T. Rangel, 1931, pp. 45-61.

FIFTEEN

INFLUENCE OF PORTUGUESE LANGUAGE AND CULTURE OF DAMAN

ATHOS FERNANDES

The discovery of the sea route to India by the Portuguese at the end of the 15th century opened a new maritime communication between Europe and Asia. Vasco da Gama, arrived in India in 1498, and the ship carrying Diogo de Melo, sailing towards Hormuz, caught in a big storm was driven off to the shore of Daman in 1523.

Daman in those days was one of the main centres of trade and commerce and when the Portuguese came to know about the importance of the city and of its port which could harbour big ships they wanted to conquer it.

António de Silveira, on his way to conquer Surat, by an order of the Viceroy D. Nuno da Cunha marched towards the city of Daman in 1529 but it was only in 1559, 30 years later, that D. Constantino de Bragança conquered and brought it under the Portuguese domination, which remained so till 1961, when Portugal lost all its colonies in India.

This big blow which broke all political and economic interest of Portugal, left behind a vestige of its culture, which had deep roots for four centuries of its domination. During that period, experiences, knowledge, new values, products of all kinds, were exchanged. New realities were learnt. East and West came closer.

This Chapter deals with this aspect of Portuguese culture in Daman which I propose to analyze in respect of its development and progress, its linguistic form, its dialects, uses, customs that even today, people of faith and hope remember with nostalgia.

Mais do que prometia a força humana,

Entre gente remota edificarão
Novo reino que tanto sublimarão

(Camões, Canto I)

Camões thus sang the glory of Portugal, beginning his epic with the maritime discoveries. Such a fact was so important that with the discoveries, the Portuguese gave new worlds to the world, and established contacts with the unknown kingdoms, implanting their culture wherever they passed.

The Portuguese discovery has been a subject, for many years, of a detailed study in different forms, the documents of such studies are well known and generally of easy access, at least to the historians. However, the same is not the case with respect to studies related to the context of the Portuguese, and of the influence at various levels of activities in Daman. There is a lot to reveal.

Daman, an ancient city was unknown to the Portuguese, and according to an old version, King Scita Rudra Daman, after conquering Konkan from his father-in-law, king Andra Palumaio, established in the middle of the 2nd century the city of Daman on the banks of the Damanganga. In the 4th century Daman was incorporated into the empire of Chandragupta II. Later on it came under the rule of various rajas, the last being the king of Cambay who had its headquarters at Ahmedabad. As he could not fight his enemies, and knowing about the utility of the beautiful port and of the topographical conditions of the city, he conquered it, built a small fort there and became autonomous.

It was at this juncture, i.e. at the end of the 15th century, that Vasco da Gama came to India. Afonso de Albuquerque, having conquered Goa in 1510, began to outline his administration in order to establish his commercial domain in the Indian Ocean, building settlements in some cities from where he sent spices to Portugal. Daman was still in the dark in his mind and in the minds of other viceroys of India. But destiny was different. In 1523, D. Nuno da Cunha became the Viceroy of India, and ordered that Portuguese ships should set sail in the direction of Hormuz, and Diogo de Melo, sailing in one of them in that direction, was caught in a big storm in the Indian Ocean and driven off to the coast of Daman, and was forced to land on the bank of the river, thus, becoming the first

Portuguese to set foot on that unknown kingdom - Daman. And Camões narrates:

"...Quem to trouxe a est' outro mundo
Tão longe da tua Pátria Lusitana?
Abrindo, Ile responde o mar profundo.
Por onde nunca veio gente humana
Vimos buscar do Indo a grão corrente,
Por onde a Lei divina se acrescenta."

(Camões, Canto VII, Est. XXV)

Diogo de Melo, seeing the grandeur of the city, which was one of the main centres of commerce in India, and its beautiful port which was capable of harbouring big ships, brought this to the notice of the Viceroy in Goa, who later on wanted to conquer it. Many attempts were made in that direction, but it was only in 1559, when D. Constantino de Bragança took over as Viceroy of India that the Portuguese conquered it on 2 February, 1559. Thus, Daman came under the Portuguese rule for four centuries till December 1961, when, having failed all diplomatic negotiations with India for a peaceful solution, Portugal had to face the Indian armed forces, and in this encounter lost all its colonies in India which were under its domination. In this context the contemporary Portuguese poet Fernando Pessoa recalls in his collection of poems *Mensagem*.

O Mar Salgado, quanto do teu Sal
São lágrimas de Portugal!

(Oh salty sea, how much of your salt
Are tears of Portugal)

Those were the tears of the last Portuguese soldiers and of the last Governor of Daman, Major António Costa Pinto, who wounded during the fight, fell on the hard rocks of the Daman fort and till today the memory of the deeds of the Portuguese in the North Province, stands firm in memory.

And a little further Pessoa narrates:

"Valeu a pena? Tudo vale a pena
Se a alma não é pequena"

(Was it worthwhile? Everything is worthwhile
If the soul is not small)

It was. It is because the soul of Portuguese people is well reflected in its culture — a culture of a nation that gave new worlds to the world, and that remains to this day in the memory of the people of Daman, who remember it with nostalgia.

Daman: Four Centuries of Portuguese Domination—A Review

According to some historians, the jurisdiction of Daman comprised the territory from Bulsar till Bassein. This vast extension of territory with its excellent maritime ports, helped Daman progress during the first centuries of Portuguese domination, i.e. 16th to 18th centuries. Commerce, was the main source of income. From the Daman port, the best in Cambay, many ships sailed to the different ports of Brazil, Africa, China and Japan. In the market of Daman there were various types of woolen clothes. In Daman de Cima alone, in 1630, there were more than 200 weavers, manufacturing various types of clothes for export. This activity in the docks was so intense that it lasted for decades and reached its climax during the administration of Julião Vieira at the beginning of the 19th century.

Daman had also its own mints, the first established by the Senate in the 16th century. Later on, in 17th century, D. Lourenço de Távora gave license to mint copper coins known as *bazarucos*. The second mint was established by the Jesuits in 1617, and the third in 1769. It is worth mentioning that even today we can hear some old people saying: *Num tê bazaruc* — I don't have money.

In the field of religion and education Daman reached its climax with the construction of many colleges, convents, seminaries and churches which became centres of attraction for neighbouring kingdoms. To name a few: the Convents of São Paulo, São Domingos, Colégio de Onze Mil Virgens, Sé Cathedral, the churches of Nossa Senhora dos Remedios and Nossa Senhora do Mar. These contributed to the development, progress and grandeur of Daman. But with the expulsion of Jesuits by Marques of Pombal, secondary education began to decline, and only those who had money could send their children to Goa or Mumbai. And, as was to be expected, the poor were the worst affected.

The reminiscences of the Portuguese are not only preserved by words or by verses inherited from generation to generation and recited orally, but are immortalized in the rocks, everlasting signs of civilization that marked the history of that people, and that today constitute a reflection of the real questions and are demonstrations of their own culture. This reflection while looking at the monuments is worth mentioning. The gigantic forts built by the Portuguese in those days, on the banks of the Damanganga, even today exalt the glory of Portugal.

The two forts of S. Jeronimo and da Praça have stood firm against all forces and calamities of nature. Any visitor on entering the city becomes perplexed to see the magnitude of the works of the Portuguese, tries to decipher the words written therein and becomes curious to know about their past. Who will tell us today about the victorious battles that the black and ancient forts of the city had witnessed? The Damanganga perhaps.

But the Damanganga or Sandalcalo, as it is known today, is long and narrow, not very deep, so much so that during low tide, it is difficult for certain types of boats to cross it. But, in spite of this, the port of Daman was, in those days, one of the best on the coast of Cambay, had the best shipyard where during 18th and 19th centuries many frigates and other types of ships were constructed and sent to Goa, Mozambique and Portugal. This shipyard was famous and their masters were sons of the soil, among them the distinguished Yeodo Samogi who was given the title of Lieutenant of the Sea.

It is worth mentioning that in 1773, Marques of Pombal, the then Prime Minister of Portugal remarked that while in Goa during the last hundred years only three boats had been constructed, the famous shipyard, *Caliana*, had done more than the entire maritime unit at Goa. He endowed it with the name of Royal Shipyard. Great was the fame of the Daman Shipyard and of their directors.

The frigate D. Fernando e Glória, constructed at Daman in the 19th century, and which during the 33 years it sailed from India to Angola and Mozambique and back transporting military personnel and people, and was destroyed in a fire 1960, is today under repairs in the shipyard at Aveiro in Portugal. The newspaper *Diário de Notícias* dated 29 April 1994 had published the following: "A última fragata da carreira das Indias a D. Fernando e Glória está a ser recuperada em Aveiro. O Mestre Alberto Costa orgalha-se da sua obra. A fragata foi construida pelo mestre Português Gil José da Conceição e pelo mestre mouro Yeoda Samogi".

Daman had distinguished men, sons of the soil, like João Francisco Xavier de Seixas, who took over as Governor of Daman in 1914. Another was Luis de Melo who became a noble of the Royal House. This shows the prosperity of Daman of the Province of the North wherein the names of the sons of the soil are engraved in the history of Portugal.

The mission of the Portuguese in the East was not only to conquer and to trade, but also to expand the religious faith and to baptize. And with that splendour of development and progress, the Christian faith expanded even more, crossing all barriers of society, of caste and creed, and penetrating deep into the souls of the pagans. In this context it is interesting to note some of the religious curiosities of that time.

The Devotion of the People

The influence of the Christian religion, brought by the Portuguese missionaries, is reflected in the devotion of the people. This could be seen even in the non-Christians who worshipped blindly the Christian faith. It is a well-known tradition that Our Lady of Remédios (today venerated in the church of the same name at Moti Daman) was believed to be a Hindu, one of the seven sisters of goddess Laxmi, wife of Vishnu. As she converted, she lost her caste. It was a practice, in those days, for the *machins* (fishermen) to offer their newly born to Our Lady of Remédios, and prostrating on the first step of the chapel. It was also customary on every Saturday to go to that church to the accompaniment of gentile music in order to make their vows. Our Lady was known as *Ai Remed*. All these practices are not in vogue today though the devotion to Our Lady continues.

On the other side of the river is the church of Our Lady of the Sea inside the fort of S. Jerónimo. It is believed that the statue of Our Lady was found in a box floating in the Indian Ocean, and it was picked up by a Portuguese soldier who brought and kept it in this church. The statue is venerated today by the fisherfolk community with great devotion, and before they venture into the high seas, they ask Our Lady of the Sea for her protection.

Another curiosity is the devotion to São Gonçalo de Amarante, a devotion introduced by the Portuguese soon after their arrival in Daman. It is said that the devotion begins with a litany in honour of Mother Mary, and after the litany, everyone goes to the main banquet table where they are served food and drinks. After this, they come back to the oratory to sing the litany in honour of São Gonçalo. According to the tradition of those days, the litany was sung to the accompaniment of violins, where boys and girls danced in front of the oratory. It was also customary for the people of Badrapur (a ward once belonging to the Colégio de Onze Mil Virgens) that the married people who had no issues would tie a blue ribbon to the statue of São Gonçalo, as a vow, and the ribbon would be taken out soon after their vows were fulfilled. Artisans, like carpenters, masons, et al have him as their patron saint.

It is a well-known fact that the Portuguese brought with them many slaves from Africa for their domestic and agricultural works. In the 18th century there were more than 600 slaves in Daman. The Governor himself had around 40 slaves. These slaves had a devotion to São Benedito, a black saint, and they celebrated his feast with great pomp. In the Sé Cathedral, the president of the feast used to occupy the Governor's chair and all Negroes used to come to the feast wearing the best costumes of their masters. Only those who had military patents could hold the pallium. During the procession, which was solemn, all Negroes, young and old, and even children, taking part in it, sang and danced to the tune of their own music. The celebrations lasted for about a week and the Negroes were free to enjoy their festivity. This was a concession given to them during this occasion.

It so happened that in 1854 the Governor of Daman, Constantino Lopes de Azavedo e Cunha had ordered the arrest of Leão Benigno, a honest wine-merchant and president of the feast that year for occupying the Governor's chair and he made him work with his festive dress on with a spade in his hand. Later, the Governor Visconde de Vila Nova de Ourem abolished the practice of the president of the feast occupying the Governor's chair and from then on, the pomp of the feast was lost.

There are many other religious curiosities, that even today the people of Daman observe on each occasion.

São João de Damão

São João is one of the most popular saints of Daman and the people have a great affection and devotion for him. On his feast day (24 June), in spite of the heavy rains, the churches are filled with devotees, who come in their best to pay their homage to the saint of their predilection. In every house there are typical foods for this occasion, like *dampaca, espetada, bafado, gund, papary, ambotic de porco* and the traditional *val nascido*, a special dish which goes well with the *sura de cajury* (country liquor). It is the custom even today for everyone to go to the beach to have their traditional sea bath, singing and dancing imploring the saint for his celestial blessing.

São Roque, Patron Saint of Daman

He is invoked as the protector against all contagious diseases. It is said that he protected the priests at the Council of Constance against the plague. His feast was celebrated with great pomp in the Colégio de Onze Mil Virgens of the Jesuits, where all noblemen participated. But due to lack of funds, the celebrations of this feast were stopped. It so happened that Daman was struck by another plague between 1896 and 1903 which took many lives. It was at this juncture that the people of Daman began to celebrate his feast every year in December, taking out a big procession through the main streets and wards of the city singing hymns to him.

The march of progress was on and in the 19th century, due to the initiative of the Perfect, Bernardo Peres da Silva, the first Daman newspaper, *O Portugues em Damão* a weekly, was started on 18 July 1835. The editor was Prof. Solinas from Goa. As it was a political newspaper it contained sarcastic articles, and as it was very much in demand, it was distributed at night. But the newspaper was short-lived and the last edition was dated 18 August of the same year. In 1837, the second newspaper *A Sentinela da Liberdade na Guarita de Damão* also had a short run. There were also other newspapers like *Investigador Português, Pregoeiro da Liberdade, Observador*, all these published from Mumbai, and with the political and religious aims of the Portuguese in the East. After that there was not a single paper published in Daman. But it is curious to note that after the liberation of Daman in 1961, there was one weekly called *Daman* which had not enough strength for its continuity, and naturally, it disappeared forever.

Daman Today

From the Province of the North, which comprised the areas from Bassein to Bulsar, what remains today is a small part of the territory (the districts of Daman and of Dadar and Nagar-Haveli integrated in India under the direct administration of the Central government as Union Territories, having only one representative as the Member of Parliament in the Lok Sabha).

Thus the progress registered during the last four centuries of Portuguese domination in Daman is reflected today in their day-to-day life, in their linguistic forms, their music, their food habits, their customs and traditions. In order to understand it better, it is necessary for one to stay there and walk through the small lanes and wards and minutely observe everything which happens around. And the first impression that one finds is that the people of Daman are proud of their native land, and never spare any efforts to glorify the place of their birth. José Lopes and Ludovico Machado, both with nostalgic memories and distinct sons of the soil, have left a song-book for the future generation. A hymn dedicated to the Sandalcalo is today exalted at almost all festive occasions.

Rio Sandalcalo

Rio Sandalcalo, da minha Pátria,
Juro sempre lembrar de ti,
E com saudades do meu Damão;
Pátria amante, terra triunfante,
Meu rio Sandalcalo,
Sempre eu hei-de amá-lo.
Deixe, agora deixe me contar,
Dizer alguma coisa
Da minha amante Pátria.
Amo, com toda alma,
Uma praça mui formosa,
Uma bela cidade
De renome conquistador.

Daman folklore is rich and appreciated by many people. Its songs, some melancholic, others of joyful rhythm make the people live a happy life forgetting their sorrows and sadness. But when the winter season arrives, with the heavy rains during which the Damanganga is flooded with the water coming from the mountains of Nagar-Haveli bringing along with it everything, the big trees of the dense forests, as well as the wild animals who try to cross the river, the mood becomes different. In this turbulent force of nature, where the roars of thunder, the fascinating lightning flashes and the hissing sound of the winds all combined, give an impression of fear before nature. The *machins* do not go to sea and the *machanas* (fisherwomen) do not have the anxiety which they suffer from when their husbands go far on the high seas for fishing. Every body is gathered in their houses; only the peasants go to the fields to till the land. In the past, one could hear the melancholic song of *Marília* to the accompaniment of the *dol*, *chunches*, *guitars*, *violins* and *rebecas*. But today, this song is sung not only during the winter nights, but also on all festive occasions.

Canto de Marília

No Inverno rigoroso, Surumba,
Nascem florinhas no chão.
Assim nasceu meu amor, Surumba,
Dentro do meu coração.

Rosa branca bem querida, Surumba,
No peito hei-de guardar.
Ainda que eu perca a vida, Surumba,
Vosso amor não hei-de largar.

Rasgou veia do meio peito, Surumba,
Deixa sangue a correr.
Mais ingrata que tu foste, Surumba,
Hei-de amar até morrer.

Daman, situated at the sea coast, is abundant in fish. The fisherfolk community have three classes: *maglás*, who fish at the coastal zone, without going far away from the mainland and using small boats; *machins*, who fish deep on the high seas with their big boats; and the *mitnas* who fish in muddy waters of the river. They have beautiful songs on their lives.

Olá Olá

Ai olá olá
Pescador di Damanganga,
Maglá já butô rêd, ó mãi,
Já pegô Bomblá

Ai olá olá
Pescador di Cari,
Mintá já butô rêd, ó mãi,
Já pegô neuti.

Ai olá olá
Pescador di Damanganga,
Machi já butô rêd, ó mãi,
Já pegô dará.

Culinary Art

One of the typical aspects of Daman culture is undoubtedly the culinary which is a blend of oriental and western traditions. Many of the recipes vary from family to family and in certain cases the recipes are kept a secret from generation to generation. Many recipes are related to certain festivals with typical dishes prepared for the occasion. Thus, during the Christmas season, the most joyful season of the year, when children are waiting anxiously for Christmas Father, their mothers work hard in the kitchen to prepare many varieties of sweets for the Christmas gift. And in this combination of varieties one could not miss the famous *bolo de sura* which is prepared with sura, a fermented sap of the palm tree. This famous *bola de sura* is served generally after the midnight mass when people visit their friends and relatives to wish the Merry Christmas and sing the *Louvada* in praise of Jesus Christ. This tradition is very popular in Daman and even in the houses of the poor, the *bolo de sura* brings joy to the family. Other Christmas varieties are the *boroa, doce de grão, dodol, neuris, aranha do céu, pão-de-ló* and *bebinca*.

It is said that the Portuguese in order to feel at home dragged along with themselves to the seven corners of the world their famous *bacalhau, boroa* and their wine. In the same way the people of Daman do not feel at home without their famous *espetada de leitão*. On any festive occasion, especially during the religious festivals, the *espetada de leitão* is one of the main and favourite dishes.

Other varieties of Daman culinary are of daily order like *arroz e caril, alh-piment de bombilins, sêk-sêk de camarão ou caranguejo, dal bafad, dampaca, xacuti, guizado de peixe ou carne, barrad de neutis*, etc. It is curious to note that in Daman they follow the tradition of lunch, dinner and supper. All these traditions are practically seen in the Christian community who had adapted to western customs.

Daman and the Portuguese Language

As we have seen, the history of Daman dates back to the 2nd century but the first contacts of Indians with Portuguese were with the discovery of the searoute to India and later on when Diogo de Melo landed at Daman for the first time in 1523.

With this embrace of civilization and culture, a new historical epoch began to flourish in which experiences, knowledge, new values, products of all kinds, were exchanged, and new realities were learnt. The East and West came closer. All this became possible through the vehicle of communication, that is the language by which the Portuguese attempted to solidify their position for four centuries. During this encounter of civilizations, the Portuguese language began to mix up with other native languages thereby giving birth to other linguistic forms, the so-called creoles and dialects.

But to understand better the origin and development of a creole and any other language, the knowledge of historical and social and cultural datas are indispensable. And as there are no archives in Daman to gather all the data of this type, it is difficult to find out the exact sources of information. But the creole of Daman, as they call it, has a connection with the Portuguese language which is today one of the widely spoken languages of the world.

With the exception of Goa, Daman, Diu, Dadra and Nagar Haveli, Portuguese is today spoken not only in Portugal but also in Brazil, Angola, Mozambique, Cabo Verde, S. Tomé and Principe, and

Guiné Bissau, as their official languages.

For political reasons, Portuguese in the former Portuguese colonies in India, lost its official position, leaving only a trace of its memory among the older generation. Portuguese seems to have sunk into oblivion.

Last year I had the opportunity to visit Daman and Diu and had contact with many persons regarding matters related to Portuguese and its culture. I was very much impressed by the importance given to them to preserve the language and culture in those places. In this context, I think, Portugal is a country with a special responsibility in the dissemination of this language and culture, in view of the fact that its history is identified with an indisputable universal spirit of wide contacts with varied races and cultures.

Such facts determine the attention dedicated to the presence of Portugal in India, especially in Goa, with the opening of a Consulate General and a branch of the Fundação Oriente in Goa with the objective of disseminating Portuguese language and culture. The same initiative is not seen, in the same manner in other districts, like Daman, Diu, Dadra and Nagar-Haveli.

Allow me to point out here with profound respect and consideration, that Portuguese is till today the mother-tongue for the Catholics of those districts, although in its archaical form.

Fernando Pessoa, the great Portuguese poet of this century wrote: "My motherland is the Portuguese language". In the same way Portuguese, the great cultural legacy that the Portuguese transmitted for four long centuries, spread and is deeply ingrained in various latitudes of the Province of the North, becoming thus the instrument of communication among the various strata of society. In such way it is rooted in the souls of the Catholics of Daman, that made a devotion, a worship of motherland.

Allow me once again to point out my personal experiences of my stay in Daman and Diu for a few days, which left me with the sensation that the Portuguese reminiscences are still alive in the older generation, although the younger try to imitate the different cultures and societies, especially the models of the big Indian cities. From this recent contact, I give a narration of a typical dialogue, a model of Daman Portuguese, when I spoke to one of them in the following way:

A - Carlinh, vi aqui. Com vai óss.

C - Qui há falá irmão. Eu tê vai tiran di - ór bem, ór mau. I óss com vai, i cón jáeu.

A - Eu chigô ont mêm.

C - I dós muér i filh com vai?

A - Minh muér i filh vai andan - or bem, ór mau.

C - Ilôt num jáeu? Qui tê fazend na Gô. Ficô ali pâ comê bangré. Devi trazê pilôt. Aqui tê panhan muit bumbli i dará.

A - Com ad trazê pâ tud ranch. Agór tambê vid tê muit car. Ant u qui ér. Nu nóss di, tud ér barat.

C - Eu tambê vai tiran di. Mi pai, mi mãi já murreu, e eu cum minh baí, suzinh fican na cáz.

A - Agór un trabalhan óss, i quant ganhan pur di?

C - Eu num tê lugar cert. Quem chamá pármi, eu vai pâ cáz dêl. Ess gent tambê tum tê pagan bê. Algém dan cinc rupi, algém dan doi rupi, i êss caristi di hôj, num tê dan pâ batê um cóp. Si vai nu mercad dez rupi, num tê vin nad. Ess dinher num tê nêum valor.

A - Vid na Gô tambê é assi mêm. Agór tud lad é car.

C - Bem irmão Eu tê vai andan. Minh baí tê ispran pármi. Há encontrá ôtr di. Falá pâ dós muêr i filh qui eu tinh perguntan pilôt. Num isquicê di dá recad. Adeus.

As we have seen, the typical characteristic of the Portuguese language of Daman is the modulation of the phrases, which is sometimes difficult to express with clarity in writing. There are no proper rules for the grammar, like singular, plural, masculine and feminine, etc. Thus the dialect is a mixture of an archaical form of Portuguese, and there is not a single bibliography to study with accuracy the Portuguese spoken in Daman. This humiliating situation is one of the factors that may lead to a slow death of Portuguese and its dialects, although there is a great will and endeavour from many who consider this tradition which has more than four centuries of its existence, that it endures to the boundaries of the next centuries. However, on the threshold of the 21st century, what path will the Daman society follow and with what measures will they preserve the old cultural patterns?

SIXTEEN

16 MARCH 1554
Reflections of a Mid-Sixteenth Century Scene in Goa

ENGELBERT JORISSEN

In the morning there had been crowds of people as never before seen in Goa. They had been thronging the streets, straining behind the windows and gathering at the walls to have a better look. In the Rua Direita (called *Derecha* or Straight Road: the main street and pride of the city) many basins with perfumes had been placed.[1]

In the evening of that same day, 16 March 1554, there must have still been a lot of talking, rumour and gossip in the city, (of what is now known as Old Goa), in the little villages around about, villages like Ribandar situated half a mile before entering Goa and the island of Chorao on the opposite shore. There is some thrill in imagining further that exactly on that day three Portuguese of different ages and character, each of whom would leave a mark on the history of Portuguese literature and thought, might have met. It is a historical fact that these three were in Goa on that day, and that they stayed there at the same time for about a month, and there must have been much opportunity for them to have come together and to have talked to each other.

On the morning of that day, in March 1554, a dead body had been brought to Goa. For some time already its arrival had been expected since it left Malacca in December 1553. It had reached Cochin, but the calm winds had continued, and Fr. Melchior Nunes Barreto, the Jesuit vice-Provincial of India, and rector of the Jesuit college at Goa had pleaded with Viceroy D. Afonso de Noronha for a quicker ship with which he wished to meet the body, and hasten its arrival to Goa. All were in a hurry, since the Jesuits wanted the body to arrive before Easter of that year. The Viceroy finally sanctioned a *fusta* (pinnace) which took the body at Bhatkal, some 110 kms south of Goa, and on the Friday of Passion Week the *fusta* returned to Goa, it being 16th March. For the arrival the Viceroy and the important members of the Portuguese colonial administration had assembled on the bank of the river Mandovi behind the chapel of St. Catherine and the hospital. About 6,000 people had been on the roads of Goa to witness the spectacle, as the body was lifted from the boat and brought amidst much pomp to the College of St. Paul's of the Society of Jesus.[2]

The many subjects which might have been discussed on that day in Goa were, first, the question of what kind of consequences awaited religious life along the West Coast of India raided by the Portuguese colonizers; second, whether the church would use that particular day as an opportunity to further strengthen her grasp on the life of the people of Goa; and third, what measures she would use against those of other creeds.

The body which had come to Goa was, of course, that of Francisco Xavier. The three men mentioned above were Garcia da Orta (1500-1568), Fernão Mendes Pinto (1509-1583) and Luis Frois (1532-1597). All of them had been acquainted with Xavier. The three had seen how Xavier's fame had grown during his lifetime and how it had continued to increase after his death. At the same time, however, the three must have known as well how it had been Xavier himself who had proposed the institution of the Inquisition in Goa for one reads in his letter dated 16 May 1546: "The second thing necessary for India, in order that those who live here will be good Christians, is that your Majesty send the holy Inquisition, because here are many who live according to the law of Moses and the Moorish sect, without fear of God or being ashamed before the world".[3]

This consideration in which Xavier is pointing at the converted Jews and Muslims, could not be without concern for the three men, as will be shown further, or the fact that there had already been a victim of the Inquisition in 1543, a detailed report of which is found in *Lendas da India* by Gaspar Correia (1495-1564).

That year Jerónimo Dias, a bachelor of medicine, had reportedly touched on some matters which were interpreted as against the Catholic creed. He was very soon convicted of belonging to the old faith and proved to be a Jew. He was called before a panel consisting of a Franciscan preacher, a Dominican preacher, the Vicar General and some other fathers "who were all seated at the desk" (*todos assentados a mesa*). Declared guilty, he was handed over soon after to the secular law (lest the Church while demanding his death be tainted with his blood). He then found himself confronted at another desk (*outra mesa*) by the Governor, the auditor-general, several academicians and many *fidalgos*. One can read this document as an example of good co-operation between clerical and mundane justice. It was announced at that place that having been founded guilty by the holy Church and by the justice of the king of Portugal, he was condemned to be burnt alive. He was then led back to the prison (*tronco*), where he was given an opportunity to confess, and finally was brought to the pillory (*pelourinho*) accompanied by the *Misericordia*. There, because he had shown repentance, he was granted the 'immense' grace of being first strangled before his body was burnt to ashes.[4]

As becomes evident, objects (*mesa, tronco, pelourinho*) which in the future would become obligatory at the proceedings of the Inquisition in Goa, were present there.

However at this point, it will be enough to give a short synopsis of what had happened to da Orta, Pinto and Frois up to their meeting in 1554. Garcia da Orta was born at Castelo de Vide between 1498 and 1501. In his youth he studied at the Universities of Salamanca and Alcálá respectively and took a licentiate degree in medicine. Between 1530 and 1534 he worked as a doctor in Lisbon and obtained professorships in natural philosophy in 1530 at the University of Lisbon and of moral philosophy in 1531 at the same University. But on 12 March 1534 he left Portugal for Goa as a doctor to Afonso de Sousa, chief captain of the fleet that year.[5] If asked why he had come to India, he might have answered people that he was not too acquainted with things: "I have a great desire to know the medical drugs (which are called in Portugal *de botica*) and other simple medicines, which you find here, and all the fruits and spices. Of all these I wish to know their names in all languages, as well as the names of the lands where they grow, and of the trees and plants on which they grow. Further I want to know how the Indian doctors make use of them, and moreover I want to know about some other plants and fruits of this country, even when they are not of medical use, as well as about some customs of this land and things which occur therein, because all these things have to be said as they really are".[6]

It seems that da Orta in the more than thirty years that he stayed in India did not go further than Cape Comorin, but on the north West Coast and the South West Malabar Coast he would have traveled extensively, because he was involved as a jeweler too, besides his activities as a doctor and scientist. For a time he stayed in the North, becoming the owner of an orchard for his plants which made him the first owner of what is now known as the estate of the city of Mumbai.

Garcia da Orta was not only known and esteemed as erudite among a number of Jesuits, but he functioned as a member of the boards of examinations for students at the Jesuit college in Goa, too.

Fernão Mendes Pinto, as Frois would learn, must have been born between 1509 and 1511, and it is not certain whether he was born at Montemor-o-Velho or at Almada. From the end of 1521 he served for one and a half years at the house of a certain noble woman, but for some unknown reason, he had to run away from that place for his very life. He then embarked on a ship, which was very soon attacked by French corsairs, but he, along with the other Portuguese captives, however, was set free. Thereafter he entered the service of a nobleman who was related to Dom Jorge, the illegitimate son of king João II, and stayed there for four years, and finally was employed in the household of Dom Jorge himself. On 11 March 1537, he stated, "I left Portugal with a squadron of five *nãos*.[7]

1521 to 1537, as Frois would probably have reckoned, were the sixteen years Pinto describes as seven in his 'tale'. So what is one to make of the remaining nine years?[8]

In a letter Frois wrote from Macau many years later, dated 12 November 1593, one reads: "On 9 October, a year ago, we left Japan, the Father Visitor (that is Alessandro Valignano, 1530-1606) took me along to help him with his letters bound for India and Europe. And as with the help of our Lord now since 61 years. . ."[9]

According to this Frois should have been born in 1532, as it is generally held, in Lisbon. However, there is no certain proof of this, even though Georg Schurhammer in an essay written in 1929 rejects the hypothesis that Frois was born at Beja.[10]

Nothing is known about Frois' childhood and early youth, except that he probably had lived in the surroundings of the Portuguese court and that, already in his early years, had been instructed at the royal chancellery. In 1548 Frois had entered the

Society of Jesus (which had been founded and ratified by Pope Paul III just eight years before), as a fifteen or sixteen year old boy, which was not unusual at the time. In that same year he was sent to Goa in India, together with nine other Jesuits distributed on two ships, the *San Pedro* and the *Galega*. It should be mentioned here as well, that among the passengers (the name of the ship being uncertain), there was Luis de Almeida, who was to enter the Society in 1555, and who would become famous as one of the founders of the so-called *nanban igaku* (early western medicine) in Japan. Before its arrival in Goa the *Galega* (the ship on which Frois had traveled), had almost been discarded. Arriving at the Canary Islands, she had caught fire, and had been separated from the other ship, events seen as unlucky signs. After that, the *Galega* had still more hard times to face, once before arriving at Mozambique and the other between Mozambique and Goa when it almost began to sink.[11]

At the time of Frois' first arrival in Goa, Xavier was busy in South India, but in 1549 Frois could meet him. Together with Xavier and certainly at the College of St. Paul's, Frois must have met Yajiro (Anjiro) from Kagoshima, the Japanese who was to introduce Xavier soon afterwards into Japan. Later, at the time when he is writing his *History of Japan*, Frois would write, as it seems, reminiscing about his encounters with Xavier[12], an image, however that must be checked against the double image of Xavier in the *History of Japan* itself (but there is no space for that here).

Even if it may sound a personal opinion, I want to boldly consider the possibility, that Frois had thought it safer to move farther away from Europe to India after having heard several statements about the future of the missionary situation from Xavier himself.

Frois first remained in Goa as a novice, upto 1550, after which he was sent to Bassein, but from November 1551 onwards he was back again in Goa. About a year later he was given the task of writing one of the annual reports for Europe about events in India. With his letter of 1 December 1572 he began his career as one of the most prominent writers from East India of the 16th century.[13]

Now one might ask whether it was mere coincidence that the three men mentioned at this point met on that day. It would seem so. Yet another answer will lead to historical and biographical backgrounds, throwing light on certain facts that suggest that their meeting was not so totally coincidental.

First I want to go back in history to the year 1497. After the expelling of the Jews from Spain in 1492 the same year in which the converted Jew Christopher Columbus arrived for the first time in America (Guanahani), several thousand Jews fled to Portugal. A royal decree gave them the possibility to stay for some years. However, after another decree from 1497, they were expelled from Portugal as well. The humanist and chronicler Damião de Goes reports extensively and in detail about these events and about their context.[14] He was the official chronicler, but at the same time one has to consider the fact that in his later life he himself was hard pressed by the Inquisition because of his contacts with Protestants and Church-reformers whom he had met on his extensive journeys through Europe. It can be mentioned here only by the way that it was Father Simão Rodrigues, one of the founding members of the Society of Jesus and some ten years earlier a guest at de Goes' house at Padua who played a rather dirty part in the process waged against Goes.[15] These events might help us to understand and stress the fact, that his account about the reign of King Manuel I is a relatively objective report. In that way the description of the measures against the Jews becomes as well a document of the ideological indoctrination and the increasing intolerance of the Christian-European imperialism during that phase of aggressive expansionism. In detail Goes describes how it was decided, while expelling the adults, to take children under the age of fourteen away from their Jewish parents, in order to educate them as Christians. From his description it becomes evident as well, that the Portuguese name *Christão novo*, the Portuguese equivalent for the Spanish *marrano*, for converted Jews took it origin to events of that year. Goes mentions the cruelty accompanying the division of families, and he mentions that the children were taken only from the Jews and not equally from the Muslims expelled at the same time, because one had not to fear acts of revenge from Jews driven into the diaspora, as one had to fear, however, those from the Islamic countries.[16]

At the same time the Jews in Portugal (here the same pattern is present as in 1492 Spain) had still important and indispensable functions. A lively description of this is given by Gaspar Correia in his *Lendas da India*. There he reports how Vasco da Gama received important information from the Jewish astronomer Abrahão Ben Samuel Zacuto, who had come from Spain in 1492, and that the king himself had thanked him for his services.[17]

From 1497 on many of the Portuguese Jews left for India. As not a few Spanish Jews had left for America, these might have hoped to find a better living outside Europe, even in a place where the Portuguese had come, and perhaps they had not imagined at that moment how far the Portuguese would go about exporting their religious intolerance to India as well. As for India one must not forget of course the fact, that there had been a history of Jewish communities in India at least since the time of King Solomon and that there had been an exodus to the South of India after the second destruction of the temple in Jerusalem by the Romans in 70 A.D. After that community had been founded in Cranganore of Travancore in Kerala and since the fourth century there has been a Jewish kingdom in that region.[18]

Several years later on Saturday, 18 April 1506, the Indian fleet for that year departed from Lisbon under the command of Tristão da Cunha. The following day, there began a mass murder of Jews in Lisbon. One finds a detailed and analyzed description of the massacre once again in the account of Goes. In the convent of São Domingos, as Goes reports, there had been seen a certain lightening on a cross, which hurriedly had been interpreted as a wonder. When a converted Jew gave a hint, that it was nothing else than the reflection of a candle nearby, violence started: "On the following three days more than 1,900 Jews had been killed in the most cruel way". Goes does not spare the reader the most barbaric atrocities, and he seeks for explanations of the catastrophe. Here there is only space to hint at the fact that Goes points to the absence of most of the responsible people and personalities of the nobility, who were out of town because of the epidemic. Goes' description is at the same time a document about the eruption and evolution of a mass hysteria, a mass hysteria, however, which must be seen and understood against the background of an anti-Jewish and anti-new-Christian mood which had been stipulated as well by those who should have taken the responsibility, let us say at an earlier stage of the events.[19]

The harsh situation in which the Jews and new-Christians found themselves in Portugal did not calm down. In 1507 King Manuel revoked some of the restrictive measures against the Jews, but at the same time an official institution of the Inquisition was driven farther. When in 1531 there was an earthquake in Santarem there were voices who wanted to interpret this natural catastrophe as a punishment by God against the religiously obsessive Jews. On 14 July 1532 edicts were issued against the exodus of the Jews, and there were speculations already about the Jewish possessions. A papal bull of 23 May 1536 is seen historically as the official institution of the Inquisition in Portugal. On 11 March 1537, at the time of the departure of the first Indian fleet after the institution, Fernão Mendes Pinto left Portugal for Goa. In 1534 when the decision about the Inquisition must have been already very imminent, Garcia da Orta had already left for Goa. Mere coincidences?[20]

Space forces me to make some longer stories very short here. On 16 April 1554 Pinto and Frois departed on the same ship for Japan. Orta remained at Goa. There, in 1563 he published his *Coloquios*, which became at once a kind of bestseller in Europe of the time even if not in the form that he had given his book originally. Only a few years afterwards, in 1568, da Orta had died in Goa where he was subsequently buried. Once again some twelve years later his body was exhumed and burned at the stake in Goa. No word, by the way, is to be found about such events in the books written by Conde de Ficalho about the life and career of Garcia da Orta, a book which nevertheless, because nothing else was written after that, is still to this day, and must be taken as one of the most informative books about the world of Garcia da Orta. How important a figure he really was and still is, becomes somewhat understandable if one has a look at the recently published essay by Boris Catz, where one reads: "The most important physician of this group of four is Garcia da Orta, who has not received sufficient recognition in modern medicine. He is the founder of tropical medicine and the discoverer of the most important species and drugs and one of the first to describe the syndrome of cholera".[21]

Many years later and back in Portugal, Pinto would transform all his adventures into his famous novel *Peregrinação*. This, when he died in 1583, was not as yet published, and according to Pinto's will the manuscript was handed over to the Casa Pia das Penitentes in Lisbon (cf. R. Catz, *The Travel*, p. xxiv). It might be that there had been a deliberate scheme behind Pinto's considerations, and that the publishing of the novel became only possible in 1614 since it came out of a religious institution. The risks which Pinto might have feared become obvious when one has a good look at the following analysis of the motivations for the Portuguese overseas enterprise which is demonstrated exemplarily in the discovery of Japan.

As is known, Pinto claims in his novel to have been, together with two other Portuguese, one of the first Europeans to come to Japan. Back in Ningpo, on the South-China coast, they inform the Portuguese communities of that harbour town: ". . . . about the new land of Japan we had discovered, the great quantity of silver to be found there, and the huge profits that had been from goods from China, which made them so happy they could hardly contain themselves for joy".

"They immediately organized a religious procession to give thanks to our Lord for such a great blessing. . . . once this extremely pious and saintly act of devotion was over, greed soon gained control, filling the hearts of most of the men in town to such a degree that they became a community divided against themselves. . . .[22]

The overruling mixture of greed and avarice as the motives of the Portuguese 'discoverers' cannot be covered here with a religious blanket which is nothing more than an ideology. And this is expressed in terms of still more cynicism by a South-Asian king who comments "smilingly": "Would not it be better for these people, as long as they are exposing themselves to such great hardship, to go to China to get rich rather than to foreign kingdoms to preach nonsense?[23]

When resuming his life and experience in his novel, Pinto had come to the conclusion that the Portuguese in East India stole while pretending to conquer, killed while using force, scandalized while seizing power, stole while coveting and tyrannized while oppressing.[24] Still, in 1554, this same person had entered the Society of Jesus, and he seems to want to make the reader believe this, because he was so moved at the arrival of the body of Xavier on that April day, a decision which Rebecca Catz repeatedly terms "a mysterious conversion".[25]

Pinto took his decision at once, but at the same time he was asked by the merchants and administrators in Goa to travel once more to Japan as a kind of ambassador of the Viceroy, as one expected success because of the many experiences he had already had in Japan. Thus he undertook his journey to Japan officially as ambassador. However, on the way to Japan, he had to stay for several months at Malacca for onward transport. He wrote a long letter to his Jesuit brethren in Portugal as "son and servant of the Society of Jesus" (*Filho e servo da Companhia de Jesus*). This letter is one of the rarest documents of his membership in the Society. It is not possible here to make a detailed analysis of that important letter and I have to restrict myself to a very few sections of it but I dare say, that in its substance and quality it could be one of the major chapters of the *Peregrinação* itself.[26]

Pinto tells us that at the time when Xavier's body was brought to Goa he himself was thinking of returning to Portugal and that at that time he was not vexed in any way by his conscience. "Because when one did not steal the chalice or the monstrance from the Church, or when one was no Moor, one did not have for any reason to fear hell, because it was enough to be a Christian and because the mercy of God was great".[27]

If read against the background of many of the passages in the *Peregrinação* this short paragraph contains a cynical description of the mentality of the Portuguese in India of that time. They robbed the religious treasures of the island of Calempluy and desecrated the place about which the old man Hiticou comments: "There is no doubt," he exclaimed "that I now have before me something I never dreamed I would ever see or hear — inborn wickedness and feigned virtue all in one, that is — to steal and to preach.[28]

In another passage, a former Christian, who had converted to Islam for love of his wife, was drowned alive in the sea by the same Portuguese when he refused to return to Christianity. And everything was done by the Portuguese in the name of what they called their God.[29]

Pinto continues to describe how he had joined Melchior Nunes Barreto on the *fusta* to meet the body of Xavier at Bhatkal; how on seeing the entirely incorruptible body he renewed his former desire to enter the Society "because inside of the Society in my perseverance I had for sure the forgiveness of my sins,[30] and how he and the other Jesuits had then spent the last night before entering Goa at the hermitage of Our Lady of Ribandar.

After a short description of the arrival of the body in Goa Pinto tells us further how he went, again with Nunes Barreto to the nearby island of Chorão and how during the two days there he felt more urged to be a servant of "Deus Nosso Senhor", and how he nearly went insane trying to do so, and "I went through the fields without feeling any other consolation than to utter *Suspires* and cries very many."[31]

Ten days later, on 16 April he leaves with the other Jesuits for

Japan, and there begins the second part of his letter, which contains descriptions of various countries he had already visited. He informs us that he was asked for those descriptions, and at a first look this part is nothing unusual being part of the pious literature sent from the overseas missions to Europe at that time. Interesting, and even exotic descriptions accompany accounts about the progress of the missions, and strength in the belief of the newly converted so-called heathens was meant to give strength to the reader in Europe called to stand firm in his Catholic belief during the hard times of the Reformation.

However, Pinto's descriptions appear a little too exotic. I can mention, unfortunately, only his detailed descriptions of the *white elephant of the king of Burma* whose urine was gathered and with which all the nobles washed their faces, or the over-described riches of the "Venice of the East, Sacai".[32] And in that context the first part of the letter too becomes a bit doubtful in its earnestness. That is to say, it appears as a piece of very good rhetoric and literature. If I am allowed to take this document as a piece of literature, then I would like to interpret the sections cited above in an inverted way too.

A look at the old maps of Goa,. the map which is contained in the *Itinerario* by Linschotten at the end of the 16th century, for example, gives one the impression of a fortress. In the centre with the Inquisition together with the prison (*tronco*), several outer parts of the city and places of execution, it must have appeared as a religious bulwark too with the white facades of the churches appearing majestically among the soft green whispering palm groves. Seen from Ribandar, one thinks it might have been the most sure thing for a man like Pinto to have stayed in Goa as a member of the Society itself, inside which he could hide his real way of thinking best. Then again, the silhouette of Goa as seen from Chorao doubtlessly must have been much more imposing than it appears today, and why, one is tempted to ask, did not Pinto sigh inside of one of the churches he mentions.

On 16 April Frois left Goa together with Pinto. They spent time together on the ship and again for a month at Malacca, where the former was left behind while the latter continued his voyage to Japan.[33] There is no need to imagine that Frois was uninfluenced by Pinto's narrative style. Frois, of course, must have read the very first drafts of Pinto's masterpiece of a letter from Malacca. And imagination does permit that Frois must have listened during many evenings to Pintos' tale during the evenings when everything had become quiet on the ship and after the obligatory evening masses at Malacca.

In his generally more known work on Japan, Frois does not let us see these influences so directly while they are undeniably there. But in his letters from Japan there are some passages which have to be seen as chief witnesses of it.

In a letter of 19 November 1556, Frois will find plenty of time and scope to write about nature he would experience at Malacca, which is not at all a matter of fact in a Jesuit letter of that time from India. He describes the sea turtles and some of their habits, the cow-fish, which resembled physically in some way the body of a woman, and mentions the parrots, which were able to learn any language in the world.[34]

In letters dated 30 November 1557 and 14 November 1559 respectively, both written in Goa, Frois reports about events of the mission in a way in which the attentive reader cannot overlook a hidden sympathy for the so-called pagans forced to turn to Christianity, reminiscent of the intentionally ambiguous way of description in the *Peregrinação*.

In 1557 there is the report of the baptism of the daughter of Meale Khan, who is hidden by the Jesuits in order that she might not run back to her family and who is then baptized against the wish of her family. Even today one feels glad about the almost compassionate way in which Frois describes the pain and the tears of her mother.[35]

In 1559 it is a little boy who was waiting for his mother while she was buying rice in the market. During that time, the boy was made to eat cow's meat in order that he could not return to his family, after which the mother as well, in desperation became Christian. Thus, in a way, not always understandable for human beings, God seems to be leading pagans to his faith, that is, as Frois seems to want us to understand, with the evenly though not always understandable help of Christians themselves.[36]

These experiences which Frois expresses here could be summarized in his own words: "There (in the East Indies) there is much cinnamon and gold and many erring souls, which easily can be converted".[37] This is a sentence which almost reflects directly the words which Vasco da Gama should have said to the Zamorin on arriving at Calicut, that is that he had come to bring home spices and souls,[38] words which are counter-reflected once again in a comment of Mendes Pinto, which he makes one of his characters utter.[39]

I wish to mention here yet another episode in which Frois renders a vivid description of a scene in which the Portuguese are cutting off the heads of about 50 to 60 'infidels' and during which the Jesuit priest present actively defends the church with a gun in hand - an inference which is rather ambiguously defended by Frois.[40] The description of that episode, however, which by the way happened on the island of Chorao, contains too much frenzy, becomes too rhetoric, in a way that Frois' comment, that even the priests have to develop 'perfectness' in various fields, (I tend to read it thus), becomes ironic and gives his description the opposite meaning of what it intended to say. And it is no wonder that it got a reprimand from the Jesuits in Rome.[41]

As one conclusion I would like to mention the personality of Frois. The Visitor Valignano reprimanded Frois for his unwelcome contacts with persons to whom he ought not to speak to much.[42] If one considers this comment together with the rather sharp criticism against the neo-Christians in India made by Valignano elsewhere, one is inclined to consider the possibility, that Frois is blamed here for his contacts to convert some circles in Goa. And this consideration should be entertained as there are indications that Frois came from a family with a Jewish background. (Here I can only hint at this consideration to which I was led by reading *Vinculos do Fogo* by Alberto Dinis, São Paulo, Editora Schwarcz, 1992).

Space enforces me here to be very eclectic, but even so, I want to conclude with a preliminary attempt at an interpretation of the three authors mentioned here, that is of the literary aspect of their work as an answer to the negative side of 16th century European expansion, a dark side which one finds as well in bitter reflections about the colonial and missionary realities of that time which should force, especially the Western reader, to think once more about the depth of the wound inflicted on the other, in what was deliberately considered the colony of the *white man*.

And while doing so I want to concentrate especially on their identity (and here I start from the premise that all three of them had links or contacts with the world of the converted Jews) which allows me to use here the concept of counter-identity, a concept which I borrow at this moment and in the following explanations from Stephen Greenblatt's *Marvelous Possessions*.[43] And I shall start from his analysis of Michel de Montaigne's essay *Des Cannibales*.

Let us remember that Frois was born in 1532 and died in 1597. That makes him more or less a contemporary of Michel de Montaigne (1500-1500). This is, of course, no more than a mere coincidence, however, to begin with, as well as a coincidence that both were born with a relationship to the Marrano world. In Montaigne's case there is no question about the Marrano origin of his moth^r (as for Frois, there has still some proof to be found, but as I have already tried to show elsewhere his Marrano origin should, as well be accepted, and this would allow a very interesting interpretation of his work. I am trying to show this in detail in an essay to be published soon).

In his book, Greenblatt, gives an interpretation of Montaigne's essay *Des Cannibales*. He considers that one of the spiritual sources for Montaigne, who had never been to Brazil or overseas, could have been "the shadowy counter-identity embodied by his mother, born in a Jewish family (of whom Montaigne rarely wrote)".[44]

There is no need to say that long before Greenblatt's book there had been readings of Montaigne's cultural relativism, attempts however which tried to incline Montaigne in an European humanism, and not exactly beginning with his identity which makes him a French philosopher with a two-fold religious background, which again enables him to see more than what is inside the very restricted borders of Christianity. What Montaigne would further develop through his philosophy, the three authors discussed above would learn and experience through their contacts with the world of the other. As Greenblatt wants us to understand, traveling is one of the human being's main source of knowledge and of his capability to understand one's own limitedness and the phenomena of otherness in its richness.[45]

The harsh reality with which da Orta, Pinto and Frois were confronted became a catalyst for them to 'digest' what they had seen in literary forms which they each developed over the then existing limits.

For da Orta dialogue became a medium through which he could tell more than one truth. In that form, which by the way one finds in several cases of Marrano-writers of the 16th century Portugal, he had at the same time the possibility to hide himself and to show, for the understanding, that he had stepped over the limits of the normal religious and moral boundaries.

Pinto chose the *Picaro* novel, a genre which was born as a

Marrano form on the Iberian Peninsula, a genre in which he could take the role of the social underdog but which made it possible for him to say more than would have ever been allowed to any official here.

Frois wrote in 1585 a contrastive cultural description of Europe and Japan in which he would refuse to decide for the rightness or wrongness of either part.

On that night of the 16 March 1554 all the three of them might have felt something oppressive, they could not be sure about their future. At the same time they must have heard the soft beating of the Arabian Sea on the coastal shores and riverbeds of the Mandovi river. They might have thought of lands without place and time, the voices of which would come only half understandable on the waves of the wind. The coasts of western India, as Pasolini states in his fine travelogue of India, would be attacked so many times again by the devastating and marauding Europeans. Still, in the literature of da Orta, Pinto and Frois, one feels very much that freedom of thought as it would express itself with much utopian hope by one of its most important heirs, Fernando Pessoa, who dreamt of a ship leaving for a spiritual India and overcoming on its way the faults of civilization,[46] a European civilization, I want to add, that in its self-imposed self-righteousness had victimized for centuries the people of its colonies and so-called 'heretics' of any kind.

NOTES AND REFERENCES

1. Josef Wicki (ed.), *Documenta Indica* (henceforth *DI*), vol. 1, Rome, 1948; vol. 3, p. 145, doc. 32 (Ferdinandus Mendes Pinto, Nov. S.I. Sociis Lusitanis, Malacca 5 December 1554), pp. 140-155; *Fernão Mendes Pinto e Outros Documentos*, edited by Rebecca Catz, Lisbon, Biblioteca Nacional/Editorial Presenca, 1983, pp. 39-45.
2. *DI*, vol. 3, pp. 144-145; Catz, pp. 40-41; *DI*, vol. 3, doc. 23 (P. M. Nunes Barreto, Vice provincialis Indiae, P. Ignatio de Loyola in Mari inter Goam et Concinum, May 1554), pp. 71-90, especially p. 77 for the crowd in Goa ("mais de simco o seis mil animas").
3. Georg Schurhammer & J. Wicki, *Epistolae S. Francisci Xaverii aliaque eius scripta*, Rome, vols. 1-2, 1994-1995. See vol. 1, pp. 346-347, and especially p. 57 (Ioanni III, Lusitaniae Regi, ex Amboino 16 May 1546), pp. 344-348.
4. Gaspar Correia, *Lendas da India*, edited by Rodrigo José de Lima Felner, Lisbon, Academia Real das Ciencias, vol. 4, 1866, pp. 292-294.

5. *Dicionário de História de Portugal*, edited by Joel Serrão, Lisbon, Iniciativas Editoriaus, 1979, vol. 4, pp. 484-486; A. J. Andrade de Gouveia, *Garcia da Orta e Amato Lusitano na ciência de seu tempo*, Lisbon, Biblioteca Breve, 1985. For the life and career of Garcia da Orta, see Conde de Ficalho, *Garcia da Orta e o Seu Tempo*, Lisbon, Imprensa Nacional/Casa da Moeda, 1983; A. X. Soares, "Garcia D'Orta, A little Known owner of Bombay", reprinted from the Journal of B.B.R.A. Society, vol. 26, mo. 75, 1923, pp. 195-229.
6. Garcia da Orta, *Colóquios dos Simples e Drogas da India (Goa, 1563), reprodução em fac-simile da edição de 1891 dirigida e anotada pelo Conde de Ficalho*, vols. 1-2, Lisbon, Casa da Moeda, 1987. Here vol. 1, p. 19.
7. Fernão Mendes Pinto, *The Travels of Mendes Pinto*, edited and translated by Rebecca Catz, Chicago, 1989, p. 3.
8. Rebecca Catz, *A satira social de Fernão Mendes Pinto*, 1978, pp. 49-50.
9. J. Wicki, *Luis Frois, História de Japam*, vols. 1-5, Lisbon, Biblioteca Nacional, 1976-1984, vol. 1, Appendix 10, pp. 406-407.
10. Frois, *História*, vol. 1, pp. 3*, 7.
11. *DI*, vol. 1, p. 394, doc. 56.
12. Luis Frois, 25, X, 1585.
13. *DI*, vol. 2, doc. 104.
14. Damião de Goes, *Cronica do Felicissimo Rei D. Manuel (1566)*, vol. 1, pp. 38ff.
15. pp. 122ff and 245ff.
16. D. de Goes, *Cronica*, vol. 1, pp. 41-43.
17. G. Correia, *Lendas da India*, vol. 1, pp. 16, 23.
18. P. K. Peethambaran, *Life and Culture of the Jews in Cochin.*
19. D. de Goes, *Cronica*, vol. 1, pp. 253ff.
20. Alexandro Herculano, *História e estabelecimento da Inquisição em Portugal*, Lisbon, 1897, vol 1.
21. Boris Catz, "Os Medicos Judeus-Portugueses" in *Os Judeus Portugueses entre os descobrimentos e a Diaspora*, Lisbon, Fundação Gulbenkian, 1994, pp. 105-106. Here cited after the English translation, *ibid.*, pp. 262-264.
22. *The Travels of Mendes Pinto*, p. 286.
23. *Ibid.*, p. 506.
24. *Ibid.*, p. 292
25. R. Catz, ed., *Cartas*, p. 13; *A Satira*, p. 52.
26. no. 1
27. *DI*, vol. 1, p. 143; Catz, *Cartas*, p. 40.
28. *The Travels of Mendes Pinto*, p. 149.
29. *Ibid.*, p. 5.
30. *DI*, vol. 1, p. 145, no. 1; Catz, *Cartas*, p. 41.
31. *Ibid.*, pp. 41, 145-146.
32. *Ibid.*, pp. 45, 153-154.
33. *DI*, vol. 3, p. 314.
34. *DI*, vol. 3, doc. 94. p. 545.

35. *DI*, vol. 3, doc 113, pp. 743-744.
36. *DI*, vol. 4, doc. 40, pp. 345-346.
37. *DI*, vol. 3, pp. 559-560. See no. 34.
38. Luis de Camões, *Os Lusiadas*, Canto 7, 31.
39. cf. no. 28.
40. *DI*, vol. 3, p. 710
41. *DI*, vol. 4, doc. 21, p. 132.
42. *DI*. vol. 13, p. 671.
43. Stephen Greenblatt, *Marvellous Possessions: The Wonder of the New World*, Chicago, 1991, p. 150.
44. *Ibid.*
45. *Ibid.*, pp. 201-202.
46. Fernando Pessoa, "This is the First Ship bound for the Spiritual Indies" in *Obra em Prosa de Fernando Pessoa*, edited by António Quadros, Lisbon, 1980, pp. 77-78.

SEVENTEEN

FROM PEREGRINATION TO PILGRIMAGE
Tabucchi's Notturno Indiano[1]

THOMAS STRATER

In 1938 the English writer Somerset Maugham visited Goa. In his *Notebook* he drew a sketch of *tristes tropiques* in Portuguese India. Four hundred years ago Goa was intended to be the starting point for christianization of the Far East. Maugham's short description makes the failure of that enterprise evident:

> You drive through coconut groves among which you see here and there ruins of houses. On the lagoon sail fishing boats, their lateen sails shining white in the brilliant sun. The churches are large and white, their facades decorated with honeycoloured stone pilasters. Inside they are large, bare, spacious, with pulpits in Portuguese baroque carved with the utmost elaboration and altar pieces in the same style. In one at a side altar, a priest, a native was saying mass with a darkfaced acolyte to serve him. There was no one to worship. In the Franciscan church you are shown a wooden Christ on a crucifix and the guide tells you that six months before destruction of the city it wept tears. In the cathedral they were holding a service, the organ was playing and in the organ loft there was a small choir of natives singing with a harshness in which somehow the Catholic chants acquired a mysteriously heathen Indian character. It was strangely impressive to see that these great empty churches in that deserted place and to know that day by day with not a soul to listen the priest said mass in them.[2]

Nearly half a century after Maugham the Italian writer António Tabucchi, born in 1943 in Pisa, writes again about Goa. The genre of this work seems at first sight like Maugham's book to be a travel diary, yet now in a more fictional form of somewhat a novel with the title *Notturno Indiano* (1984). Tabucchi taught as a professor of Portuguese language and literature at the University of Genoa and was the director of the Italian (Culture) Institute in Lisbon. He also translated and edited the works of two of the 20th century classic poets, the Portuguese Fernando Pessoa and the Brazilian Carlos Drummond de Andrade. Therefore, one cannot be surprised at Tabucchi's close relationship to the lusophonic world and the incorporation in his narrative of characters like Pessoa or the socialist poet Antero de Quental[3], one of the most important figures of the so-called "generation of 1870" in Portugal, or as they called themselves "the defeated by life" (*vencidos da vida*). It was just a matter of time that Tabucchi would turn his interest to the great time of the Portuguese navigations, the age of the discoveries and conquests sailing around the Cape of Good Hope to India, to 'Golden Goa'. Tabucchi's book, a kind of exotic novel in the tradition of Sterne's *Sentimental Journey*, is an attempt to explore what the *Estado da India*, the ex-colonies or 'overseas provinces' — as they were euphemistically called till the formal incorporation into the Indian Union in 1961 - could mean to Europe at the end of the 20th century. The quest for Christians and spices as the much-quoted answer of a member of da Gama's crew, when he was asked, what had brought the Portuguese to India is substituted by a spiritual-metaphysical discovery of the Asian sub-continent.

To understand what *Notturno Indiano* is about, besides its metaliterary and aesthetic dimensions, its themes like the quest for identity, mirrors and mirages[4], and what kind of role Goa, the real and the imagination of it is playing in that little novel of about hundred pages, one has to have a look on its contents and basic structure. Tabucchi's *Notturno Indiano* is divided into three parts: the first consists of four, the third of five chapters, the central second part of three. The first one takes place in Mumbai; the second at Chennai and at a bus stop enroute to Mangalore and the last part in and around Goa. What is conveyed to the reader and what he gets to know durıng this travel through India is typical for a touristic point of view: hotel rooms, receptions and lounges, mainly high class, but also some functioning as brothels, hospitals, railway and bus stations. The author points out the importance of these places by giving a precise index of them in the beginning:

> Khajuraho hotel, Suklaji Street, Bombay; Breach Candy Hospital, Bhulabai Desai Road, Bombay; Taj Mahal Inter-Continental Hotel, Gateway of India, Bombay; Railway's retiring rooms, Victoria station, Central station, Bombay; Coromandel Hotel, 5 Nungambakkam Road, Madras; Theosophical Society, 12 Adyar Road, Adyar, Madras; Bus stop between Madras and Mangalore, exact place unknown; Archbishopric and College of St. Bonaventura, Goa; Zuari Hotel, Swatantrya Path, without number, Vasco da Gama, Goa; Beach of Calangute, 20 km. from Panaji, Goa; Mandovi Hotel, 28 Bandodkar Marg, Panaji, Goa and Oberoi Hotel, Bogmalo beach, Goa.[5]

Each of these places corresponds to a chapter. The reader gets acquainted with India through conversations with prostitutes, physicians, nomadic prophets, philosophers, photographers, hippies, thieves, waiters, and even the ghostly apparition of the former Portuguese Vice-king of India, Afonso de Albuquerque (1509-1515), enters the scene in an old library in Goa.[6] In the twelve chapters or episodes the narrator describes his travel through India searching for an old friend called Xavier Janata Pinto. That friend has vanished, what remains is people, who knew him, like for instance the prostitute in the first episode or a short letter given to him at the Theosophical Society in Chennai: "Dear master and friend, my circumstances don't allow me to get on with my walks at the banks of the river Adyar. I am a night bird now and therefore I prefer to believe that it was my destiny's desire. Keep me in good remembrance, as you have got to learn me once. Yours X. The date was Calangute, Goa, 23rd of September".[7] This sixth chapter together with the following one are the centre of the book and the key to an interpretation. The reader already knows that the narrator's nickname in former times was Roux, the short form for the Portuguese word *rouxinol*, the nightingale, a night bird like the person he is searching for.[8] The day is the 23rd of September, the equinox. Day and night are equal and so are the persons' identities. Narrator and Xavier are the same. There is an allusion to that date in chapter ten, when the narrator is talking to the hippies. They want to have a party because of the equinox, but it is already December,

Christmas time, the Holy Night.

As the title indicates, *Notturno Indiano* is a night piece — a piece of literature between dust and dawn, and so all the chapters take place at night. The persons who appear are merely shadows from another world, yet described in a clear language. *Notturno Indiano* in the tradition of the romantic nocturne as in paintings, music or in literature deals with the mixture of realism and imagination. Tabucchi adverts in an introductory note: "This book, beyond the fact that it comes from an insomnia is a voyage".[9] The voyage or a peregrination is in fact a pilgrimage. As the traveler confesses he wants to see the place where St. Thomas, the apostle, is supposed to have suffered a martyr's death (Meliapur, later renamed São Thomé, today a district of Chennai). The Portuguese built a church in this place. "I don't know what is left. And so I must go to Goa, I have to look for an old library, therefore I came to India". "Is it a pilgrimage?", he asked. I denied. Then I said, "may be, but not in the religious meaning of the word. It's more a private pilgrimage, [. . .], I was just looking for clues".[10] All over the text there are many other hints to be found justifying the interpretation of *Notturno Indiano* as the variations on the theme of pilgrimage. Also the man who the traveler is searching shows behind his name the idea of pilgrimage. His name mentioned above is Xavier Janata Pinto. One cannot use the name of Xavier in relation to India and Goa without remembering the figure of Francis Xavier (1506-1552), the first Jesuit missionary in Asia in 1542. M. N. Pearson writes about this time:

> In the watershed year, 1540, in order to encourage conversions all temples in Goa were destroyed. Later this was done in Bardes, in 1573, and in Salcete in 1584-7. Their no doubt distraught brahmin guardians often were able to save the holy images and install them just outside Portuguese territory; hence the several great temples in the Ponda area, acquired by the Portuguese only in the more tolerant eighteenth century. Other discrimination was legion: orphans were kidnapped and converted, rice Christianity flourished, Hindus were discriminated against by the government in a multitude of ways. In 1541 lands which had endowed the temples were turned over to the local priests and the orders. Most Hindu ceremonies were forbidden, including marriage and cremation. These now

had to be done in secret, or outside Portuguese territory. In 1623 a Portuguese complained that there were still more than 150,000 Hindus living under Portuguese protection in Goa. They should, he said, be given the choice of converting, paying a poll tax, or leaving Goa.[11]

As it is well known, the aim was to convert to Christianity. That is why Xavier traveled very widely and succeeded in converting tens of thousands of Hindus. When Xavier arrived at Goa, he was shocked at the prevalent moral laxity and the practices of the so-called Thomas Christians. This community numbered between 80,000 and 200,000 in the 16th century. It was believed that their forebears had been converted by St. Thomas himself.[12] Because their religion was tinged by Hindu and Nestorian influences it was considered sloppy, or close to heretical. But although Xavier recommended to the king that the Inquisition should be established in Goa, it was only in 1560, eight years after Xavier's death that it was introduced. The middle Indian name Janata links the Spanish-Portuguese Christian name Xavier with the typical Portuguese surname Pinto. But in Portuguese literature, especially in the so-called *literatura das viagens ultramarinas* (literature of overseas travels), the name Pinto indicates only one person, Fernão Mendes Pinto. It is not by chance that Tabucchi published his *Notturno Indiano* in 1984, just one year after the celebrations of the 400th anniversary of the death of the author of the *Peregrinação*,[13] (first published in 1614, 31 years after his death), the satiric counterpart to the heroic *Os Lusiadas* by Luis de Camões. Fernão Mendes Pinto had met the Jesuit missionary during one of his last voyages to Japan. Deeply impressed by the strong personality of St. Francis Xavier he decided to enter the Society of Jesus and to promote a mission to Japan in which he participated. It is supposed that the original *Peregrinação* suffered various cuts, because there is no mention of Pinto's participation in the Society. Nevertheless, the last chapters (113-114) of the *Peregrinação* are dedicated to the glorification and the miracles (or better what should be regarded as glory and miracles) of St. Francis Xavier, "that well adventured Father Master Francis Xavier, light of his time and all the Orient, whose virtue and holiness made him famous all over the world".[14] Rebecca Catz defends the thesis of Pinto's book as "a satire and anti-crusade", demasking and condemning the Christianization of

Asia. "By resorting to hyperbole, distortion and suppression, Mendes Pinto constructs in fact a controversial, heroic-comical portrait of St. Francis Xavier".[15] Especially in the theological disputations between St. Francis Xavier and the Japanese priests, he deconstructs the idealized portrait of the missionary. The irony lies in the difficulty for a Jesuit saint who voted for poverty to convert the Japanese people who were convinced that God only loves the rich and it often seems that He really does? Poverty looked upon as a divine punishment is one of the fundamental themes of the *Peregrinação*. Full of irony is the episode about the Japanese Bonzos' complaint that Francis Xavier uses in his sermons ugly names (to the Japanese), when he says *Deus* (God) or prays in his litany to the saints: "*Sancte Petre ora pro nobis, Sancte Paule. . .*". By order of the king Francis Xavier had to suppress the word *sancte* and to substitute it by *beate*. But what about the word *Deus* which in Japanese sounds similar to *diusa*, the word for "lie". The reader has to assume blasphemically that Xavier had to suppress the mention of God.

Tabucchi's *Notturno Indiano* is a book on religion, not at least a spiritual text. Logically there is no longer any interest in the conquest of wealth or the mission for converting people who have already created a highly developed religion like Hinduism. Now we have a new type of missionary, not one who is convinced to teach the right way in believing in the one and only Christian God. The narrator of *Notturno Indiano* is a character, a 'person' (*pessoa* in Portuguese) in the Latin sense of the word: an actor's mask. He is hiding himself behind the disguise of different names like Roux(inol), nightingale, Xavier, Janata, Pinto and even the author's name Tabucchi.[16] Through his conversations with the different persons he meets on his way to Goa he learns about Indian philosophy and thinking: the love story between Vimala, the prostitute, and Xavier; the visit to the hospital and the tragicomic talk with Ganesh, a cardiologist in a land where death is always present but nobody dies of heart attack: "Do you believe in anything?', I asked. 'No', he said, "I am an atheist. Atheist is the worst cure here in India".[17] The dialogue with the death bound Jain in the retiring rooms of a railway station goes even further: "It seems you are a Catholic?", my travel companion said, 'All Europeans are in a sense Catholics', I said, 'or at least Christians, it's practically the same."[18] A climax is reached in the above mentioned chapter 6 at the Theosophical Society in

Chennai. In the impassive distinguished conversation with one of its members one literary allusion follows the other. It begins with a quotation from Victor Hugo's *Les travailleurs de la mer*, goes on with authors who have written about India like Friedrich von Schlegel, Swedenborg, Hermann Hesse, Annie Besant and culminates in the evocation of Fernando Pessoa: "Pessoa believed in Gnosticism", I said. "He was a Rosicrucian. He has written a series of esoteric poems with the title *Steps of the Cross*".

Pessoa is one of Tabucchi's preferred authors he always returns to. Pessoa's game with his heteronyms Alvaro de Campos, Alberto Caeiro and Ricardo Reis had a strong influence on Tabucchi's theoretical background and his fictions. Also the person whose fictitious name is Xavier Janata Pinto is an *alter ego*, a heteronym of Tabucchi: a man whose profession is to write short stories.[19] At the same time the narrator is searching for this man and hiding behind his name. Fitting to the season, December, when *Notturno Indiano* is playing, the member of the Theosophical Society quotes Pessoa's poem *Natal* (Christmas) saying goodbye to the narrator:

> "Blind science ploughs the vane soil
> The mad faith lives in the dream of its cult
> A new god is only a word
> Do not believe and do not search: everything lies in darkness."[20]

In this poetical meditation and advice of four lines lies the quintessence of *Notturno Indiano*. At the end of the novel the narrator has found his friend Xavier. Or better, in other words: Xavier has found the person (his own mask) he is writing about. Narrator and narrated person have changed their roles and merged into one in that highly intellectual literary puzzle. The narrator tells the story of *Notturno Indiano* but now from Xavier's point of view. *Roux* is nightingale now. He is dining with Christine (!), a photographer on the terrace of the Oberoi Hotel in Goa. For her book about South Africa she chose the French title *Mefiez-vouz de morceaux choisis* (Don't trust in selected parts). One of her photos shows a young Negro with his arms raised like a sprinter in the finish. But the impression eludes. It is the second in which he is hit by a bullet, the moment of his death. Don't trust in what you see!

That's what the reader of the novel might do as well. The German translation of *Notturno Indiano* for instance offers a kind of supplement which is not included in the original edition: an exchange of two letters each between the member of the Theosophical Society at Chennai and Tabucchi in Italy now after the book was published. What at the first sight seems to be a self-interpretation by the author, an 'authentic' discussion between both a fictitious person of the novel, the reader of it and the authentic author called Tabucchi is in fact also a fiction. This narrative with Epimenides' paradox as the title "The following phrase is false. The preceding phrase is true"[21] is a part of one of Tabucchi's books.[22] Here the theosophist signs his name — Xavier Janata Monroy. Is he the wanted man? There are some hints that forbid such an interpretation. Especially when he refers to their discussion about the words 'practically' and 'actually'. In *Notturno Indiano* it is the Jain in chapter 4 who paid attention to that linguistic phenomenon and not the theosophist. It seems as the author wants to give us the advice: Don't trust in what you read!

Notturno Indiano is a cat-and-mouse game, a do-it-yourself kit, a riddle. When the reader assembles all the different parts and fits them together, he gets an imaginative novel on several levels. António Tabucchi is an Italian author who adopted and incorporated voluntarily a new culture in his literary work, the Lusitanian world. To come to a deeper understanding of the literary background of his fictions one has to follow Tabucchi's spiritual peregrination through the ages of Portuguese history and so he will discover India, the 'golden Goa' again.

NOTES AND REFERENCES

1. I wish to thank Victor Coelho, Hanna Kessler, Maria do Céu Mascarenhas, Reinhard Monssen, P. P. Shirodkar, Teotónio de Souza and Cristina Braga Ramalho for their critical comments and translation suggestions.
2. W. Somerset Maugham, *A writer's notebook*, Harmondsworth, Middlesex, Penguin, 1949/1987, pp. 268-269.
3. The original title of Tabucchi's narrative concerned with Portuguese literature are *Antero de Quental: Uma vita*; "*L'amore di don Pedro*; *Gli archivi di Macau*; *Passato composto: Tre lettere (La donna de Porto Pim.*, Palermo, 1983); *Sostiene Pereira* (Milano, 1994); *Requiem: Uma alucinação* (Lisbon, 1991) was originally written in Portuguese. *Un*

baule pieno di gente: Scritti su Fernando Pessoa, Milano, 1990, is a collection of essays on Fernando Pessoa.

4. Gunde Kurtz has analyzed such topics in her book, *Die Literatur im Spiegel ihrer selbst: I. Calvino, A. Tabucchi -- Zwei Beispiele* (The literature in the mirror of itself: I, Calvino, A. Tabucchi — two examples), Tubingen, 1992. Nevertheless the whole cultural-historical Indian-Portuguese background does not play any role in her interpretation.
5. *Notturno Indiano*, 1994, p. 11. Translations from the Italian, Portuguese and German are the author's.
6. This happens in the third part, chapter 8. The guardian of the library, described as an old man (*vecchietto*, 73) is called Teotónio. One of the participants of the symposium (at Cologne) was Teotónio de Souza, a librarian but far from being called an old man. As he also referred to Tabucchi's *Notturno Indiano* in his contribution, I was interested in his opinion on the book. He told me that he liked it very much, and that he got the impression that Tabucchi came to a deeper understanding of India. When I asked him if he had ever met Tabucchi, he smiled and moved his head like the guardian ("... mi fece grandi sorrisi dondolando la testa. . .", 73). "I met him, without knowing who he was", Teotónio told me. "I have the honour to appear in Tabucchi's novel. But as you can see, he has changed many things", the real Teotónio confessed with his characteristic humility. I like to reveal this fact here less for its anecdotic quality but for giving me the chance to show how Tabucchi bases his fictions on real facts and persons.
7. *Notturno Indiano*, 1984, p. 59.
8. "Between you and me I was Roux, and it was fine with me" (the initial letters of "*rouxinol*" (Port. nightingale), Tabucchi 1984, p. 36.
9. *Notturno Indiano*, 1984, p. 9.
10. *Ibid.*, pp. 40, 41.
11. Michael N. Pearson, *The Cambridge History of India*, I.1: The Portuguese In India. Cambridge, Cambridge Univ. Press, 1987, 117sq.
12. I wish to thank P. Shirodkar for his valuable remark, that there were Thomas Christians to be found only in the more southern regions of India and not in Goa at that time.
13. The original Portuguese title *Peregrinaçam de Fernam Mendez Pinto* was translated for the first English edition as *The voyages and adventures of Fernand Mendez Pinto* (London, 1653). There are two implications of the Portuguese word *peregrinação* in English: 'peregrination', the archaic and jocular word for travel or journey, especially extensively or at leisure and second 'pilgrimage', a journey to a sacred place for religious reasons (cf. *The Concise Oxford Dictionary*, 9th ed. Oxford, 1995). Both words have the same origin in the Latin word for stranger *peregrinus*.
14. António José Saraiva (ed.), *Peregrinação e outras obras*, 1961, vol. 2, ch. 113, p. 246.
15. Rebecca Catz, *Fernão Mendes Pinto: Sátira e anti-cruzada na*

"Peregrinação", Lisbon, Instituto de Cultura e Lingua Portuguesa, 1981, pp. 94-95.

16. Cf. the fictitious exchange of letters between a reader of *Notturno Indiano*, the theosophist from Chennai called Xavier Janata Monroy and the author A. T. of *La frase che seque é falsa. La frase che precede é vera. I volatili del beato Angelico*, Palermo, 1986.
17. *Notturno Indiano*, 1984, p. 31.
18. *Ibid.*, p. 41.
19. *Notturno Indiano*, "cf. *Scriveva dei racconti*", p. 28.
20. Fernando Pessoa, *Obra poetica*, Rio de Janeiro, Nova Aguilar, 1987, p. 73.
21. "La frase che segue é falsa. La frase che precede é vera". *I volatili del beato Angelico*, Palermo, 1986.
22. *I volatili del beato Angelico*, It may be that this book and also *I treni che vanno a Madras* (*Piccoli equivoci senza importanza*, 1985) share with *Notturno Indiano* the same time of their creation.

EIGHTEEN

GOA IN THE NOVEL "O SIGNO DA IRA" BY ORLANDO DA COSTA*

HELMUT SIEPMANN

A scene of realistic tenor in literature is relatively recent. It exists since the age of Romanticism and follows the scene stylized and typically idealized in literature since the Middle Ages till the 17th century.

It is clear that there had already been descriptions of scenes mainly of distant and unknown locations in travel literature and in texts of epic and encyclopedic character, but the preoccupation of understanding what the human being is as a social entity in one's milieu has its origin in romantic and realistic literatures of the 20th century.

The literary genres most appropriate to convey this preoccupation are the novel and short story. *As Viagens na minha terra* by Almeida Garrett, the *Novelas do Minho* of Camilo Castelo Branco, *A Morgadinha dos Canaviais* of Júlio Dinis and *A Cidade e as Serras* of Eça de Queiros are among the first efforts of this style of literature in Portugal. Neo-realistic literature, on the other hand, interprets the human conduct as an expression of conditioning of the economic order and explains the misery, the satisfaction, but also the hopes of the desperate in their conditions of work in agrarian settings in various parts of Portugal.

The novel *O Signo da Ira* of Orlando da Costa issues from a neo-realistic position in its conceptual orientation, although it has drawn much from the ideological positions of its predecessors. It is not an atemporal novel[1] in the sense of a creation without historicity or of a philosophical construction. Its reference cover is a time historically defined, in which Japanese troops stationed in South

* Translated from the Portuguese by Charles J. Borges.

East Asia and in Bengal portray the defense of Japanese interests during the Second World War, and of a region spatially demarcated: a village and a small city of Goa, where the presence of Portuguese troops, like a reaction to changes in the centre of world political forces, excites a certain disquiet within the local population. The scene, the time and the climatic conditions, these are what structure the novel.

The time of action is reduced to about six months. It begins with the heavy rains of the monsoon of November, covers the time of irrigating the fields, the planting of rice, the time of ripening and growing, the harvest and the three months of waiting under the suffocating sun, in which the situation of feeding becomes dramatic, and ends with the first showers of July.

The curve of the epic tension follows an impulse of nature, from one rainy season to another. It encompasses a tragic happening, that unfolds in a dusty colonial village close to the small city and has as a backdrop a semi-feudal traditionalism, that leads to serious conflicts, finishing, however, with a resurgence of new life, to give place to an included hope.

In the midst of this happening comes an indefinite idea of what is unknown and strange and this excites fears and provokes unforeseen reactions. This idea concretizes itself in divisions of caste, marginalizations and xenophobia. The dependency of the inhabitants of the village, the *kurumbins*, on the brahmin landowners, is on one hand accepted by the villagers, on the other is looked with distrust. The village *comunidade* feels within itself, for example, threatened when one of its members has to go to serve directly in the house of the lord, although this could mean the beginning of a good economic base and of a better future. The fear lives in the fact of the day labourers who like free workers, are used to working hard in the field and returning to their village *comunidade* after work, now having to give up a life of liberty from the moment in which they enter the house of the lord. The work here implies, for the female workers, the loss of physical innocence: sexual abuse by the master and humiliations associated with the type of work and work conditions. And although they do not seem to be only objections of a moral character that exist in relation to the manner of living in the master's house, yet what is criticized, is the mixture of castes. For the menial works in the house of a stranger, there is the inferior caste of the sudras.

However, in the village community there is a second aversion. It is true that this is not felt by all the villagers in the same manner but at the time of crisis, it rears itself for the older people, for Rumão, the tavern keeper, is an outsider. It is true that he lives with the villagers ever since his father took charge of the tavern, but it is also true that he has humiliated them on countless occasions with his utopian plans of living in distant places. He is only partially accepted by the older people, more so since he is calculative and keeps contacts with the Portuguese soldiers, who for their part, appear like a superior threat that enters the more intimate circles of life.

The character of Rumão with his tavern turns the central point of the story that in its spatial-temporal concentration is structured like a novel. His tavern is the social centre of the village. It is at the moment when he finally is taken into quarantine, being suspected of having leprosy, that his existence changes fatally for himself and for the others around him. He had paid a night visit to Coincão, daughter of Pedrú, before she had to go to serve in the house of the lord, without violating her, as the lord himself confirms. Father Antú, to whom Rumão, arrested by the soldiers, has confessed his relations with Coincão, to impede a possible epidemic from spreading, breaks the seal of confession. Antú warns the lord, who full of fear and anger, inspects the body of Coincão, who in an act of solidarity had made a part of the crop she has usurped, reach the hands of the hungry village, and she thinks that her robbery has been discovered and she hangs herself. Pedrú with uncontrollable fury follows those responsible for the death of his daughter. As a frequent visitor of the tavern, he knows the illicit business of petrol between Rumão and the soldiers. He accuses Rumão, who is in the quarantine of the garrison, of being the author of the robbery and the banned dealings. A soldier implicated in the incident of the petrol forces Rumão to destroy at night the stored petrol in the bar, with the object of removing the evidence. He shoots the hesitant Rumão and sets fire to the tavern. With the destruction of the tavern and the death of the owner of the same, the subsequent poverty of the village is interconnected. In the absence of Rumão the bar will serve as a barn for the rice stolen by Coincão. This rice, for which the villagers have worked in vain at the time of harvest and for which Coincão had sacrificed a life, also is burnt.

The novel ends, taking up an incident at the beginning, in a circular movement. Coincão had left the village to work in the house of the lord, to substitute another village-girl. The one who was supposed to go to work in the house was her friend Natél. For her, however, the promise of marriage with a young man of the village was too important that she opposed the invitation of the lord. Some time later, however, she felt the pang of passion and mute admiration for a soldier of clear eyes, whose mute language she could not understand. When this soldier is unjustly accused of robbery and of the fire, as a result of all the hatred for foreigners in the village, it is Natél who stops one more injustice, explaining that the visits of the soldier to the village were due to the love that he had for her. With this in mind, raising herself from the conspiracy of hatred and of anger, she goes into self-exile. In the end, she abandons the village with a heavy heart, climbing the slope that separates the manor house and the foreign soldiers of the village, so that she may dedicate herself to the work that originally she was destined in the house of the lord. She sacrifices herself, abandons the circle of hatred, precinding consciously a familiar happiness that she never questioned and breaks thus with the knowledge of caste that started the tragedy of the story.

Together with rain that promises new fertility, the birth of a child that announces new life, the path of Natél to an unknown future is more than a dream of hope. Her painful path perhaps may permit the breaking with the "fate of anger".

My theme is Goa in the novel *O Signo da Ira*. Little is so far spoken about Goa. For this reason, let us speak in the second part of the reality of the scene evoked in the novel. It is clear that in fiction one cannot probe the ethno-geographical or socio-historical setting. Rather it is a realistic scene that becomes the object of reflection and fictional personages are perceived as significant and to the narrator appear necessary for the characterization of the motives and of the plot. And it is for this reason that one speaks of climbing the mountain at the end of the novel. This climbing shows itself in a realistic way: from the cashew grove, through the dry grass to the stones and cliffs without vegetation where the dry roots do not show any difference between living nature and the dead. However, the climb shows itself necessary in this part of the novel because the protagonist Natél, by virtue of an unbounded effort frees herself of her ties to family, village and caste without knowing if she will free herself of the fire and hatred that had illuminated the dawn of her life,[2] "a new sentiment, born in that instant, a hatred, a revolt, the spirit disturbed her, implanting itself in her afflicted heart".[3] The climb to the mountain is the path that the author uses to turn uneasy the strong effort that Natél has to put in get herself away from her previous life.

We come across the ambit of the monsoon winds, that come in October from the Northeast, and carry fertile showers for the regions of the south east India. As the cashew trees, the mango trees and the coconut trees, so also the large sections of the irrigated lands use it for the sowing of rice, and the herd of buffaloes who manage to outlive the dry season. With the end of the rains comes the sowing of the rice (and as we know the time of romance) and with the end of the monsoon, the second sowing of the year. The water which accumulates itself in the canals is left in the sluices of the earth that is going to receive the seeds of rice. Near the river, every eight years a part of the terrain is not cultivated so that it is able to recuperate.

Between the sowing and the harvest, the land dries up, the plants germinate in the slush. After the harvest, the earth rests for three months. The harvest succeeds under conditions of hard work and a system of strict vigilance. The following treatment of the rice takes place in the house of the owner of the lands.

At Easter (in spring) the heat continues for three months, the heat dries the earth, gives the extremities of the coconut trees a yellow colour and lets the earth become cracked. The burning earth[4] and the dry plants turn people and animals aggressive. In the viewpoint of the narrator who feels moved by the disgrace of the people, the ground is burning and in agony.[5] Under the form of renovation that the novel evokes in the end (this land, flat, red and brown will become covered by a green mantle),[6] there is an insinuation of the hope to an end of anger among men following the example of nature.

The villagers live in poor houses of mud walls covered by coconut palms and tiles between the bamboo grove and the grass. The houses are dark, the persons sleep flat on the ground, and sit on their haunches. Besides their work in the cultivation of rice, they make articles of bamboo. The women look after the garden, the fruits and vegetables (ladyfingers, brinjals, and peas) and are sold in the city close by. They travel in groups to the city with bamboo baskets on their heads. For these orchards they use the natural manure which the buffaloes leave on the way and they carry it in bamboo baskets home. The water is removed from the well and carried on the heads to their homes. For a cheaper removal of the tall coconuts there are pluckers. In the dry season, the men depend on other works like, for example, sawing wood, covering the roofs and digging the wells, work for which they are needed off and on.

The tavern in the settlement is the centre of communication for the men. In it they drink aguardente of cashew or of coconut. One cooks on stones in clay pots. Dry fish and rice, dried kokum, pieces of dried coconut kernel and cashew are the more important foods. The rice is cooked, one drinks the water of the rice and rice is eaten at meals. The husks of the coconut are used as fuel. One drinks buffalo milk, water through the neck of the copper pot, and aguardente from the bottle. For the feasts, one makes rice with fish curry on banana leaves, and for the children there is roasted grams and a sweet of jaggery and coconut.

The master who lives in a manor house a good distance away from the village is intimately connected with the settlement. He exercises an unchallenged power. No one dares to go contrary to his wishes. He negotiates with the farmers through the senior of the village. All resent his right of abusing his servant-girls, but no one challenges him for fear of being expelled from the lands. The master of the lands considers this right a necessity to impose obedience. During religious feasts he exercises the function of paying the expenses. In the procession he walks in the front position and organizes the fireworks; at the reception in the manor house he gets together his dependent workers who owe him homage, as inferior castes owe their superiors. The master gets together his family and the subordinates in the manner of a grandseigneur in the chapel for prayer. The relations between the master and the servants are only placed in question the moment when the workers are deceived in their share of the rice harvest. The theft of Coincão is then, a type of reconquest of the rights of the farmers.

It is in this static order existing for centuries that the results of the world political situation in 1942 arise. Besides the poor harvests, there were rumours of war, and signs of the Japanese presence in Bengal, from where the annual supplies of rice were guaranteed the population in the dry season. Many fled through the frontier close by, others settled for dealing in the black market so that the military contingents in the distant mission who had to guarantee silence and order, at the same time provoked and spread ill-will and anger. The unlimited power of the brahmin owners was sensibly put down. They left the rice to rot in the fields so that only the fruits and the pasture remained. Hunger and desperation were the result, and an economic decay of the latifundary whose properties were often mortgaged. The Portuguese troops lived in the barracks besides the mountain, their jeeps used the rural roads to the city. Their behaviour, bold and arrogant, increased the suspicions of the inhabitants who did not understand their language. They are whites, like the Christian saints. But contrary to approaching the saints, the people approached the soldiers with anger and fury when they showed their presence through their firings and detonations. But one tended to copy their style of life. Their goggles would sell in the Christmas fair. In spite of the mutual distance, conflicts occurred between the soldiers and the farmers. The ethnic barrier between the white soldiers and the locals was considered invincible. In the village one feared unhealthy contacts between the soldiers and the daughters in the same way as the economic interests of the tavern keeper who inspite of the prohibition of the officials, wanted to attract the soldiers more and more to the tavern.

The presence of the soldiers in the settlement coincides with the economic decadence, the failure of the rice harvest and the desperation of the inhabitants during the months that will end the rice harvest in the winter. The fault of the disappearance of a part of the rice harvest and the consequent loss that the master pins on the workers, the fact of the owners being forced to mortgage their goods and give the profits to foreign merchants, the lack of sugar and kerosene, this is, all the result of the war, and appear to be the responsibility of the soldiers, who have food, money and power. With hunger, incrimination, suspicions, hatred, a protest and fury begin to take shape. They turn themselves against all that is alien especially against the soldiers, but also against their unjust master who gives them a share of alms instead of their due. The group of beggars that walk through the city once a week to collect their weekly charity each time is bigger. In exchange of a promise of prayer, the masters give material help to the humble of the land. But the aggravation of the misery also affects this option, the charity of rice is already not guaranteed.

In this situation of collective tension tragic happenings come together that end in death, arson and flight: one soldier notices with benevolence for some time a girl who is promised to a farmer; the tavern-owner, an outsider and of another caste, seeks sex with another girl who then enters the service of the latifundary and is deflowered.

Parallel crimes take place, believed to be just restitution, like the theft of rice in the manor house and the shady business of the tavern owner that harms five drunk soldiers, and takes part in the theft of the petrol. The sudden imprisonment of the tavern owner by the troops with the hint of his possible contagious sickness, introduces a dramatic turn in the direction of a catastrophe.

There is a shock (collision) between the world of the natives and the visible colonizer, the army, in a concentrated form. Between both there is the church that Father Antú represents with dignity, but also with human foibles. The village of the *kurumbins* is made up of Christian as also of the brahmin master. The merchants who make profits from the misery are considered non-Christians. The soldiers are equally Christian and the priest gives them a sermon during the midnight mass on Christmas day in Portuguese. Thus the father has the function of intermediary and as a man of colour (is in the place where he was born).[7] He takes on as intercessor of his fellow farmers. These are the devout ones, they participate actively in all the religious feasts, although the men prefer to be in the public square instead of in the church. For Christmas they put up a star of bamboo sticks in the village, for Easter they proclaim the Easter message from door to door and in exchange collect by donations some money for their living. In houses are found images of saints and graphic representations of a religious character to whom a petition is directed in times of misery.

The firm conviction of Antú with reference to the accusation of leprosy that caused the imprisonment of Rumão, leads him to diffuse the panic. The army seeks persons of contact and having more than one, accusations follow, due to fear and anger, against the infatuated soldier (of blue eyes) and against the traffickers of kerosene and the visiting soldiers to the tavern, against Rumão and Coincão, dishonoured by him. Wrongly understood messages provoke a suicide, in spite of the fact of the health department proclaiming through the priest of the disinfection and of the end of the danger to health. But the suspicions and the fury over what took place and what has not taken place already are not left to fade. The general hatred is concretized. The chaste soldier who follows the beautiful girl with his stare turns himself into an angel of evil that was to be destroyed.[8] The nocturnal embrace of Rumão results in relations that would threaten the master of the lands through infection. Coincão presumes the discovery of the theft in consequence of the control of health by the landowner and kills herself. The fury of her humiliated father has as consequence the bringing to light the trafficking of petrol, the concealing of the evidence and elimination of the accomplices of the arson: "the destiny of the collective desperation . . . kills the hopes and the collective hatred".

In the end the priest is confronted with death and dissatisfaction like "fruits of hatred".[9] The farmers and soldiers confront themselves and a foothold opens among themselves. But in place of the hour of judgment[10] and of the tribunal of rebel hearts, of the torrent of passions of the occult, hatred and heightened spirits, surges finally the voice of human truth. The bride who was never unfaithful to her groom declares that the incriminated fire-setter is no more than an infatuated youth who admired her from a distance. The conditions of preparation for a marriage — the pure approach, the familiar agreements and the public announcement of the engagement in the community — do not permit the presence of a third as an alternative to the bridegroom chosen in the thought of the bride. The simple approach to the truth means renunciation and exile for a girl. Would that her sacrifice be . . . the sign of anger would end?

The novel shows through a theme of renunciation its favour for an ideal humanism in the world woven by regional and historical elements. These structure the novel and explain the behaviour of persons. The author has managed to concentrate in a few figures many aspects and problems of social life in Goa in the middle of the 20th century.

NOTES AND REFERENCES

1. Júlio Conrado, *Jornal de Letras* (Lisbon), 24 April 1996, p. 24.
2. Orlando da Costa, *O Signo da Ira*, Lisbon, Edições Temas de Actualidade, 4th ed., 1996, p. 258.
3. *Ibid.*, p. 236
4. *Ibid.*, p. 203.
5. *Ibid.*

6. *Ibid.*, p. 236.
7. *Ibid.*, p. 158.
8. *Ibid.*, p. 117.
9. *Ibid.*, p. 228.
10. *Ibid.*, p. 231.

NINETEEN

ANTAM DE PROENÇA'S TAMIL-PORTUGUESE DICTIONARY, PRINTED IN INDIA IN 1679

THOMAS MALTEN

The aim of this Chapter is to examine the linguistic contact of the Portuguese with Tamil, a major literary language of India, in the 16th and 17th centuries as exemplified by the earliest printed lexicographical works. The study is intended as a contribution to the general study of the early development of Asian European lexicography was well as the development of the language of modern Tamil prose.

The *Tamil Portuguese Dictionary* by Antam de Proença or *Vocabulário Tamulico (VT)*, printed in the Jesuit missionary station of Ambalakad in South India in 1679 is the earliest specimen of a printed dictionary of any Indian language of which only one copy has survived. On the Portuguese side it contains the collected lexicographical knowledge of over 150 years of linguistic contact with the main language and literature of South India and is a first attempt to define a prose standard of Tamil based on text corpora. This perceived standard is more closely linked to the spoken language of the time than the standard of today's prose which is based mainly on classical commentators's prose and purist reform efforts which excluded spoken elements and were not based on an analysis of modern language corpora. It is doubtlessly the most important Tamil linguistic monument of its time, which enables us to fix a large part of the pre-17th century non-poetic vocabulary of Tamil (apart from inscriptions) which then was still free from European influence.

A manuscript version of the *VT* discovered by S. Rajamanickam in the Central Library of Goa shows that the printed dictionary contains only a mutilated version of the original dictionary and also leaves out other, mostly grammatical portions. Moreover, some details of the innovative system of the alphabetical ordering of the entries in the *VT* can only be understood from the missing parts.

There still remain many open questions regarding the printing history of the book as well as its sources which have yet to be answered by further research. The photo mechanic reprint of the book in 1966 has not led to any appreciable research of the linguistic contents over the past thirty years. The reason for this may be found in the inaccessibility of the data in the original form, which on the one hand, is due to the low readability of the print and on the other, to the language used in the dictionary entries, viz. Portuguese.

The Tamil language of South India is spoken today by some 60 million people in several countries of South and Southeast Asia and is the main language of South India. It developed the most distinguished and extensive literature in India besides Sanskrit which can be traced back to more than 2,000 years. The first literary products of Portuguese cultural interaction with India are related to Tamil. Though most linguistic work of the Portuguese Jesuit missionaries is still in manuscript form and though there is an important indigenous scholarly tradition, it can be shown that all modern grammars and dictionaries are based on the works of the Portuguese period. It goes without saying that this historical research on the Portuguese contribution to Indology has not received the attention it merits as there exist - to my knowledge — not even descriptive lists of relevant Mss. held in the archives of Portugal, Goa and other places. One of the reasons for this neglect is seen in the fact that there seem to be no qualified scholars equally at home in Tamil and Portuguese studies. As long as this is the case, any progress, in this field can thus be expected only from a cooperation of specialists.

Portuguese in India between the 16th and 18th centuries is characterized by its function as a *lingua franҫa* in the trade along the coast and the absence of a territorial base excepting Goa and parts of Sri Lanka. Its relation to the languages of India is marked by its close association with Christian missionary efforts, mainly of Jesuits. In coastal areas dominated by the Portuguese, local minority populations (*topaz, topas*) developed through marriage and conversion. Their language remained Portuguese even after the Dutch Protestant became the leading maritime power in Asia from the middle of the 17th century. Although the fall of Cochin in 1663 marks the end of Portuguese military and political power in South India and Sri Lanka, books written in Portuguese continued to be printed at Tranquebar till at least the middle of the 18th century and in the local trade on the Coromandel coast, Portuguese families were still prominent in 1782.[1]

The latest, most important and — apart from Christian religious treatises –– the only printed contribution of the Portuguese to the linguistic study of South India is without doubt the *Tamil Portuguese Dictionary* of Antam de Proença (1625-1666), posthumously published in 1679. It summarises the linguistic and, to some extent, literary knowledge the Europeans had of Tamil.

Proença and his Dictionary: Background, Genesis and History of the Work

Apart from numerous later dictionary and other mss. in European and Indian archives, we find mss. by Jesuits writing in Portuguese that describe the cultural-religious background of Hinduism. Prominent among these is a treatise on Indian mythology and literature written by an unknown author at roughly the same time (*c*. 1670) as the *TT*.[2] This description gives us a good idea of contemporary European knowledge of Indian literature and religion though it does not seem to be explicitly based on South Indian traditions. It is however, quite remarkable, that all the main characters in the short reproduction of the Indian national epic *Ramayana* in chapters 5-7 and 25, are to be found as entries in the *TT*. The fact that the version of the *Ramayana* summarized in the text is obviously derived from popular sources and contains unusual details that are still found in various South Indian local versions, needs further research.[3]

Antam de Proença[4] compiled his dictionary which contains about 16,000 main entries, as a Jesuit missionary in India between 1653 until his early death in 1666. The troubled times in which all Portuguese trading stations along the coast fell into Dutch hands, must have also led to a decline in the material support of the missionary work so that we may surmise that the delay of 13 years in publishing his manuscript may have been due to economic reasons.

When it was finally printed in 1679, some passages of the manuscript that went beyond the mere dictionary were deleted.[5] The deletions included passages of the preface as well as grammatical essays of the author. Most important of all, some parts which explain the transliteration of the Tamil head word entries, and without which the alphabetic order of the dictionary cannot be properly understood, were left out. Moreover, his innovative introduction of using diacritical signs to express vowel lengths in Tamil were ignored in typesetting, but possibly for technical reasons. All this leads to the obscurity surrounding the historical importance of de Proença with regard to innovations leading to the modern Tamil writing system as used today.

Only one complete copy of *VT* is known to exist in the Vatican Library from which a facsimile print was produced in 1966. In the literature we find only two more copies mentioned, one existing only in a few remaining pages, and about the other nothing is known.[6] It is quite remarkable that the German Protestant missionaries who came to Tranquebar in 1706 do not mention the *VT* even though B. Ziegenbalg, who compiled a Tamil-German Dictionary manuscript (now lost) of about the same size as the *VT* does not mention it in his detailed reports from Tranquebar between 1706-1719.[7] Therefore it may be concluded that only a few copies had been printed in the first place. What makes the printing history even more mysterious is the fact that no moveable letters were used for the Tamil portion of the book, but only woodcut letters, even though, more than a hundred years earlier, such type had been already available. Manuscript copies of the *VT* mentioned in bibliographies of Tamil dictionaries Dhamotharan (1978), James (1991) and Rajamanickam (1995) are far more numerous, but their relationship to the printed work has not been investigated so far. Most of them appear to be 18th century copies of the printed work which also points to an early unavailability of the book. The most interesting manuscript is mentioned by Rajamanickam (1995) as it appears to be dated 1670 (Central Library, Panaji M.34). It contains the diacritical marks left out in the published version and, so, may either be the original manuscript on which the print is based, or the manuscript copy by João de Magalhaens mentioned in the front portion of the *VT*. According to his own words de Magalhaens had been working intensively with this manuscript for many years. His report states the complete conformity of the printed book with de Proença's manuscript. It needs to be found out how to reconcile this statement with the apparent omissions from the *VT*. It is to be hoped that, to solve this problem references can also be found in the archives of Goa or those of the Society.

The *Mss. Indien 221 and 222* in the Bibliotheque Nationale, Paris, have to be regarded as later copies of *VT* and de Bourzes' *Tamil-French MS Dictionary* is also based on *VT*.

The first description of the only existing copy of the *VT* in the library of the Society of Jesus in Rome was written by San Bartholomeo (1792) more than a century after its publication. Again after almost another century had passed Burnell[8] reported that "Prof. de Gubernatis has made a fruitless search in the library of the Propaganda" for the book. This statement is repeated in the Tamil Lexicon[9] and with reference to Grierson's *Linguistic Survey of India*[10] it is written: "Of this Dictionary by Father Antam (sic) de Proença, no trace is found". But around 1900 Jules Vinson had proved the existence of the *VT* in the Vatican Library, Museum Borgia, to which the library of the Society belongs (*Fondo Indiano, no.12*) and had given a new detailed description of the work including a facsimile reproduction of its title page. It seems however, that he did not see the *VT* in Rome himself but that he owes his report to the information supplied by others (Vinson 1910: 78). Vinson's report again is unknown to Thani Nayagam (1954) who reported the (re)discovery of the *VT* ca. 1954, and published a photo mechanic reprint in 1966. At the same time the Indian Jesuits Sauliere and Rajamanickam produced a typewritten copy of the *VT* which at that time was used by the latter for his edition of de Nobili's Tamil writings and has now been used in the first stage of producing an electronic version of the dictionary. Considering the extremely bad quality of the print of *VT* coupled with the omission of vowel lengths in the Tamil portions, this typed copy represents a considerable advance towards the final edition of the *VT*.

The Censors' Remarks on the VT

Whatever we know about the sources and contents of the *VT* is contained in the introduction where Proença describes in detail the reason for his compilation and the work of his predecessors. Preceding this compiler's introduction, we find, on the first seven pages, twelve reports and letters documenting the lengthy process of censoring the *VT* by the church authorities mainly in Goa during fifteen months's period between 20.09.1678 and 06.12.1679. These certificates, firstly, relate to the teaching of the Catholic church and, secondly, to the complete identity of Proença's original manuscript dictionary with the printed version. In this process four censors of Goa who are explicitly named as Tamil experts, give their opinion on the dictionary.

The most important among these is João de Magalhaens, S.J., procurator of the (Jesuit) provinces of Malabar and Goa, who is described as "reviser" in Goa. On 21.02.1679 he writes[11] that he has examined again the book called *Tamil Dictionary* by Antam de Proença which he used intensively for (many) years in studying and practising the Tamil language. He states that he copied it with his own hand and used it for teaching and translating. More information on the life of Magalhaens may show whether we can infer from this comment that Tamil was practised and taught in Goa itself and also whether the reference to his copy of Proença's Ms. is in fact, to the said Central Library Ms. 34 of 1670. He also states that the *VT* forms the completion of the work attempted by many scholars and that the *VT* has reduced the Tamil lexicography to a simpler method, a more convenient arrangement of the matter in a more agreeable and easy style of this "difficult and most eloquent language".

Three more Jesuit Tamil experts are mentioned in the censors' section, viz., A. Pereira, at Ambalakad, Valeriano Cataneo, also at Ambalakad, and João Pessoa, professor of theology at the colleges of Goa and Cochin.

The Introduction by Proença to the VT

The general introduction to the *VT* which treats the prerequisites of the dictionary covers about two and a half pages of the book. It is followed by a chapter on the alphabetical order used in the dictionary and a a chapter on phonetics.

Proença first gives his reasons for compiling the *VT* and describes the scope of the entries and their origins. He then shows the criteria for adding certain types of words and meanings to the dictionary and finally tells us what kind of words have been left out.

The *VT* is written for European missionaries who have to learn Tamil as a precondition for their work (*cultinaçam*) in South India. Even though a dictionary is the most important aid to learning Tamil not one had been printed so far, even though many attempts have been made to produce one for publication. The *VT* has been compiled upon the wish of many missionaries and supersedes all previous Ms. dictionaries in all respects.

The entries to the dictionary have been collected primarily from Father Bruno's Ms. dictionary which merits special mention because it is the most voluminous of the existing Ms. vocabularies. To Bruno's collection all words from the works of de Nobili[12] and Martins are added as well as many words from indigenous Tamil words. To this are added words collected in conversation with Tamil speakers.

The meanings of Tamil words are ascertained by taking them from literary contexts and, in addition, the explanation of native scholars. Even then the meaning of words is not always certain and has to be further investigated by people much learned in both languages.

The selection of words from particular regions as well as books give them an assured quality so that the words contained in the dictionary can be used in (missionary) conversation.

Proença is conscious of the fact that Tamil has a much greater vocabulary which can be collected only through the study of Tamil literature by many scholars over a long period.

Proença confesses that even after 12 years of studying Tamil he still has uncertainties about the meaning of some words especially as the native scholars themselves are not unanimous with regard to their meanings. Therefore many meanings in the *VT* would have to be corrected later.

Proença leaves out many words spoken in different groups of Tamil society, especially those of the lower and rural castes and fishermen. The exploration of this type of vocabulary is left for later research. (If any of these dialectal expressions occur in the above-mentioned Christian works they are, however, included in the *VT*). At the same time also the words, that occur only in classical poetry are deliberately left out as they are useless for practical purposes and there exist special dictionaries that list them. Many Sanskrit words are included to facilitate the reading of de Nobili's books and because these words connote a high social status.

Proença's introduction may allow us to state that his dictionary is mainly based on preceding Jesuit Tamil Ms. works — among which we find a number of dictionaries — since the beginnings of the Christian mission in the Tamil-speaking areas from about 1535. The compiler seeks to define a 'standard' of prose Tamil (written and spoken) which he may be said to have created himself, largely on the basis of selecting suitable words from an available Tamil corpus. The question arises whether this was generally an intentional procedure in the linguistic effort of the Jesuits in Asia or other regions of the world. If there was a coordinated effort in any way, it could, to some extent, explain the decision to print the work despite the lack of movable type and the generally extremely difficult or turbulent times in India.

It is quite remarkable that Proença is aware of numerous dialectal and other variants in Tamil that characterize it today.[13] These variants include classical Tamil, conversational Tamil, regional and caste dialects, Jaffna Tamil, Standard Madurai Tamil, Christian Tamil, High Tamil, Low Tamil, as well as the dichotomy pure and corrupt. Words borrowed from Sanskrit and specified as such are included as they are considered to be associated with the highest social prestige.

Even though Proença consciously does not use a transliteration of the Tamil script, he achieves, by using the Portuguese alphabetical order, not only a more efficient use of the dictionary but, more importantly, this method also gives him a possibility to implicitly express the pronunciation of certain letters that otherwise would have to be separately indicated. It is still to be studied to what extent his expression of standard pronunciation can throw light on the phonetic development of Tamil. Proença's mentioning of prose literature[14] can either refer to Christian missionary works, to the prose works commentating classical literature, or to some early narrative prose literature that is lost today. In the almost complete absence of any critical editions of Tamil texts it is nearly impossible to make any statements regarding the linguistic history of the Tamil lexicon. Only by having such editions at our disposal we can evaluate the implicit historical statements made by Proença in his dictionary.

A new edition of *VT* which will have to include a translation into English, is the precondition to any well-based conclusion. It will have to take into account the existing Mss. and must be embedded in a wider context of Tamil lexicography on the one hand and a study of early Asian European lexicography on the other. In order to be successful, certain computerized procedures will have to be adopted, that allow us to fix the position of each word in the modern corpus-based lexicon as well as in the *VT*.

NOTES AND REFERENCES

1. H. Dodwell, *The Nabobs of Madras*, Chennai, 1926, p. 126 (reprint New Delhi, 1986).
2. First published by the Royal Academy of Sciences at Lisbon in 1812 in the series *Colecção de Noticias para a História e Geografia das Nações ultramarinas que vivem nos Dominios Portugueses ou lhes são vizinhas* of which a partial translation (ch. 1-26) into English was published in *Anthropos* 1, 1906, pp. 864-876; 2, 1907, pp. 128-132 and 275-281; 3, 1908, pp. 771-772.
3. Thomas Malten, "Die Geschichte von Rama und Laksman" in *Sudasien Anthologie*, Hrsg. von G.D. Sontheimer Stuttgart, Steiner, 1993, pp. 98-107; Theodor Zachariae, *De Open-Deure tot het verborgen Heydendom door Abraham Rogerius*, 1916, pp. 584ff.
4. S. Rajamanickam, "Antam Proença's Tamil Portuguese Dictionary · Discovery of the Missing Link". Seminar on "Jesuits in India: Sources and Problems" (Xavier Centre of Historical Research, Alto Porvorim, Goa 1-2 December 1995).
5. *Ibid.*
6. D. Ferroli, *The Jesuits in Malabar*, vol. 2, Bangalore, p. 470.
7. H. Beythan, *Praktische Grammatik der Tamilsprache in Umschrift*, Leipez, Harrassowitz,1943, pp. 6ff; Zedlei, J.H. *Grosses vollstandiges Universal-Lexikon*, vol. 62, Leipzig & Halle, 1749, p. 488.
8. A.C. Burnell, *Elements of South Indian Palaeography from the fourth to seventeenth century A.D.*, Varanasi, Indological Book House, 1968, p. 44 (reprint London, Trubner 1878).
9. *Tamil Lexicon*, vol. 1, Chennai, Chennai Univ. , 1924, p. xxxvi.
10. G.A. Grierson, vol. 4, 1927, p. 301.
11. *VT*, pp. 5-6.
12. S. Rajamanickam, *The First Oriental Scholar*, Tirunelveli, De Nobili Research Institute, 1972.
13. Francis Britto, *Diglossia: A Study of the Theory with Application to Tamil*, Washington D.C., Georgetown Univ. Press 1986, pp. 127ff.
14. *VT*, p. 9.

TWENTY

DRAVIDIAN BORROWINGS FROM PORTUGUESE (Kannada and Telugu)

DIETER B. KAPP

I

Portuguese was the first European language with which the Dravidian-speaking peoples of the Indian sub-continent came into contact. Even though the Portuguese period in South India was comparatively short — it lasted not even a hundred years — its influence, particularly on the languages of the peoples of South India was remarkable.

> "Portuguese was spoken in its pure or corrupt form throughout the whole of India, in Malaysia, Pegu, Burma, Siam, Tonquin, Cochin-China, China, in Kamaran in Persia, in Basra of the Turkish Vilayet, and in Mecca in Arabia. And it was spoken not only by the Portuguese and their descendants but by Hindus, Mohammedans, Jews and by Europeans of other nationalities in their intercourse with one another or with the indigenous people. It was employed by the Dutch missionaries in their own dominions and, even to this day, English Protestant ministers make use of it in Ceylon. It was therefore for a long time the lingua franca of the East".
>
> It is true that to-day the radius of the circulation of Portuguese in Asia is no longer what it used to be; it is much reduced. It has ceased to be the lingua franca, and of its several dialects, some are extinct, others are in articulo mortis, and it may well be that yet others shall, after the lapse of ages, have entirely

disappeared. But when perchance Portuguese shall have ceased to be spoken in the East, the words from the beautiful tongue of Camoens, adopted and naturalized in a hundred and one of the vernaculars of the East, will continue to exist as long as the vernaculars themselves endure and stand as living and abiding monuments of the Portuguese dominion and civilization in those parts". (Soares 1936: xxxiii)

Thanks to Sebastião Rodolfo Dalgado who, in 1913, published his outstanding dictionary, entitled *Influencia do Vocabulário Portugues em Linguas Asiáticas* and to Anthony Xavier Soares who brought out an enlarged English edition of Dalgado's dictionary in 1936 under the title *Portuguese Vocables in Asiatic Languages*, we are provided with the most comprehensive source for loan-words from Portuguese in Dravidian languages. So, for studies dealing with Dravidian borrowings from Portuguese, the data supplied by Dalgado/Soares serve as an excellent starting-point.

While in the case of Tamil, we have, at least, three studies at our disposal which are devoted to its linguistic contact with Portuguese,[1] no attempts have to my knowledge, been made so far with regard to studies on the borrowings of other Dravidian languages from Portuguese. Bearing this in mind, I decided to devote the present paper to Portuguese loan-words in Kannada and Telugu, disregarding here Malayalam borrowings from Portuguese as they ought to be given a separate treatment, with the object of closely scrutinizing all the Kannada and Telugu words listed in Dalgado/Soares as presumable loan-words from Portuguese.

According to the Kannada and Telugu word lists to be found in Soares, the Kannada borrowings from Portuguese amount to 89 words and the Telugu borrowings to 77. A counter-check with the dictionary, however, resulted in the Kannada words amounting to 85 and the Telugu words to 83.[2]

The whole of the Kannada and Telugu borrowings from Portuguese can be divided into two distinct groups: (a) Christian expressions and terms, and (b) cultural words in general. Thereby the latter group comprises words belonging to the following spheres viz.

— commerce and industry
— house (outside and inside),

— dishes, tools and instruments,
— shoes, clothes and bathroom items,
— food, flora and fauna, and
— various.

Since the Christian expressions and terms which by the way, are known to comparatively small minorities of Christian Kannada and Telugu speakers only, do not pose any problems with regard to their Portuguese origin, they have been neglected in the present study. So, the following analysis concentrates on the remaining 57 Kannada (i.e. 85 minus 28 Christian terms) and 68 Telugu (i.e. 83 minus 15 Christian terms) cultural words all of which are according to Dalgado/Soares, presumed to be of Portuguese origin.

The investigation led to the surprising and, therefore, noteworthy results that, from among the examined 57 Kannada and 68 Telugu words.

(a) only 15 Kannada and 14 Telugu words,[3] can be safely regarded as true loan words from Portuguese (Port. >Ka/Te).
(b) in the case of 18 Kannada and 14 Telugu words, Portuguese fulfilled the function of an agent language (other language > Port. > Ka/Te).
(c) in the case of 4 Kannada and 8 Telugu words, the Portuguese origin is doubtful (?Port. > Ka/Te).
(d) in the case of 6 Kannada and 2 Telugu words, the Portuguese words given in Dalgado/Soares prove to be Portuguese borrowings from a New Indo-Aryan or a Dravidian language (NIA/Dravidian > Port).
(e) in the case of 5 Kannada and 2 Telugu words, an etymological connection with the Portuguese words given in D/S does not exist (Port. >· Ka/Te).
(f) with regard to the remaining 9 Kannada and 28 Telugu words, the standard dictionaries of Kannada (Kittel) and Telugu (Brown; also drawn upon Galletti) are silent for which reason these words had to be left out of the discussion since there is no evidence of their being in common use (Port > ? Ka/? Te).

In the following, the 57 Kannada and 68 Telugu words, subdivided into the above sections will be discussed one by one.

Thereby, in each section, the Portuguese words appear in alphabetical order along with their English meanings as listed in Dalgado/Soares (D/S). Next, the corresponding Kannada (Ka) and/or Telugu (Te) words are given as quoted in D/S. They are then followed by corresponding quotations from the respective standard dictionaries (Kittel = K; Brown = B; Galletti = G) whenever they could be verified by checking on these sources. Occasionally, references, notes and/or comments have been added wherever it was found useful.

II

A. Port. > Ka./ Te.

1. Port. *aia* "dry nurse"
   Te. *āyá* (D/S)
   āyā "a waiting woman, a maid servant, an ayah" (B)
   áyá, áyamma "lady's maid or children's nurse" (G)
   Cf. H-J s.v. *ayah*
2. Port. *armário*, (archaic form) *almário* "cupboard"
   Ka. *almārí, almáru* (D/S)
   almaira "an almira, a cabinet, a chart of drawers, a wardrobe" (K)
   Te. *almár(a)* (D/S)
   almāra, almāru "a wardrobe, almirah" (B)
   almáru "wardrobe" (G)
   Cf. H-J s.v. *almyra*
3. Port. *amarra* "cable (of a ship)"
   Te. *amáru, amárutádu* (D/S)
   amāru, amārutādu "a cable" (B)
   — (G)
4. Port. *bomba* "water-pump"
   Ka. *bámba* (D/S)
   bamba "a pump; a fire-engine" (K)
   Te. *bombásu, bombása* (from *bombas*, the pl. of *bomba*) (D/S)
   — (B and G)
   Cf. H-J s.v. *bumba*
5. Port. *botão* "button"
   Te. *butaum, bottam* (D/S)

bottāmu "a button" (B)
bottámu "button" (G)

6. Port. *camisa* "shirt"
Ka. *kamisu* (D/S)
- (K)
Te. *kamisu, kamsu* (D/S)
- (B)
camízu, "shirt" (G)
Cf. H-J *s.v. cameeze*; but cf. Littmann (22): Kamisol, chemise, Chemisett, Chemisett, Kluge s.v. *Kamisol*: "Zu mlat. *camisia* 'Hemd'. . ..".

7. Port. *chave* "key"
Ka. *chávi* (D/S)
cāvi (*sāvi*) "a key" (K)
Te. *sávi*, chevi (D/S)
— (B and G)

8. Port. *couve* "cabbage"
Ka. *kōbisu* (D/S)
kōsu "cabbage" (K) (=evidently a contracted form of the word quoted in D/S)

9. Port. *estirar* "to extend; stretch out"
Ka. *istri* "to pass the iron over" (D/S)
istari, istrī "A smoothing iron; ironing (K)
Te. *istiri* "the act of passing the iron over" (D/S)
istiri "ironing of clothes" (B)
istiri "ironing" (G)

10. Port. *hospital* "hospital" (influenced by English)
Ka. *āspatri* (D/S)
āspatri "the English hospital" (K)
Te. *āspatri* (D/S)
— (B)
áspatri "hospital" (G)
cf. Hindi *aspatāl*

11. Port. *jogar* "(in the sense of) a game of chance or game with stakes; a raffle"
Ka. *jugáru* "game of chance"; jugáru aḍuvava "gambler"; *jugáru áḍu* "to gamble" (D/S)
jugāru "gambling" (K)
All other forms quoted in D/S are to be derived from Sanskrit dyūtá "gambling; cf. Emeneau/Burrow 172,

CDIAL 6608.

12. Port. *meia(s)* "sock(s), hose"
    Ka. *mējōḍu* (D/S)
    mē-jōḍu "a stocking, a pair of stockings" (K); the second part of this compound, jōdu, means "a pair" and is a borrowing from Indo-Aryan (cf. Emeneau/ Burrow 179)
    Te. *mējóḍu, mejóḷḷu* (D/S)
    mējōḍu "stockings" (B)
    méjódu (*sic*!) "stockings" (G)
13. Port. *mesa* "table"
    Ka. *méju* "(also) ration, confused with English "mess" (D/S)
    mēju "a table; dinner; the stake or sum played for at dice" (K)
    Te. *méja; méjar* "a big table" (D/S)
    mējā, mēdzu "a table, dinner, mess" (B)
    - (G)
14. Port. *mestre* "master"
    Ka. *mestre* "carpenter, stone-cutter, mason" (D/S)
    mēstri "a head workman" (K)
    Te. *mestrí, mestarí* "a foreman"
    mēstri "a master workman, a head-workman" (B)
    méstri "foreman" (G)
    Cf. H-J. *s.v. maistry, mistry, mystery*
15. Port. *pena* "quill, writing-pen"
    Ka. *pénu* (D/S)
    - (K)
    Te. *pēná* (D/S)
    pēnā "a pen" (B)
    péna "pen" (G)
16. Port. *pera* "Psidium, guayava, guava"
    Ka. *pērla* (*-mara*) (the tree); *pērla (-haṇṇu)* (the fruit) (D/S)
    pērala, pēraḷa, pērle "the guava, *Psidium guyava*, Linn" (K)
17. Port. *pipa* "a cask; (also) a barrel"
    Ka. *pipe, pipái, pīpáyi* (D/S)
    pīpu, pīpāyi "a cask, a barrel, a tub" (K)
    Te. *pípaya* (D/S)
    - (B)
    pipá "cask" (G)

18. Port. *prato* "a plate; dish"
    Ka. *paráta* (D/S)
    parāta, parātu "a circular or edged dish" (K)
19. Port. *sabão* "soap"
    Ka. *sabbu, sābúnu* (D/S)
    cavu, saba, sabu, sabbu "soap" (K)
    Te. *sabbu* (D/S)
    sabbu "soap" (B and G)
20. Port. *toalha* "towel"
    Ka. - (D/S)
    tuvāl "a towel, a touaille" (K)
    Te. *tuvālā, tuvālāguṭṭa* (D/S)
    tuvāla, tuvālu "a towel" (B)
    tuválu "towel" (G)
    Cf. H-J. *s.v. towleea*

B. Other language > Port. > Ka./Te.

21. Port. *ananás* "pine-apple"
    Ka. *ananásu* (D/S)
    - (K)
    Te. *anānásu, anásu, anás-paṇṭu, anāsavanasa-paṇṭu* (D/S)
    anāsa "Ananas sativa or the Pine Apple, or Bromelia *sativa* (B) anása "pine-apple" (G)
    Origin: A Brazilian language (cf. H-J *s.v. ananas* < Brazilian *nana*(s); Littmann (146 f.) < Brazilian; Kluge s.v. *Ananas* < Tupi); Messner 1987, 95: most likely < Guarani *naná*
22. Port. *arrátel* "a pound weight"
    Ka. *rátalu* (D/S)
    rātal "a weight of twelve, fifteen, or sixteen ounces (in Mysore = 16 ounces or 1 lb)" (K)
    rātal, rātalu "a weight of fifteen or sixteen ounces" (Kedilaya 338)
    Origin: Arabic (Cf. Lokotsch 1708: < arabiach raṭl
23. Port. *cafre* "(in the sense of) negro"
    Ka. *káphri* (D/S)
    - (K)
    Te. *káppiri* (D/S)
    kappiri "dusky" (B)

- (G)

Origin: Arabic (cf. H-J *s.v. caffer, caffre, coffree*: < Arabic *kāfir*, pl. *kofra* "an infidel, an unbeliever in Islām"; Lokotsch 997: "Cf. also Kluge *s.v. Kaffer.*)

24. Port. *candil* "(in the old acceptation of:) a lamp (now obsolete)"

Ka. *kandíla* (D/S)

kandil "a candle, a lantern, a globe of glass" (K)

kandil, kandīl, kandīlu "a lantern" (Kedilaya 66)

Origin: Arabic (c.f Lokotsch 1053: < arabisch *kandil.*

25. Port. *chá* "tea"

Ka. *chá* "tea" (D/S)

cā, cahā, cāha "the China tea-plant, *Camellia therifera* Griff' (K)

Origin: Chinese (cf. H-J s.v. tea: < Chinese, mandarin dialect chha; Lokotsch 415.

26. Port. *damasco* "damask" (i.e. a variety of fabric from Damascus)

Ka. *damásu* (D/S)

damāsu "damask" (K)

Origin: Arabic (cf. Lokotsch 476: < arabisch *Damaskus.*

27. Port. *fulano* "such a one"

Ka. *phaláni* (D/S)

- (K)

phalāni "such a one" (Kedilaya 241)

Te. *phulána, phaláni* (D/S)

palāna "such and such, such a one" (B)

paláná, paláni "such and such" (G)

Origin: Arabic (cf. Lokotsch 614: < arabisch *fulan.*

28. Port. *goiaba* "*Psidium guayava*, guava fruit" Ka. - (D/S)

koyyā "guava Psidium pyriferum L." (Emeneau/Burrow 119)

Te. *gōvā-panḍu* (D/S) (? cf. Te. *gōva* "the town Goa" (B)

goyyā-panḍu "the fruit called guava" (B)

goyya (pandu) (*sic*!) "guava (fruit) (G)

Origin: A Brazilian language (cf. H-J *s.v. guava*: < Brazilian *guayaba*; Littmann (148): do.; Emeneau/ Burrow 119.

29. Port. *batata* "potato, not sweet"

Ka. *batāṭé* (D/S)

baṭāṭi "a potato" (K)
Origin: A Central (Haiti) or South American language (cf. H-J *s.v. sweet potato*; Littmann (147); Kedilaya 247: wrongly < Arabic *baṭāṭah*). The retroflex *ṭ* is due to the influence of English *potato.*

30. Port. *jalapa* "jalap root"
Ka. *julábu* (D/S)
julābu "a purgative; a purge" (K)
Origin: The name of the Mexican town *Jalapa*; *jalap* = the dried root of any of several Mexican plants of the morning-glory family (especially *Exogonium purga*) used in medicine as a hydragog (Funk & Wagnalls).

31. Port. *leilão* "auction, sale"
Ka. *leylam, lilámu, yálam, yélamu* (D/S)
- (K)
Te. *lélam, yálam, yalam, yélamu* (D/S)
yālamu, ēlamu, lēlamu "an auction" (B)
élamu, vulgarly pronounced *yálam* "auction" (G)
Origin: Arabic (cf. H-J *s.v. neelám, leelám*: < Arabic *i'lām* "proclamation, advertisement"; the correct Arabic source word, however, is *i'lān* "do"; Kedilaya).

32. Port. *limão "Citrus medica,* var. *Limonum*, H.; lemon"
Ka. *limbe, nimbe* (D/S)
limbe, nimbi, nimbe "the acid lime, *Citrus medica* L., var. acida" (K)
Te. *nimma* (D/S)
nimma "appertaining to the lime tree";
nimma-kaya, nimma-pandu "a lime" (B)
nimmacáyi 'lime (unripe)" (G)
Origin: Persian, but originally < Sanskrit (cf. H-J *s.v. lemon*; Lokotsch 1322: < persisch *limūn* "Zitrone, *Citrus limonum*", ebenso arabisch *laimūm*; Littmann 83: Cf. Emeneau/Burrow 229 where all forms are explained by Sanskrit *nimbū(ka);* cf. *CDIAL*, 7247).

33. Port. *palangana* "a flat dish"
Ka. *pingáni* (D/S)
pingāni "crockery, porcelain, China-ware dishes, plates, etc" (K)
Te. *pingáni, pīngáni* (D/S)
pingāṇi "a china plate" (B)

pingáni "crockery" (G)
Origin: Persian (cf. Kedilaya 347: < Persian *fiñjan* "small cup of porcelain; glass"; Steingass: *finjān* (for Persian *pingan* "a bowl, a cup"),"porcelain dish, tea, or coffee-cup"; > Arabic *fingān*, "Tasse"; *fanag*.

34. Port. *papaia* "*Carica papaya*, Linn., the papaw tree and its fruit"
Ka. - (D/S)
pappam, pappāyi "the Papaya (cf. Haiti) or Papaw" (K)
Origin: A Caribbean language (cf. H-J *s.v. papaya, papaw*: "the Carib name was *ababai*").

35. Port. *papuses* "a sort of sandals"
Ka. *papósu* (D/S)
pāpāsu, pāpōsu "a shoe or slipper" (K)
Te. *pāpásum* (D/S)
pāpāpōsu, pāpōsu "a shoe" (B)
pápósulu "slippers (G)
Origin: Persian (cf. Kedilaya 343: < Persian *pāpōs* "slipper"; Lokotsch 1625; Persian *pāpūs*; "Fubbekleidung" > arabisch *bābūs*; Steingass: *pā-poś* (footcover) "a shoe, slipper").

36. Port. *pato* "gander; drake"
Ka. *bátu* (D/S)
bātu, bāte "a duck" (K)
Te. *bátu; pedda bátā* (big drake) "gander"
bātu, bātupu "a duck"; *pedda-bātu* "a goose"; *gūḍa-bātu* "the smaller pelican" (B)
bátu "duck"; *pedda bátu* "a goose"; *gúda-bátu* "pelican" (G)
Origin: Arabic (cf. Lokotsch 276: Harder: baṯṯ "Ente"; Kedilaya: cf. Emeneau/Burrow 328 where this word is derived < Persian).

37. Port. *resma* "a ream"
Ka *rejmu* (D/S)
rēśami, rēśimi, rēśmi, rēśme, rēśne, rēśime "silk, silken" (K)
Origin: Arabic (cf. Lokotsch 1723: < arabisch *rizma;* Littmann (98): < arabic *rizma* "Paket, Ballen, Bündel", später auch "Ries Papier"; Harder: *rizam* "Paket, Bündel, Ries Papier"; Kedilaya: -).

38. Port. *sagu* "sago"
Ka *sāgo, seigo* (D/S)
sāgū, sabbu "sago" (K)
Te. *saggu* (D/S)
sabbu-biyyamu, saggu-biyyamu "sago" (*biyyamu* "rice when cleared from the husk") (B)
- (G)
Origin: Malay (cf. H-J *s.v. sago*: < Malay *sāgū*, Littmann (130): do.; Kluge *s.v. Sago*: "Mal(ayisch) *sāgū*".

39. Port. *tabaco* "tobacco"
Ka. *tambaku* (D/S)
tambāka, tambāku "tobacco" (K)
Origin: A Caribbean language (Taino or Tupi) (cf. H-J *s.v. tobacco*; Littmann 149).

40. Port. *tambor* "tambour, drum"
Ka. *tambúre* (D/S)
tambūra, tambūri "a kind of guitar with three to five strings" (K)
Te. - (D/S)
tambura, tamburā "a kind of stringed instrument like the guitar, a tambourine" (B)
tambura "a kind of guitar" (G)
Origin: Persian or Arabic (cf. Lokotsch 483: Kedilaya 225: < Persian *ṭāmbūrah* "tambourine; Steingass: *dunba-bara* (lambs' tails, often contracted into *dunbara*, a guitar"; Harder: *ṭunbūr* "Laute, Mandoline"; Cf. also Kluge *s.v. Tambour*. This is obviously a case of semantic contamination of two nearly homonymous words both of which denote a musical instrument, viz. a drum and a stringed instrument respectively.

41. Port. *tara* "tare, abatement from the gross weight of goods".
Te. *táramu* (D/S)
tāramu "tare in merchandise: the sum allowed for the packing case" (B)
- (G)
Origin: Arabic (cf. Lokotsch 2024: Littmann (99).

42. Port. *tufão* "hurricane"
Ka. *tuphánu* "hurricane; groundless accusation; calamity" (D/S)

tupāni, tupānu "a storm, a typhoon; slander, calumny" (K)

Te. *tuphánu* (D/S)

tupānu "a storm, a cyclone" (B)

tupánu "storm, cyclone" (G)

Origin: Chinese or Arabic (cf. H-J *s.v. typhoon*: < Chinese *t'a-fung* "great wind", Arabic *ṭūfān* "an overpowering rain. . . Noah's flood"; Lokotsch 1990: < chinesisch *t'ai-fung*, Kedilaya 192: < Arabic *ṭūfān (sic)* "storm"; Littmann (132): ". . . Ef. also Messner 1987: 90, 98.)

43. Port. *verruma* "gimlet"

Te. *buruma, baramá* (D/S)

baramā, barmā, burumā "a bradawl, a drill, a kind of augar or gimlet worked with a string" (B)

- (G)

Origin: Arabic (cf. Harder: *barīme* (*barrīme*).

C. ?Port. > Ka./ Te

44. Port. *bordo* "board, ship's side"

Te. *boḍa* (D/S)

bōḍa (in sea language) a board, i.e, a side (B)

- (G)

This word may as well be a borrowing from English.

45. Port. *café* "coffee"

Ka. *káphi* (D/S)

kāpi "coffee" (K)

Te. *kápi* (D/S)

- (B and G)

Origin: Arabic or the name *Kaffa* (cf. H-J *s.v. coffee:* < Arabic *kahwa* or *Kaffa*, a district in South Abyssinia; Littmann (82): do.; The Ka. word for *coffee* cannot be regarded as a borrowing from Portuguese; it is certainly an English loan-word.

46. Port. *canal* "canal"

Te. *kanáli* (D/S)

kanālu "a canal" (B)

canálu "canal" (G)

Origin: Latin < Old Babylonian (cf. Littmann (18): Kluge

s.v. Kanal: This Te. word may as well as a borrowing from French or English.

47. Port. *copo* "a drinking cup"
Te. *kōpá* (D/S)
kōpa "a cup" (B)
- (G)
Origin: This Te. word may as well be a borrowing from Dutch *kop* or English *cup*.

48. Port. *cozinha* "kitchen"
Ka. *kuśni* (D/S)
- (K) (!)
Te. *kusini-kára, kusini-vádu* "a cook" (D/S)
kuśîni "a kitchen, cook-room" (B)
cuśîni "kitchen" (G)
This Te. word might as well be a borrowing from French cuisine, but cf. Galletti *s.v. cusini* (see note 3)

49. Port. *esponja* "a sponge"
Ka. *spanju* (D/S)
- (K)
Te. *spanji* (D/S)
- (B)
spanji "sponge" (G)
Origin: These Ka. and Te. words are certainly borrowings from English.

50. Port. *estado* "state, condition"
Te. *istuva, istuvu* "property"
istuva, istuvu "an estate" (B)
- (G)
Origin: The origin of this Te. word is not clear; a connection with Port. *estado* is possible, but questionable.

51. Port. *lanterna* "lantern"
lántaru (D/S)
lāndara, lāndra "a lantern" (K)
Te. *lántaru, lándaru* (D/S)
- (B)
lánṭaru "lantern" (G)
These Ka. and Te. words might as well be borrowings from French *lanterne*; the Te. word given by G reveals a clear English influence which is indicated by the

retroflex *t*.

52. Port. *pistola* "a pistol"
Ka. *pistúlu* (D/S)
pistūlu "a pistol" (K)
Te. *pistólu* (D/S)
- (B)
pisṭólu "pistol" (G)
Origin: These Ka. and Te. words might as well be a borrowing from Dutch *pistool* or French *pistole*; the Te. word given by G reveals English influence which is indicated by the retroflex *t*.

53. Port. *policia* "police"
Ka. *pólis* (D/S)
- (K)
Te. *polisu* (D/S)
pōlisu "belonging to the police" (B)
pólisu "police" (G)
Origin: These Ka. and Te. words are certainly not borrowings from Portuguese, but from English.

54. Port. *visagra* "hinge"
Ka. *bijágri* (D/S)
bijāgari "a jointed hinge, jummers" (K)
The origin of Ka. *bijagari* as well as of Port. *visagra* (cf. Machado: "de origem obscura") is ascertainable; likewise, which of the two languages has to be regarded as the borrowing language.

D. NIA/Dravidian > Port.

55. Port. *andor* "palanquin, litter"
Ka. *andaṇa,* (D/S)
andaṇa, andaḷa "a litter, a palankeen" (K)
Origin: Sanskrit (cf. H-J *s.v. andor*: < Marathi *hinḍolā*, Hindi *hinḍolā, hanḍolā* < Sanskrit *hindola*; Monier-Williams: *andolana* "swinging, oscillating", *hindola, hindolā* "a swing, swinging cradle or hammock"). cf. *CDIAL* 14094.) This word is most likely a Portuguese borrowing from NIA through a Dravidian language; cf. Machado: "do malaiala *andola*, que, como outros termos sinonimos e divergentes de dialectos

hindustanicos, entronca no sansc. *hindola*".

56. Port. *chapa* "seal, impression, stamp, brand"

Ka *chāpé* "stamp, print, impression, customs-mark"; *chāpisu* "to print, stamp, mark; *chāppa, tubákiya chápu* "trigger of a gun" (D/S).

cappe "an impression, a stamp, a seal"; *cāpa, cāpe, chāpe* "a stamp; a type of printing letter; an impression"; *cāpa, cāpu* "the cock of a gun"; *capisu, chāpisu* "to stamp, to print" (K)

Te. *chhappá* (for *chāpa*) "seal, stamp, impression"; *chhámp* (for chámpu) "trigger" (D/S)

tṣappa "a seal" (B)

- (G)

Origin: Sanskrit (cf. H-J *s.v. chop* "it might be of Portuguese origin"; Lokotsch 417: Hind(ustani) *chhāp* (=*chāp*) "Siegel, Stempel" (vom Verbum *chhāpnā* (=*chāpnā*) "drucken"); Sanskrit *chapp* "to press, cover, hide". (*CDIAL* 4994). This word is clearly a Portuguese borrowing from New Indo-Aryan through a Dravidian language.

57. Port. *gudão* "a warehouse for goods and stores"

Ka. *gaḍangu* (D/S)

gaḍaṇga, gaḍaṇgu, giḍḍaṇgi "a godown, a store room, especially also a spirit-shop" (K)

Te. *gaḍangu, giḍḍingi* (D/S)

giḍḍangi "a godown, a ware-house, a store-room" (B)

giḍḍangi "ware-house" (G)

Origin: Dravidian (cf. Tamil *kiṭaṇku, kiṭaṇki* "a storehouse", etc. (*DEDR* 1525); cf. H-J *s.v. godown*: < Malay *gadong*; Winstedt: *gudang, gedong*; Lokotsch: -. Port. *gudão* is a borrowing from Malay *gudang* which itself is a borrowing from Dravidian.

58. Port. *jangada* "a raft; two boats latched together, with a planking laid across them"

Ka. - (D/S)

jaṇgāl "a platform with railings placed on two boats, used at ferries" (Emeneau/Burrow 130)

Origin: Sanskrit (cf. H-J *s.v. jancada*; Emeneau/Burrow 130; Sanskrit *saṁghāṭa* "joining of timber", etc.; Marathi *sāgaḍ* "double-canoe"; cf. *CDIAL* 12859.) Port.

jaganda is most likely a direct borrowing from a Dravidian language (which has borrowed it from Indo-Aryan); cf. Tamil *caṇkaṭam* "ferryboat of two canoes with a platform thereon"; *caṇkaṭam* "a kind of boat"; Malayalam *caṇṇaṭam* "ferryboat, made of two boats" (Emeneau/Burrow 130). Cf. also Messner 1987: 96 : < Malayalam.

59. Port. *ripa* "the thin laths laid across the rafters of a roof to bear tiles"
Ka. *ripu* (D/S)
rīpar, rīpar "lath work or lathing of a roof" (K)
Origin: Most likely Marathi *rip* "a lath (especially for the roof of a house, lathing or lath-work (of a roof etc.)" (Molesworth); *CDIAL*: -. Cf. H-J *s.v. reaper*; Machado: "doubtful origin".

60. Port. *varanda* "verandah"
Ka. *varaṇḍa* (D/S)
varaṇḍa "a veranda, a portico; a multitude; an eruption on the face" (K)
Origin: Sanskrit or Persian. Sanskrit (cf. H-J *s.v. veranda*; Lokotsch 223: < Sanskrit *baraṇḍa*, Sanskrit *varaṇḍaka-* "small mound of earth"; Hindi *barāḍa, baraṇḍā* "veranda" (*CDIAL* 11317); Steingass: *bar-amada* "a balcony verandah, porch"; Kedilaya 522: < Persian *barāmadah* "a projected thing"; Littmann (121f.): Thus Portuguese *varanda* is in all probability a borrowing from NIA.

E. Port. > Ka./Te.

61. Port. *buraco* "hole"
biráku, biríku, birúku (D/S)
biraku, biriku, biruku, birku "a crack, a cleft a fissure" (K).
Origin: Of the Ka. word: Dravidian; cf. *DEDR* 5411.

62. Port. *doce* "a sweet"
Ka. *dôse* "cake, fritter" (D/S)
dōse "a holed, i.e. spongy, cake of rice-flour, uddu, etc., baked on a potsherd or iron plate" (K)
Origin: Ka. word; Dravidian; cd. *DEDR* 3542.

63. Port. *foguete* "(in the sense of) Chinese cracker"
    Ka. *phaṭóki* (D/S)
    paṭaki, paṭakṣi "a cracker, a squib" (K)
    Te. *phaṭóki* (D/S)
    paṭaki "a cracker, a kind of firework" (B)
    - (G)
    Origin: Of the Ka. and Te words: a NIA language; cf. *CDIAL* 9038; Sanskrit *phaṭ* - "sudden movement"; Hindi *paṭāk* "Knall, Krach"; *paṭākā, pataxa,* "Knallfrosch"; *phataka* "Knall, explosion" (Sharma/ Vermeer).
64. Port. *paga* "salary, payment"; *pagar* "to pay" (used as a subst.)
    Ka. *pagadi* "tax, customs-duty" (D/S)
    pagadi, pogadi "tribute, tax" (K).
    Origin: Of the Ka. word: Dravidian; cf. *DEDR* 3808.
65. Port. *recibo* "receipt"
    Ka. *rasídi, rasídi, rasidu* (D/S)
    rasīti, rasīdī, raṣīdu "a receipt" (K)
    Te. *radiśu* (D/S)
    rasīdu, raśīdu "a receipt, an acknowledgement in writing " (B)
    rasíḍu "receipt" (G)
    Origin: Of Ka. and Te. words: Persian, or English, influenced by Persian (cf. H-J *s.v. raseed*; "a native corruption of the English `receipt', shaped, probably, by the Persian *rasīda*, 'arrived'; *viz*, an acknowledgement that a thing has 'come to hand'; cf. Kedilaya 491: < Perśian *rasida* "what has been received; a receipt; the acknowledgement of receipt"; Steingass: *rasīd* "an acknowledgement of arrival or receiving; a receipt").

F. Port. > Ka / Te.

66. Port. *ama* "wet-nurse"
    Ka. *āmá* (D/S)
    - (K)
67. Port. *bacia, bacio* "dinner plate"
    Ka. *bási* (D/S)

- (K)
Te. *bási* (D/S)
- (B and G)

68. Port. *balde* "a bucket"
Te. *baldí, bādlí* (D/S)
- (B and G)

69. Port. *banco* "wooden seat, bench"
Te. *bankatí* (D/S)
- (B and G)

70. Port. *baralho* "a pack of cards"
Te. *baredo* (D/S)
- (B and G)

71. Port. *bateria* "battery, set of guns"
Te. *battéri, phattéri* (D/S)
- (B and G)

72. Port. *biscoito* "biscuit"
Te. *biskotthu* (D/S)
- (B and G)

73. Port. *bruça* "clothes brush"
Te. *barusu* (D/S)
- (B and G)

74. Port. *calafate* "a caulker"
Te. *kalapati* (D/S)
- (B and G)

75. Port. *câmara* "a room"
Te. *kāmará, kāmerá, kāmrá, kāmiri* (D/S)
- (B and G)

76. Port. *capa* "a cloak"
Te. *kappu* "a superscription" (D/S)
- (B and G)

77. Port. *cartucho* "a cartridge"
Te. *kātarusu, kātanusu* (D/S)
- (B and G)

78. Port. *comandante* "a commander"
Te. *kumumdán* (D/S)
- (B and G)

79. Port. *comando* "command"
Te. *kómánu* (D/S)
- (B and G)

80. Port. *fita* "ribbon"
    Te. *phita, pita* (D/S)
    - (B and G)
81. Port. *funil* "a funnel"
    Ka. *phannále* (D/S)
    - (K)
82. Port. *galão* "gold-lace"
    Te. *galan* (D/S)
    - (B and G)
83. Port. *granadeiro* "grenadier"
    Te. *garandílu* (D/S)
    - (B and G)
84. Port. *janela* "window"
    Te. *janalu* (D/S)
    - (B and G)
85. Port. *madeira* "wood, timber"
    Te. *mádiri* "teak wood" (D/S)
    - (B and G)
86. Port. *major* "major, an army officer"
    Te. *mayóru* (D/S)
    - (B and G)
87. Port. *melão* "melon"
    Te. *meláma* (D/S)
    - (B and G)
88. Port. *pangaio* " a two-masted barge with lateen sails"
    Ka. *pangayu* (D/S)
    - (K)
89. Port. *pateca* "(archaic for:) water-melon"
    Te. *batéka* (D/S)
    - (B and G)
90. Port. *poial* " a raised platform on which people sit, usually under the verandah, or on either side of the door of the house"
    Te. *payal, payálu* (D/S)
    - (B and G)
91. Port. *prova* "proof"
    Te. *puroya* (D/S)
    - (B and G)
92. Port. *rabeca* "a fiddle"
    Ka. *rabaku* (D/S)

- (K)

93. Port. *salada* "salad"
    Ka. *saládu* "lettuce" (D/S)
    - (K)
    Te. *salladam* (D/S)
    - (B and G)
94. Port. *sapato* "shoe"
    Te. *sapáth* (D/S)
    - (B and G)
95. Port. *sopa* "soup, or bread soaked in broth, or wine"
    Te. *sópa* (D/S)
    - (B and G)
96. Port. *sorte* "a lottery-coupon"
    Ka. *soḍti* (D/S)
    - (K)
97. Port. *toranja* "Citrus decumana, the shaddock or the pomelo"
    Te. *turanj, turánju* (D/S)
    - (B and G)
98. Port. *tubo* "tube"
    Ka. *tubu* "sluice, bore, hole" (D/S)
    - (K)
99. Port. *vara* "a linear measure, a yard"
    Ka. *váru* (D/S)
    - (K)
100. Port. *vinho* "wine"
    Te. *vínu* (D/S)
    - (B and G)

ABBREVIATIONS

afrz.	Old French
B	Brown
CDIAL	A Comparative Dictionary of the Indo-Aryan Languages
D/S	Dalgado/Soares
DEDR	A Dravidian Etymological Dictionary, Second Edition
G	Galletti

H-J	Hobson-Jobson
K	Kittel
Ka.	Kannada
lat.	Latin
mlat.	Middle Latin
NIA	New Indo-Aryan
Port.	Portuguese
Te.	Telugu

TWENTY-ONE

AN AFTERWORD

THE CHURCHES OF GOA
World Heritage Programme of UNESCO

MICHAEL JANSEN

Since the late 1960s, Goa has become known as a paradise for young Europeans who want to escape their own way of living. Today, it is a booming tourist holiday resort with 5-star hotels and charter flights during the season. Not only Europeans but expatriate Goans and "Mumbaikars" have started to settle down here, the former to invest their foreign money in property, and the latter to escape the exploding metropolis through a 45-minute flight exchanging the overcrowded hot and polluted streets for the swaying palm trees, wind surfing and for Kingfisher beer at low prices.

In 1961 Goa was annexed by India and developed during the past 30 years into a modern member state of the Union. It, formerly a largely Christian oriented Portuguese colony with a history of almost 500 years, soon had to face multi-ethnic and multi-cultural competitions. Political and economic power from outside Goa became more and more influential.

Though there are proposals for a regional plan for Goa till 2001, including the protection of the coastline, in Bardez at least, the coastal strip seems to have been spoilt by uncontrolled building activities. The former romantic hippie beaches are crowded by low cost charter tourists; new and rather ugly edifices grow like mushrooms even within the 500 meters of the coastal protected zone. In opposition to this development, which brings some money to the local people, in Salcete, exclusive holiday resorts (mostly owned by non-Goan financial groups) charge 250 US dollars and more a night and are often fully booked. Hardly any money remains with the local employees.

Within the process of extraordinary development of modern Goa the cultural property of the former Portuguese colony appears like both a wanted and an unwanted relic of former days. Many old houses have been "taken care of" now privately, a quarter of Panaji has been protected. But the most precious (and oldest) part of colonial Goa is the former capital, Old Goa, which was abandoned in the 18th century.

Being aware of the importance of the most valuable monuments, in 1982 the Government of India made an application to UNESCO to register seven of the most prominent and existing churches of Old Goa on the World Heritage List, the convention of which was sanctioned in 1972. In 1986 the monuments were included in the list under number 234.

With this registration the monuments now fall under the responsibility of the world community. The conservation and maintenance should follow international standards. This seems to be a problem which has been raised several times by members of the India Heritage Society (Goa Chapter) who feel responsible for the Goan cultural heritage. A seminar jointly organized by the Archaeological Survey of India, the Consulate General of Portugal in Goa and the Indian Heritage Society (Goa Chapter) was held (11-14 December 1995) during which recommendations were passed to identify a "heritage zone". i.e. the area within the walls of the outer fortification of Old Goa to serve as a cultural, historical and tourism node. The seminar also stressed that the original architectural and structural equilibrium of the Old Goa monuments should be maintained at all costs and nothing should be done to damage or alter the balance of architectural and structural elements that have faced the onslaught of nature for centuries. (*Navhind Times* (Panaji), 21 March 1996).

For a secular state like Indian respect for the various cultures should be a basic necessity of political behaviour. This also accounts for the post Portuguese-Christian tradition in Goa, but it is equally important for all other cultural traits in Goa. i.e. Islam, Hinduism and other religions along with their material manifestation.

Being aware of the 500th anniversary in 1998 of the discovery of the sea route to India by Vasco da Gama it will be advisable to celebrate Goa as a multi-cultural society of which the European component was (and is) but one part. Of this component with its extremely rich cultural past, hundreds of Goan churches still stand as a living monument out of which only a few have been especially selected to be on the World Heritage List. Many more could be added.

Most of them have hardly been scientifically documented and studied, a prerequisite for scientific conservation. While cultural tourism is one aspect, the other is the authenticity of monuments as historic testimony and scientific source. This has led the world community to formulate through UNESCO the Charter of Venice and many more charters, including the Convention for the World Heritage List. With its registration on such a list, a country is honoured and receives prestige for cultural tourism as is the case at Borobodour, Abu Simble and the Cultural Triangle in Sri Lanka to name but a few. But it also takes over responsibility for the maintenance according to international standards which should be applied to each monument to be protected.

BIBLIOGRAPHY

Angle, Prabhakar, *Goa: An economic review*, Mumbai, Goa Hindu Association Kala Vibhag, 1983.

Angle, Prabhakar, *Goa: Concepts and Misconcepts*, Mumbai, Goa-Hindu Association Kala Vibhag, 1994.

Asher, Catherine B., *The New Cambridge History of India*, Cambridge Univ. Press.

Auboyer, Jeannine, *Landmarks of the World Art (The Oriental World)*, London, Paul Hamlyn.

Barreto, Adeodato, "Aposteose", "Redenção" in *Livro da Vida (Fala Ishwara)*, eds. Vimala Devi & Manuel de Seabra, Panaji, Swatwa, 1940.

Barreto, Floriano, "A Bailadeira da India", in *Phalenas: com uma parte sobre assuntos indianos*, Bastora, T. Rangel, 1898.

Barreto, Floriano, "Coqueiro" in *Colecção de Versos*, Bastora, T. Rangel, 1931, pp. 45-61.

Barroco, J. Ferreira, *Memória Histórica do actual estabelecimento dos dizimos prediais nas Ilhas de Goa...*, 1793.

Barros, Joseph de, "Discoveries and Martyrs of Missionary Expansion in the East", in *Discoveries, Missionary Expansion and Asian Cultures*, ed. Teotónio R. de Souza, New Delhi, Concept Publishing Co., 1994, pp. 85-90.

Bausinger, H., *Zur Kulturalen Dimension der Identitat*, Stuttgart, 1971.

Bausinger, H., *Kulturelle Identitat*, Bonn, 1982.

Beythan, H., *Praktische Grammatik der Tamilsprache in Umschrift*, Leipez, Harrassowitz, 1943.

Bhat, M. Mariappa (ed.), *Kittel's Kannada-English Dictionary*, vols. 1-4, Chennai, 1968-71.

Borg, Paul, "The Polyphonic Music in the Guatemalan Music Manuscripts of the Lilly Library", Ph.D. dissertation, Indiana Univ. , 1985.

Borges, Charles J., "Popular Expressions of Religiosity in 6th century

Catholic Goa", *Souvenir of the Holy Family Chapel*, Goa, 1992.

Borges, Charles, *The Economics of the Goa Jesuits 1542-1759: An Explanation of their rise and fall*, New Delhi, Concept, 1994.

Borkar, B.B., "The Secret and Significance of Goa's Scenic Beauty", *Boletim do Instituto Menezes Braganza (BIMB)* (Panaji), no. 112, 1976, pp. 151-154.

Boxer, Charles R., "Fidalgos Portugueses e Bailadeiras Indianas (séculos xvii e xviii)", *Revista da História*, 22 (no. 45), January-March 1961, pp. 83-105.

Boxer, Charles R., *Relações raciais no império colonial português 1415-1825*, Porto, Ed. Afrontamento, 1988.

Bragança Pereira, A. B. de, (ed.), *Arquivo Português Oriental*, Tomo 4, vol. 2, Part I, Bastora, 1937.

Braudel, F., *The Structures of Everyday Life: Civilization and Capitalism, 15th-18th Century*, vol. I, New York, Harper & Row, Publ., 1981.

Britto, Francis, *Diglossia: A Study of the Theory with Application to Tamil*, Washington D.C., Georgetown Univ. Press, 1986.

Brown, Charles Philip, *A Telugu-English Dictionary*, 2nd ed. Chennai, 1903.

Brown, Percy, *Indian Architecture (Buddhist and Hindu Periods)*, Mumbai, D.B. Taraporevala & Sons.

Bulhão Pato R.A. de (ed.), *Cartas de Afonso de Albuquerque*, vol. I, Lisbon, 1884.

Burnell, A.C., *Elements of South Indian Palaeography from the Fourth to Seventeenth Century A.D.*, Varanasi, Indological Book House 1968, (repr. of London, Trubner 1878).

Burrow, T. & Emeneau, M.B., *Dravidian Borrowings from Indo-Aryan*, Berkeley & Los Angeles, Univ. of California, vol. 26, 1962.

Burrow, T. & Emeneau, M.B., *A Dravidian Etymological Dictionary* 2nd ed. Oxford, 1984.

Cabral, António Carlos Pereira, *Pequeno Dicionário de Moçambique*, Lourenço Marques, A. C. P. Cabral, 1972.

Caland, W. and Fokker, A.A., "Drie oude Portugeesche Verhandelingen over het Hindoeisme toegelicht en vertaald door Caland en Fokker", in *Verhandelingen der Koninklijke Akademie van Wetenschappen te Amsterdam*, Afdeeling Letterkunde, Nieuwe Reeks, 16, no. 2, 1915, Amsterdam.

Camões, Luis de, *Lírica*, ed. Nassaud Moises, São Paulo, Cultrix,

1981.

Castanheda, Fernão Lopes, *História de Descobrimentos e Conquista da India pelos Portugueses*, Coimbra, 1833.

Catz, Rebecca, *Fernão Mendes Pinto: Sátira e anti-cruzada na "Peregrinação"*, Lisbon, Instituto de Cultura e Lingua Portuguesa, 1981.

Chabal, Patrick, "Literatura e Nacionalidade", *Vozes Moçambicanas*, Lisbon, Vega, 1994.

Clyne, Michael (ed.) *Pluricentirc Languages: Differing Norms in Different Nations*, Berlin/New York, Mouton de Gruyter, 1992.

Coelho, George V., "Images of Woman in Goan Portuguese Poetry: The Bailadeira theme and variations", in *Actas II Congresso Internacional: Rosto Feminino da Expansão Portuguesa*, Lisbon, Comissão para a Igualdade e para os Direitos das Mulheres, pp. 365-379.

Coelho, George V., "Nostalgia in Seven Goan Poets", *BIMB*, no. 171, 1994, pp. 79-112.

Coelho, Victor, "Cross-Cultural Repertories and the Politics of Music in Renaissance Goa" in *Encomium Musicae: A Festschrift for Robert Snow*. ed. D. Crawford, New York, Stuyvesant, 1977.

Coelho, Victor, "Kapsberger, Giovanni Girolamo" in *The New Grove Dictionary of Opera*, ed. S. Sadie, London, MacMillan, 1992.

Coelho, Victor, "The Apotheosis... of Francis Xavier and the Conquering of India", in *The Work of Opera: Gender, Nation and Genre*. eds. D. Fishling & R. Dellamore (forthcoming).

Conrado, Júlio, "Um romance intemporal" in *Jornal de Letras* (Lisbon), 24 April 1996.

Cortesão, Armando (ed.), *A Suma Oriental de Tomé Pires e o Livro de Francisco Rodrigues*, Coimbra, Univ. of Coimbra, 1978.

Costa, Balthasar da *De Arte Tamulica*, 1650.

Costa, João Paulo Oliveira e, "A rivalidade luso-espanhola no Extremo Oriente e a quereia missionológica no Japão" in *O Século Cristão do Japão*, ed. Roberto Carneiro & Teodoro de Matos, Lisbon, 1994.

Costa, Orlando da, "A lingua Portuguesa em Goa - um valor cultural em vias de total extinção", *BIMB*, no. 170, 1994.

Costa, Orlando da, *O Signo da Ira*, Lisbon, Edições Temas de Actualidade, 4th ed., 1996.

Dalgado, Sebastião R., *Influencia do Vocabulário Portugues em Linguas Asiáticas*, Lisbon, 1913.

Dalgado, Sebastião R., *Glossário Luso-Asiático*, vols. 1-2, Coimbra, 1919/1921.

D'Costa, Anthony, *The Christianisation of the Goa Islands (1510-1567)*, Mumbai, St. Xavier's College, 1965.

D'Souza, Carmo, *Legal System in Goa — Judicial Institutions (1510-1982)*, Vol. 1, 1994; *Legal System in Goa - Laws and Legal trends (1510-1969)*, Vol. 2, 1995.

Desai, Kalpana, "Images of Christianity: Ivory and wood icons from Goa", *India Magazine*, June 1985, pp. 40-47.

Devi, Vimala & Seabra, Manuel de, *A Literatura Indo-Portuguesa*, vols. 1-2, Lisbon, Junta de Investigações do Ultramar, 1971.

Dias, Paulino, "A Lira de Ciencia" in *A Literatura Indo-Portuguesa: Antologia*, eds. Vimala Devi & Manuel de Seabra, 1971, pp. 137-139.

Dodwell, H., *The Nabobs of Madras*, Chennai, 1926.

Doshi, Saryu (ed.), *Goa: Cultural Patterns*, Mumbai, Marg Publications, 1983.

Fabri, Charles, *An Introduction to Indian Architecture*, Mumbai, Asian Publishing House.

Feio, Mariano, *As Castas Hindus de Goa*, Lisbon, 1979.

Fernandes, José Manuel, "Vestígios do Manuelino na Arquitectura Religiosa de Influencia Portuguesa na India: Malabar, Coromandel, Goa", in *Oceanos*, no. 19/20, 1994. pp. 136-154.

Ferroli, D., *The Jesuits in Malabar*, vol. 1, Bangalore 1939, vol. 2, 1951.

Figueiredo, Pacheco de, "Goa Pre-Portuguesa", *Studia* (OEHU), nos. 13-14.

Fletcher, Banister, *A History of Architecture*, 18th ed., Athlone Press, 1975.

Fonseca, José Nicolau da, *An Historical and Archaeological Sketch of the City of Goa*, New Delhi, Asian Educational Services, 1994 (reprint).

Freire, Gilberto, *O Luso e o Trópico*, Lisbon, Comemorações do Quinto Centenário da Morte do Infante D. Henrique, 1961.

Funk & Wagnalls, *Funk and Wagnalls Standard Dictionary of the English Language*, vols. 1-2, New York, 1966.

Furtado, J., "Nunca Pensei", in *Primeiros Versos*, Bastora, T. Rangel, 1927.

Galletti, A. di Cadilhac, *Galletti's Telugu Dictionary, a Dictionary of Current Telugu*, London, 1935.

Gracias, Fátima da Silva, *Health and Hygiene in Colonial Goa 1510-1961*, New Delhi, Concept Publishing Co., 1994.

Gracias, F. da Silva, *Kaleidoscope of Women in India*, New Delhi, Concept, 1996.

Gracias, Mariano, in *Colectanea de Escritos do Doutor António Colaço*, Margao, 1988.

Grey, Edward (ed.), *The Travels of Pietro della Valle in India*, vols. 1-2, London, Hakluyt Society, 1892. New Delhi, Asian Educational Services, 1991 (reprint).

Grierson, G.A., *Linguistic Survey of India*, vol. 4, Calcutta, 1927.

Guimarães, J.M. Teixeira, *As Comunidades Indianas das Velhas Conquistas*, Panaji, Imprensa Nacional, 1885.

Hambye, E.R., "Goa", in R. Aubert (ed.), *Dictionnaire d'Histoire et de Géographie Ecclèstiastiques*, fasc. 121, Paris, Letouzey & Ané.

Heras, Henry, "Indian Christian Art", *Examiner* (Mumbai), Nov 19, 1949.

Honwana, Luís Bernardo, *Nós matámos o cão-tinhoso*, Porto, Edições Afrontamento, 1972.

Hoppe, Fritz, *A Africa Oriental Portuguesa no tempo do Marques de Pombal (1750-1777)*, Lisbon, Agencia Geral do Ultramar, 1970.

Houtart, François, *Religion and Ideology in Sri Lanka*, Bangalore, TPI, 1974.

Houtart, François & Lemercinier, Genevieve, *Genesis and Institutionalization of the Indian Catholicism*, Louvain-la-Neuve, Universite Catholique de Louvain, 1981.

Isaacman, Allen e Barbara, "Os Prazeiros como Trans-Raianos: Um Estudo sobre Transforma Social e Cultural" in *Boletim do Arquivo Histórico de Moçambique. Tete*, no. 19, October 1991, pp. 5-48.

James, Gregory, *Tamil Lexicography*, Tubingen, Niemeyer, 1991.

James, Gregory, "Some Lexicographical Records in Western Europe" (Part 2) in *Journal of the Institute of Asian Studies*, vol. 8, no. 2, 1991, pp. 97-129.

Joshi, L.M., *Shri Navnath Tatvadnyan ani Upasana*, Mumbai, Gajan Book Depot.

Kedilaya, A. Shanker, *Foreign Loan words in Kannada (Arabic and Persian)*, Chennai, 1970.

Keil, Luis, *Distrito de Portalegre. Inventário Artístico de Portugal*, vol. I, Lisbon, Academia Nacional de Belas Artes, 1943.

Knowlton, Edgar C. & Xavier, S. Thani Nayagam, "Preface to the Tamil Portuguese Dictionary", in *Tamil Culture*, vol. 11, no. 2, 1979, pp. 127-128.

Knowlton, Edgar C., "Antão de Proença's Vocabulário Tamulico-Lusitano: Indo-Portuguese Elements", *Tamil Culture"*, 11, no. 2, 1964, pp. 135-164.

Knowlton, Edgar C., "Portuguese-Tamil Linguistic Contacts", *Proceedings of the First International Seminar of Tamil Studies*, Kuala Lumpur, vol. 2, 1969, pp. 607-617.

Kosambi, D.D. *The Culture and Civilisation of Ancient India in Historical Outline*, London, 1965.

Kubler, George, *A Arquitectura Portuguesa Chã. Entre as Especiarias e os diamantes 1521-1706*, Lisbon.

Kurtz, Gunde, *Die Literatur im Spiegel ihrer selbst: Italo Calvino, António Tabucchi — Zwei Beispiele* (The literature in the mirror of itself: Italo Calvino, António Tabucchi — two examples), Tubingen, 1992.

Lemmon, Alfred E., "Jesuits and Music in Mexico", *Archivum Historicum Societatis Iesu*, vol. 46, 1977.

Littmann, Enno, *Morgenlandische Worter im Deutschen. Zweite, vermehrte und verbesserte Auflage nebst einem Anhang uber dis amerikanischen Worter*, Tubingen, 1924.

Lobato, Alexandre, *Lourenço Marques, Xilunguine. Biografia da cidade*, Lisbon, Agencia Geral Ultramar, 1970.

Lokotsch, Karl, *Etymologisches Worterbuch der europaischen (germanischen, romanischen und slavischen) Worter orientalischen Ursprungs*, Heidelberg, 1927.

Lopes, Maria Jesus dos Martires, *Goa na Segunda Metade do Século xviii: Esboço de um Ensaio Cultural*, Lisbon, 1993.

Machado, José Pedro, *Dicionário Etimológico da Língua Portuguesa*, Lisbon, vols. 1-5, 1977.

Malten, Thomas, "Die Geschichte von Rama und Laksman" in *Sudasien-Anthologie*, Hrsg. von G.D. Sontheimer Stuttgart, Steiner, 1993, pp. 98-107.

Marques, A.H. Oliveira, *História de Portugal: Das origens as revoluções liberais*, vol I, Lisbon, Palas Editores, 1974.

Mascarenhas, Lambert, *Sorrowing lies my Land*, Mumbai, Hind Kitabs, 1955.

Mascarenhas, Lambert, *The Greater Tragedy or the Death of a Nationalist*, Dona Paula, Lamas Publications.

Mascarenhas, Mira, "The Impact of the West on Goan Music" in *Goa: Cultural Trends*, ed. P. P. Shirodkar, Panaji, Casa Packmaster, 1988, pp. 189-204.

Maugham, W. Somerset, *A Writer's Notebook*, Harmondsworth, Middlesex, Penguin, 1949/1987.

McNab, Gregory, "Porque mataram o Cão-Tinhoso", in *Africa*, no. 14, 1977, pp. 61-74.

Melo, Carlos M. de, *The Recruitment and Formation of the Native Clergy in India (16th-19th century): An Historico-Canonical Study*, Lisbon, Agencia Geral do Ultramar, 1955.

Mendes, António Lopes, *A India Portuguesa*, 2 vols., New Delhi, Asian Educational Services, 1989 (reprint).

Messner, Dieter, "A Difusão de Palavras Portuguesas, Problemas e Métodos", *Linguistica*, vol. 27, 1987, pp. 87-98.

Minakshisundaram, T.P & Shanmugam, M., "Portuguese Influence revealed by the Tamil Words, *Journal of the Annamalai Univ.* , 16 (no. 3), 1951, pp. 11-25.

Miranda, J.C. Barreto, *Quadros Historicos de Goa*, Margao, 1864.

Mitchell, David, *The Jesuits: A History*, New York, Franklim Watts, 1981.

Mitter, Patha, *Much Maligned Monsters: A History of European Reactions to Indian Art*, 2nd ed., Chicago, Univ. of Chicago Press, 1992.

Mitterwallner, Gritli, "The Hindu Past", *Goa: Cultural Patterns*, Mumbai, Marg Publications, 1984, pp. 21-40.

Molesworth, James Thomas, *Molesworth's Marathi-English Dictionary*, Pune, 1975.

Monier-Williams, *A Sanskrit-English Dictionary*, Delhi, Patna, Varanasi, 1974.

Morais, Carlos Alexandre de, *Cronologia Geral da India Portuguesa*, Macau, Instituto Cultural de Macau e Instituto Rainha Dona Leonor, 1993.

Morais, Henrique Bravo de, *Noticia de como e quando se erigio a Cathedral de Goa, e dos Bispos, e Arcebispos que nella houve antes, e depois da sua erecçam com outras cousas mais pertencentes ao dito Arcebispado*, 1772, pp. 97-179, F. G. 176, (Microfilm 2527), Biblioteca Nacional (Lisbon).

Moreira, Rafael, "Goa em 1535: Uma cidade manuelina", *Revista da Faculdade de Ciências Sociais e Humanas*, II, 8 (1995), pp. 177-221.

Muhlmann, W.E., "Kultur" in *Dicionário da Sociologia*, Bernsdorf, 1969.

Mulackal, Thomas, "The Christian Paintings in Arab-ki-Sarai", *Examiner*, 22 February 1975.

Nazareth, Peter, "The end of exile, or why should Goans read Goan literature", in *Goa: Continuity and Change*, eds. Narendra K, Wagle & George V. Coelho, Toronto, Centre for South Asian Studies, 1995, pp. 35-50.

Nery, Rui Vieira, "The Music Manuscripts in the Library of King D. João IV of Portugal (1604-1656): A Study of Iberian Music in the Sixteenth and Seventeenth Centuries", Ph. D. diss., Univ. of Texas, Austin, 1990.

Noronha, Carmo de, "Contracorrente", Goa: Fundação Oriente, 1991.

Noronha, Percival, "O Mobilário Indo-Portugues" in *Revista de Macau a Goa*.

Paiva Manso, V. de, (ed.), *Bullarium Patronatus in ecclesiis Africae, Asiae atque Oceaniae*, Tomo 1, Lisbon, 1889.

Pascoães, Teixeira de, *A Saudade e o saudosismo*, Lisbon, Assirio e Alvin, 1988.

Pearson, Michael N., *The Cambridge History of India* I.1: *The Portuguese In India*, Cambridge, Cambridge Univ. Press, 1987.

Pereira, António, *Konknni Oparinchem Bhanddar*, Panaji, 1985.

Pereira, José, "A Sheaf of Deknnis", in *Konkani Folk Songs*, Mumbai, Konkan Cultural Association, 1967.

Pereira, José, *Golden Goa*, Mumbai, Marg Publications, 1980.

Pereira, José, "The Art Historiography of Baroque India", *Indica* (Mumbai), 23 (nos. 1-2), 1986.

Pereira, José., "Some Mandos of yearning", in *Proceedings of the 1st International Goan Convention* (Toronto), August 1988.

Pereira, José, *Baroque Goa: The Architecture of Portuguese India*, New Delhi, Books & Books, 1995.

Pereira, Rui Gomes, *Goa - Hindu Temples and Deities*, Panaji, Printwell Press, 1978.

Perniola, V., *The Catholic Church in Sri Lanka* (The Portuguese, Dutch and English Periods 1505-1844), Dehiwala (Sri Lanka), Tisara Prakasakayo, 1989-1992.

Pessoa, Fernando, *Obra Poetica*, Rio de Janeiro, Nova Aguilar, 1987.

Pinto, Floriano, "Bailadeira", in *Brísas do Mandovi*, Bastora, T. Rangel, 1931.

Pischel, Gina, *The Golden History of Art*, London, Paul Hamlyn.

Pissurlencar, P.S.S., *Portugues-Maratha Sambandh*, Pune, Univ. of Poona, 1967.

Plattner, Felix, *Christian India*, London, Thames and Hudson, 1957.

Platts, John T. *A Dictionary of Urdu, Classical Hindi, and English*, Oxford, 1965.

Priolkar, A.K., *The Goa Inquisition*, Mumbai, Univ. of Mumbai, 1961.

Quadros, António *Critica e Verdade*, Lisbon, Livraria Classica Editora, 1964.

Quivy, Raymond, *Manual de Investigação em Ciências Sociais*, Lisbon, Gradiva, 1992.

Rajamanickam, S., *The First Oriental Scholar*, Tirunelveli, De Nobili Research Institute, 1972.

Rajamanickam, S., "Antam Proença's Tamil Portuguese Dictionary - Discovery of the Missing Link" (Xavier Centre of Historical Research, Goa, Seminar 1995).

Ramirez, Ricardo, "The Question of Columbus: Evaluation of the Result", *Boletim Cehila* (São Paulo), nos. 43-44, January 1993.

Rebello, Fenelon, "Cruz de São Tomé no reinado de D. João III", *Moeda* (Lisbon), 15 (no. 2) 1990.

Rees, Owen, *Polyphony in Portugal, c.1530-c.1620: Sources from the Monastery of Santa Cruz, Coimbra*, New York, Garland, 1995.

Rego, António da Silva (ed.), *Documentação para a história das missões do Padroado Portugues do Oriente*, vols. 1-12, Lisbon, SARL, 1947-58.

Reis, António, *Portugal Contemporaneo*, Lisbon, Publicações Alfa, vol. 5, 1990.

Rivara, J.H da. Cunha (ed.), *Archivo Portuguez Oriental*, vols. 1-10; Panaji, 1857-77.

Rita-Ferreira, A., "Moçambique e os naturais da India Portuguesa", *II Seminário Internacional História Indo-Portuguesa*, (Actas), Lisbon, 1985, pp. 617-648.

Rocha, Leopoldo da, *As Confrarias de Goa*, Lisbon, 1973.

Rodrigues, Eusebio, "Stray Thoughts on Goan Exile, in *Goa: Continuity and Change*, ed. Narendra K. Wagle & Geroge V. Coelho, Univ. of Toronto, Centre for south Asian Studies, 1995, pp. 51-58.

Rodrigues, Lucio, "Mando — the Song of Love; Dulpod — the Song of Joy; Dakni — the Song of the Dancing God", in *Folklore*, 4 (no. 11), November 1963, pp. 361-68.

Saldanha, M.J. Gabriel de, *História de Goa, Politica e Arqueológica*, vols. 1-2, New Delhi, Asian Educational Services, 1990 (reprint).

Saldanha, J., "Indian Christian Art", *Indian Missiological Review*, October 1980, pp. 271-327.

San Bartholomeo, Paulino, *Examen historico-criticum codicum indicorum bibliothecae sacrae congregationis de Propaganda Fide*. Rome, 1792.

Santa Maria, Joseph di (Giuseppe Sebastiani), *Seconda Speditione all'Indie Orientali*, Venice, 1683.

Saraiva, António José (ed.), *Peregrinação e outras obras*, 2 vols, 1961.

Sardessai, Libia Lobo, *Glimpses of family laws of Goa, Daman and Diu*, Seva Samiti, 1982.

Sardessai, Manohar, "Poemas", *BIMB*, no. 96, 1971.

Sardo, Susana, "Sons e Silencios", in *Oceanos* (Lisbon), nos. 19-20, September-December 1994, pp. 246-256.

Sauerwein, Astrid, *Mission und Kolonialismus in Simbabwe 1840-1940: Kollisionenm, Konflikt Kooperation*, Gieben, Focus, 1990.

Schutte, Josef F., *Valignano's Mission Principles for Japan*, vol. 1, Part 1, Anand, Gujarat Sahitya Prakash, 1980.

Sequeira, Gustavo de Matos, *Distrito de Leiria. Inventário Artistico de Portugal*, vol. 5, Lisbon, Academia Nacional de Belas Artes, 1955.

Sharma, Aryendra & Vermeer, Hans J., *Hindi-Deutsches Worterbuch*, vols. 1-3, Heidelberg, 1987.

Shaw, Graham W., "The Copenhagen copy of Henriques' *Flos Sanctorum*" in *Fund og Forskning i Det kongelige Biblioteks samlinger*, vol. 32, 1993, pp. 39-50.

Silva, Anthony da, "The Discovered versus the Discovered: Psychological perspectives on Portuguese-Goan Prejudices in the 16th-18th centuries", in *Discoveries, Missionary Expansion and Asian Cultures*, pp. 45-54.

Snow, Robert, "Music by Francisco Guerrero in Guatemala", *Nassarre Revista Aragonesa de Musicologia 3*, 1987, pp. 153-202.

Snow, Robert, *Gaspar Fernandes: Obras Sacres. Portugaliae Musica 49*, Lisbon, Fundação Calouste Gulbenkian, 1990.

Soares, Anthony Xavier, *Portuguese Vocables in Asiatic Languages from the Portuguese Original of Monsignor Sebastião Rodolfo*

Dalgado, trans. with notes, additions, comments, Baroda, 1936.

Souza, Caetano F. de , *Estudos Históricos Archaeologicos Instituições Portugueses de Educação e Instrucção no Oriente*, Mumbai, 1980.

Souza, Francisco de, *Oriente Conquistado a Jesu Christo*, Mumbai, Examiner.

Souza, Teotónio R. de, *Medieval Goa*, New Delhi, Concept Publishing Company, 1979.

Souza, T. R. de, "The Voiceless in Goan Historiography: A Case for the source-value of Church Records in Goa", in *Indo-Portuguese History: Sources and Problems*, ed. John Correia-Afonso, Mumbai, OUP, 1981, pp. 114-31.

Souza, T.R. de & Borges, Charles J. (eds.), *Jesuits in India: In Historical Perspective*, Macau, Instituto Cultural de Macau, 1992.

Souza, T. R. de, "Christianization and Cultural Conflicts in Goa 16th—19th Centuries", *BIMB* (Panaji), no. 170, 1994.

Souza, T. R. de, "Christianisation and cultural conflict in Goa: 16th - 19th centuries", *Congresso internacional de história: Missionação portuguesa e encontro de culturas — Actas*, vol. 4, Braga, 1993.

Souza, T. R. de, "Gonçalo Martins: A Jesuit procurator, businessman and diplomat in the Estado da India", *Mare Liberum*, no. 5, Lisbon, 1993, pp. 119-128.

Souza, T. R. de, "The Christian Missions in the Aftermath of Discoveries: Tools for shaping the Colonial Other" in *Discoveries, Missionary Expansion and Asian Cultures*, New Delhi, Concept, 1994, pp. 33-44.

Souza, T. R. de, "Uns confessionários inéditos: Instrumentos de missionação e fontes para a história de Goa", *Amar, Sentir e Viver a História: Estudos de Homenagem a Joaquim Verissimo Serrão*, ed. Colibri, Lisbon, 1995.

Steingass, Francis Joseph, *A Comprehensive Persian-English Dictionary*, London, 1892

Strasser, Robert, "Paradies am Indischen Ozean-Goa", *Verlag Indo-Culture*, 1992.

Subramanian, P.R. *et al*, *Kriyavin Tarakalat Tamil Akarati, Tamil-Tamil-Ankilam*, Chennai, 1992.

Tabucchi, António, *Un baule peino di gente: Scritti su Fernando Pessoa*, Milan, 1990.

Telles, M. Balthasar,*Chronica da Companhia de Iesu da Provincia de Portugal*, 2 vols., Lisbon, 1645-47.

Telles, Michael Ricardo, "Igrejas, Conventos e Capelas na Velha Cidade de Goa", *O Oriente Português*, no. 1, Dec. 1931.

Thapar, Romila, *Time as Metaphor of History: Early India*, Delhi, Oxford India Paperbacks, 1996.

Thomaz, Luis Filipe F. Reis, *De Ceuta a Timor*, Lisbon, Difel.

Thomaz, Luis Filipe F. Reis, "O Cristianismo e as Tradições Pagcs na India Portuguesa", *Actas do Congresso Internacional de Etnografia* (Camara Municipal de Santo Tirso, Julho 1963, vol. IV, Lisbon, Junta de Investigação do Ultramar, 1965).

Turner, Ralph Lilley, *A Comparative Dictionary of the Indo-Aryan Languages*, vol. 1. London, 1966.

Vaz, Carmo, "A Diaspora Goesa no Mundo" in *Goa* (Revista of Casa de Goa), Lisbon, March-June, 1991.

Vasconcelos, Carolini Michaelis da, *A Saudade Portuguesa*, Lisbon, Guimaraes, 1996.

Vinson, Julien, "Le premier vocabulaire tamoul imprimé" in *Revue de Linguistique*, vol. 43, 1910, Paris, pp. 74-82.

Watson, Francis, *India - A Concise History*, New York, Thames & Hudson, 1979.

Wicki, Josef (ed.), *Documenta Indica*, vols. 1-18, Rome, Institutum Historicum Societatis Iesu, 1948/1988.

Wicki, J. (ed.), *O Livro do Pai dos Cristãos*, Lisbon, Centro de Estudos Ultramarinos, 1969.

Winius, George D., *The Black Legend of Portuguese India*, New Delhi, Concept Publ. Co., 1985.

Winstedt, Richard, *A Practical Modern English-Malay Dictionary*, Singapore, 1960.

Woodfield, Ian, *English Musicians in the Age of Exploration*, Stuyvesant, Pendragon Press, 1995.

Xavier, Felippe Nery, *Colecção das Leis Peculiares das Comunidades agricolas dos Concelhos das Ilhas, Salcete e Bardez*, Panaji, Imprensa Nacional, 1852.

Xavier, F. N., *Bosquejo Histórico das Comunidades das Aldeas dos Concelhos das Ilhas, Salcete e Bardez*, vol. 1, Bastora, Rangel, 1903.

Yules, Henry & Burnell, A.C, *Hobson-Jobson: A Glossary of Colloquial Anglo-Indian Words and Phrases and of Kindred Terms*, Etymological, Historical, Geographical and Discursive, new ed. London, 1903.

Zachariae, Theodor, *De Open-Deure tot het verborgen Heydendom door Abraham Rogerius*, ed. W. Caland, Gravenhage, Martinus Nijhoff, 1915.

Zedler, J. H., *Grosses vollstandiges Universal-Lexikon*, vol. 62, Leipzig & Halle, 1749.

INDEX